BLOODSHOT REBORN

COLORADO

JEFF LEMIRE | MICO SUAYAN | RAÚL ALLÉN | DAVID BARON

CONTENTS

Collection Cover Art: Mico Suayan

Associate Editor: Kyle Andrukiewicz
Editor: Warren Simons

VALIANT.

Peter Cuneo
Chairman

Dinesh Shamdasani
CEO & Chief Creative Officer

Gavin Cuneo
Chief Operating Officer & CFO

Fred Pierce
Publisher

Warren Simons
Editor-in-Chief

Walter Black
VP Operations

Hunter Gorinson
VP Marketing & Communications

Atom! Freeman
Director of Sales

Matthew Klein
Andy Liegl
John Petrie
Sales Managers

Josh Johns
Associate Director of Digital Media and Development

Travis Escarfullery
Jeff Walker
Production & Design Managers

Tom Brennan
Editor

Kyle Andrukiewicz
Editor and Creative Executive

Robert Meyers
Managing Editor

Peter Stern
Publishing & Operations Manager

Andrew Steinbeiser
Marketing & Communications Manager

Lauren Hitzhusen
Danny Khazem
Assistant Editors

Ivan Cohen
Collection Editor

Steve Blackwell
Collection Designer

Rian Hughes/Device
Trade Dress & Book Design

Russell Brown
President, Consumer Products,
Promotions and Ad Sales

BLOODSHOT REBORN

JEFF LEMIRE

MICO SUAYAN

DAVID BARON

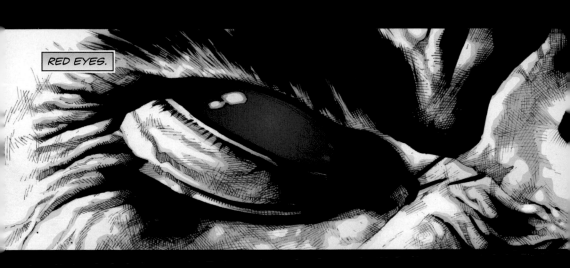

WHO WAS
BLOODSHOT?

RED EYES.

WHITE SKIN.

GUNS...LOTS
OF GUNS.

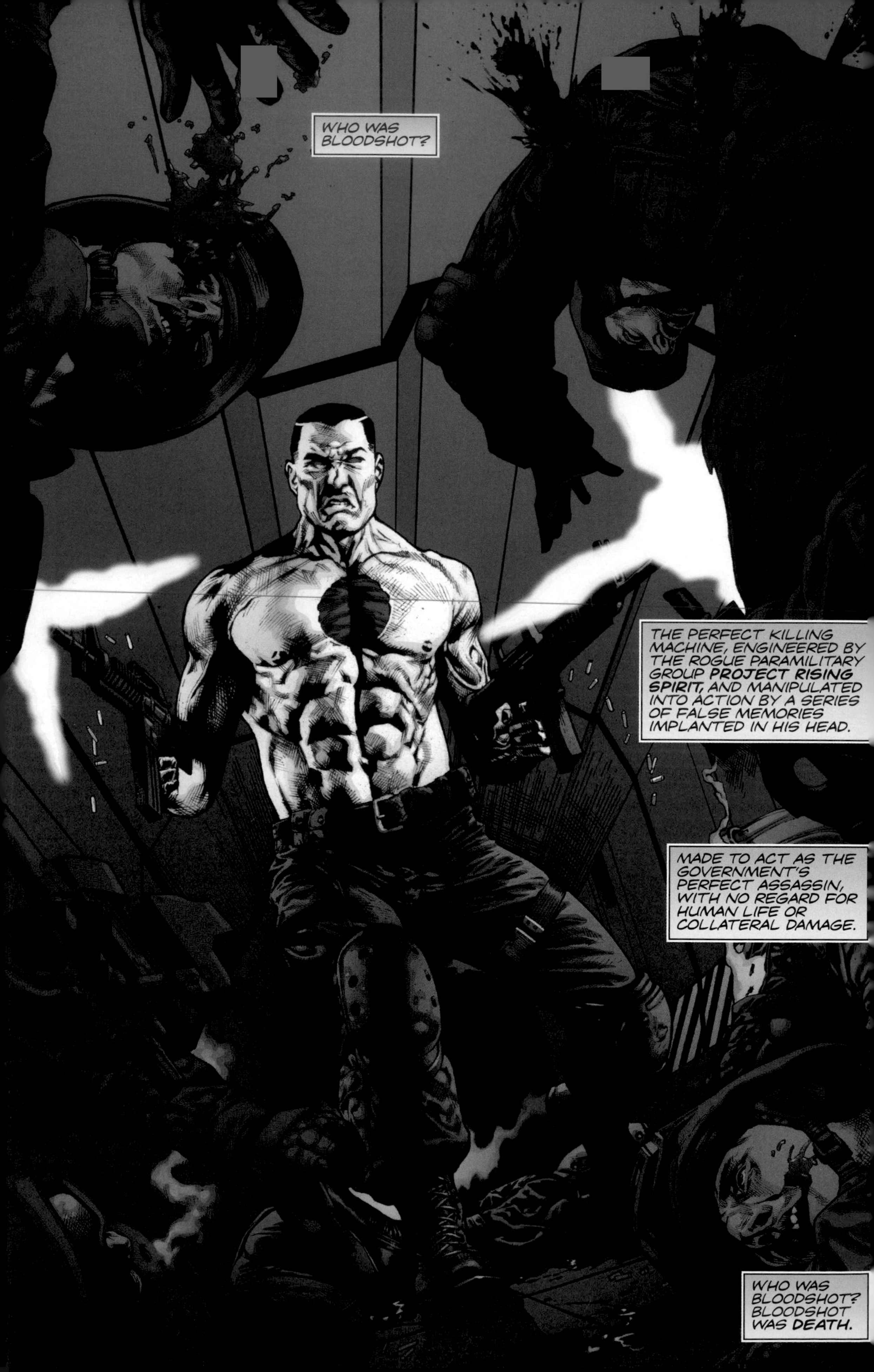
WHO WAS BLOODSHOT?
THE PERFECT KILLING MACHINE, ENGINEERED BY THE ROGUE PARAMILITARY GROUP **PROJECT RISING SPIRIT,** AND MANIPULATED INTO ACTION BY A SERIES OF FALSE MEMORIES IMPLANTED IN HIS HEAD.
MADE TO ACT AS THE GOVERNMENT'S PERFECT ASSASSIN, WITH NO REGARD FOR HUMAN LIFE OR COLLATERAL DAMAGE.
WHO WAS BLOODSHOT? BLOODSHOT WAS **DEATH.**

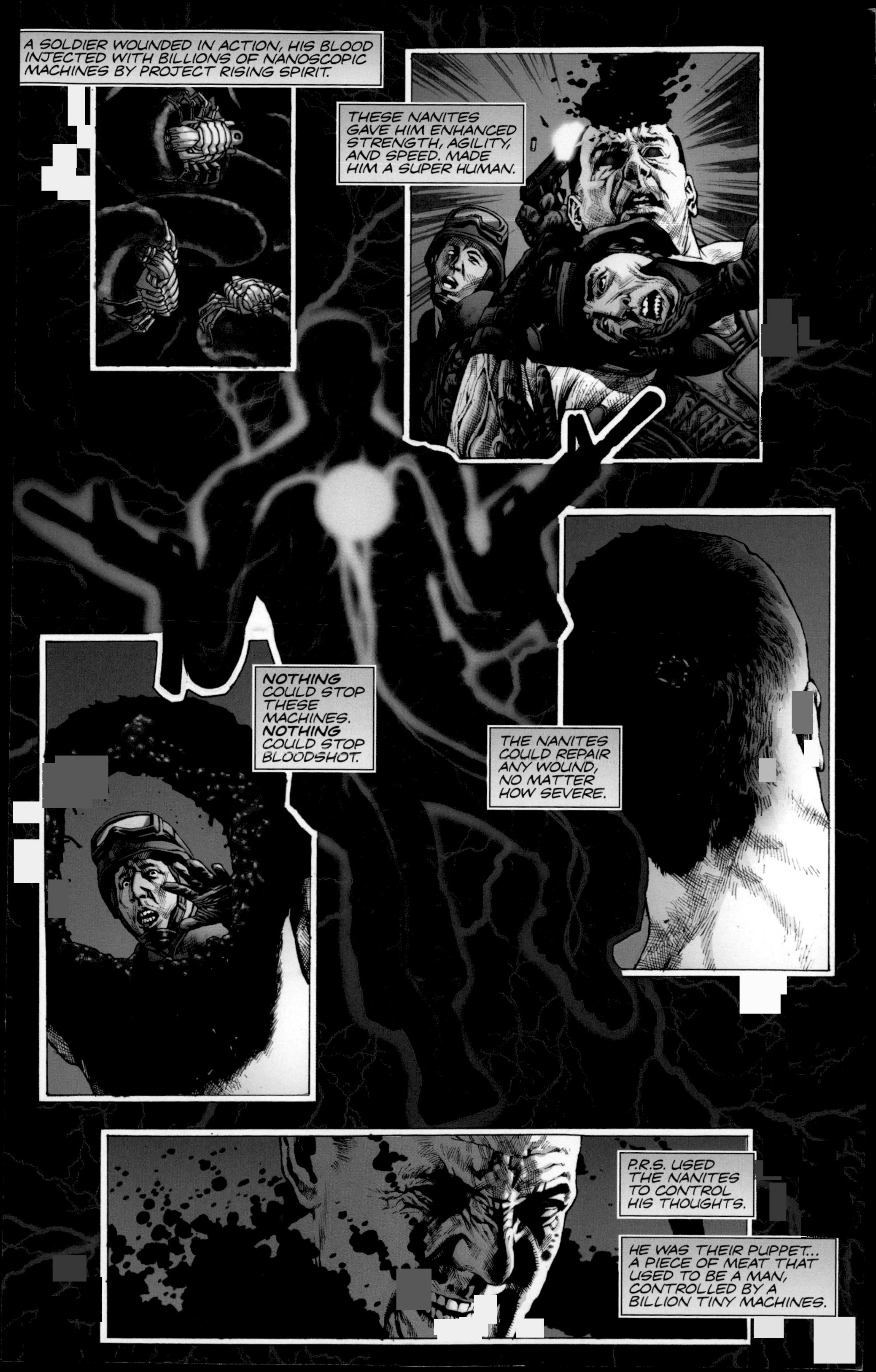
A SOLDIER WOUNDED IN ACTION, HIS BLOOD INJECTED WITH BILLIONS OF NANOSCOPIC MACHINES BY PROJECT RISING SPIRIT.
THESE NANITES GAVE HIM ENHANCED STRENGTH, AGILITY, AND SPEED. MADE HIM A SUPER HUMAN.
NOTHING COULD STOP THESE MACHINES. NOTHING COULD STOP BLOODSHOT.
THE NANITES COULD REPAIR ANY WOUND, NO MATTER HOW SEVERE.
P.R.S. USED THE NANITES TO CONTROL HIS THOUGHTS.
HE WAS THEIR PUPPET... A PIECE OF MEAT THAT USED TO BE A MAN, CONTROLLED BY A BILLION TINY MACHINES.

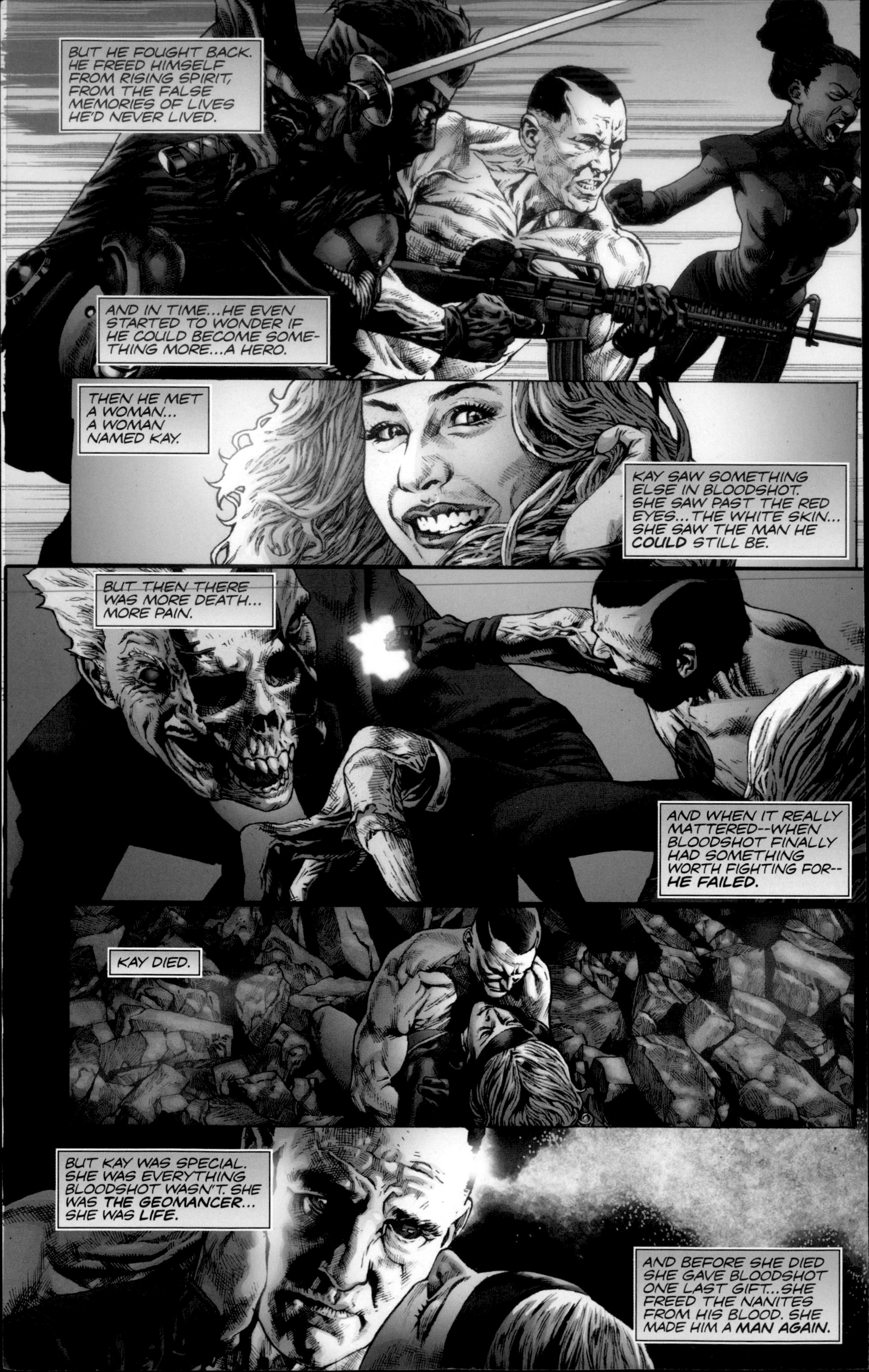
BUT HE FOUGHT BACK. HE FREED HIMSELF FROM RISING SPIRIT, FROM THE FALSE MEMORIES OF LIVES HE'D NEVER LIVED.
AND IN TIME...HE EVEN STARTED TO WONDER IF HE COULD BECOME SOMETHING MORE...A HERO.
THEN HE MET A WOMAN... A WOMAN NAMED KAY.
KAY SAW SOMETHING ELSE IN BLOODSHOT. SHE SAW PAST THE RED EYES...THE WHITE SKIN... SHE SAW THE MAN HE **COULD** STILL BE.
BUT THEN THERE WAS MORE DEATH... MORE PAIN.
AND WHEN IT REALLY MATTERED--WHEN BLOODSHOT FINALLY HAD SOMETHING WORTH FIGHTING FOR-- **HE FAILED.**
KAY DIED.
BUT KAY WAS SPECIAL. SHE WAS EVERYTHING BLOODSHOT WASN'T. SHE WAS **THE GEOMANCER**... SHE WAS **LIFE.**
AND BEFORE SHE DIED SHE GAVE BLOODSHOT ONE LAST GIFT...SHE FREED THE NANITES FROM HIS BLOOD. SHE MADE HIM A **MAN AGAIN.**

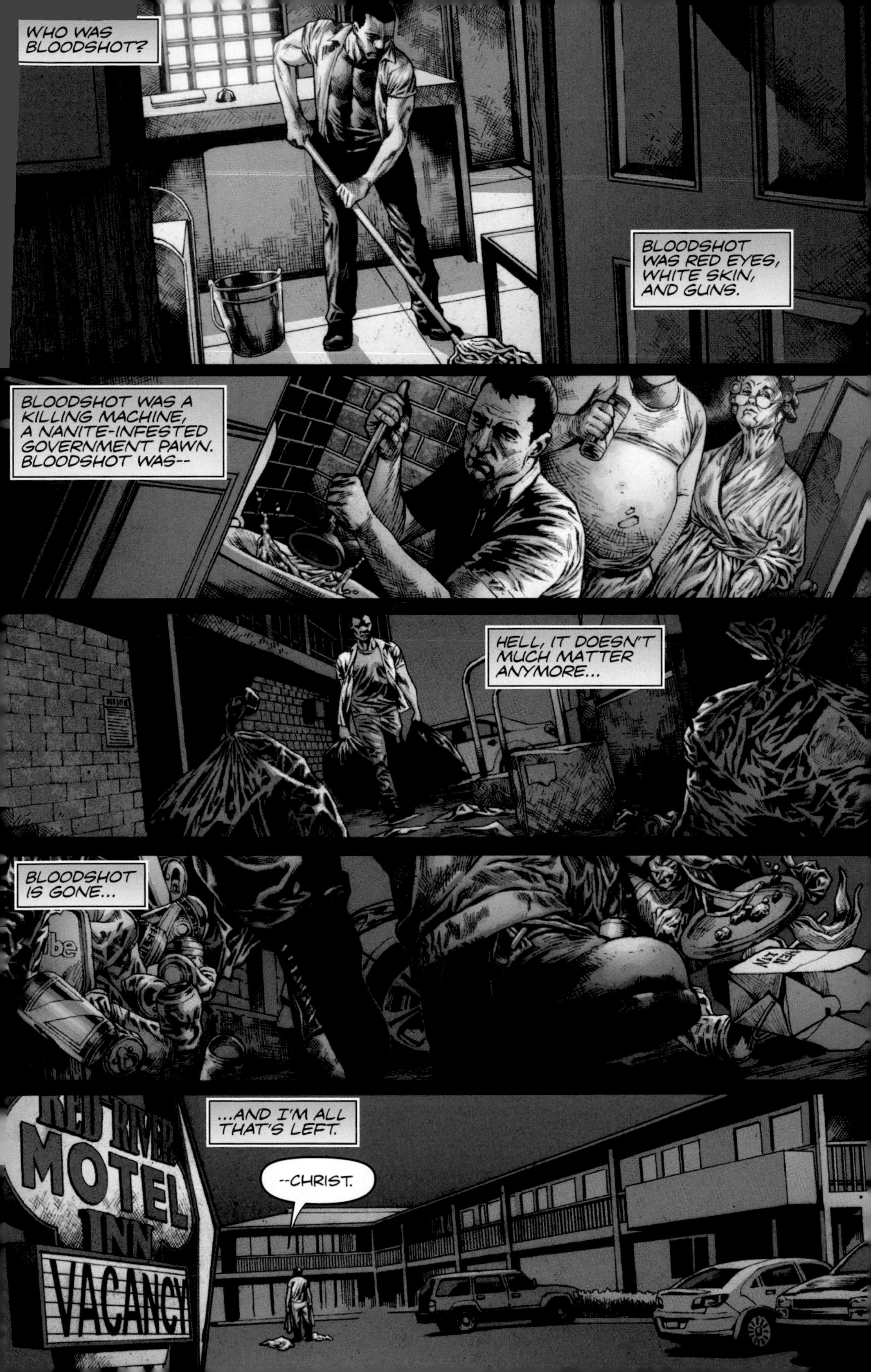
WHO WAS BLOODSHOT?
BLOODSHOT WAS RED EYES, WHITE SKIN, AND GUNS.
BLOODSHOT WAS A KILLING MACHINE, A NANITE-INFESTED GOVERNMENT PAWN. BLOODSHOT WAS--
HELL, IT DOESN'T MUCH MATTER ANYMORE...
BLOODSHOT IS GONE...
...AND I'M ALL THAT'S LEFT.
--CHRIST.
RED RIVER MOTEL INN
VACANCY

BLOODSHOT

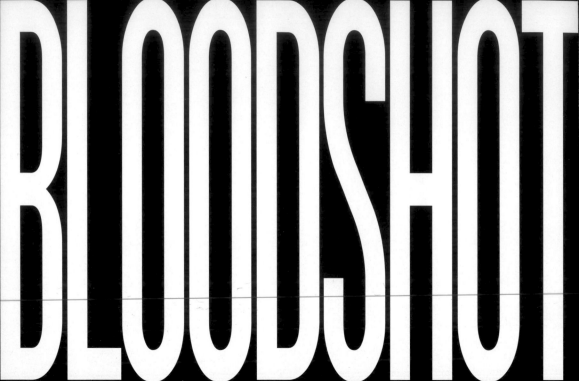

REBORN:
COLORADO

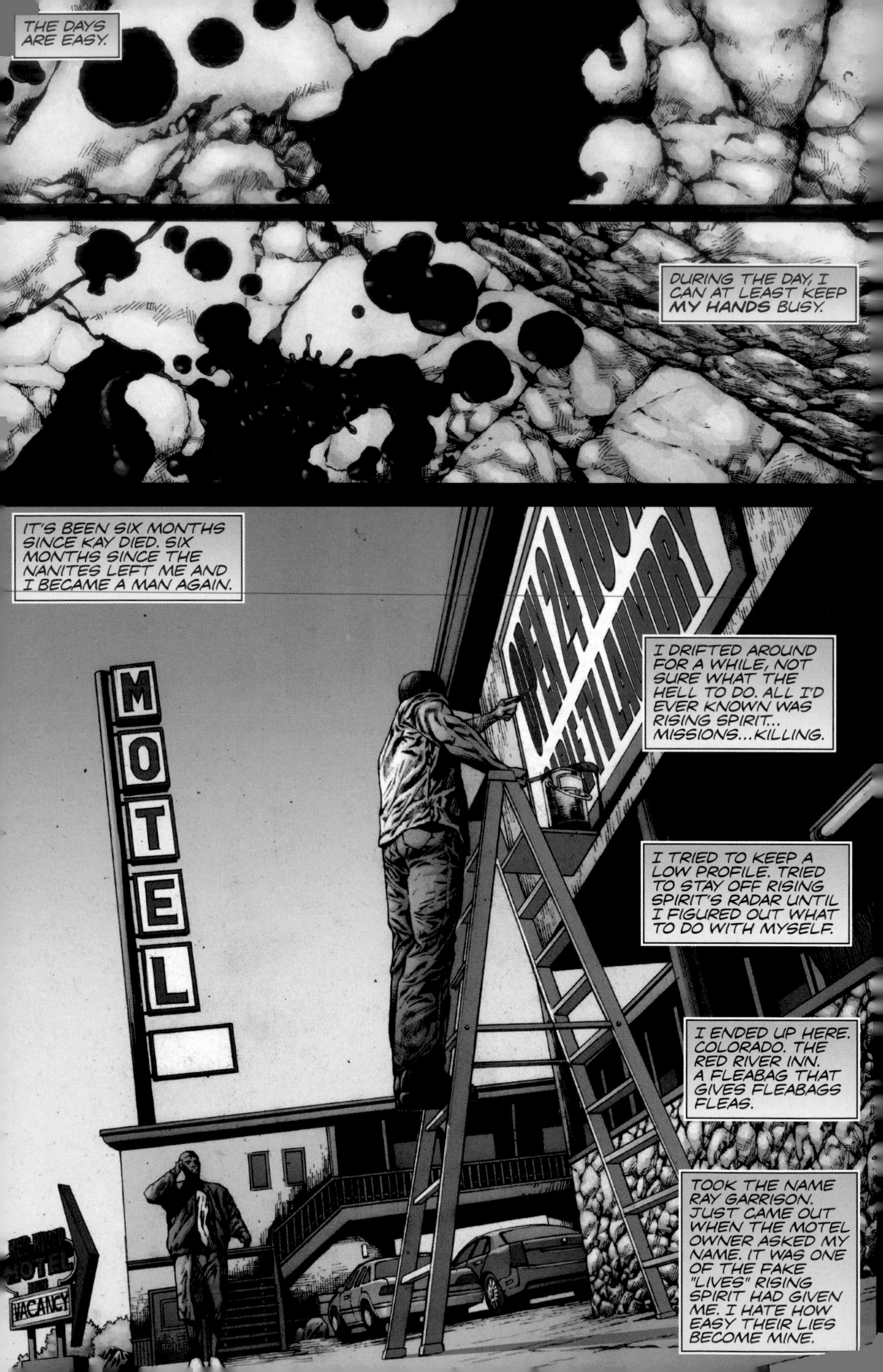
THE DAYS ARE EASY.
DURING THE DAY, I CAN AT LEAST KEEP MY HANDS BUSY.
IT'S BEEN SIX MONTHS SINCE KAY DIED. SIX MONTHS SINCE THE NANITES LEFT ME AND I BECAME A MAN AGAIN.
MOTEL
I DRIFTED AROUND FOR A WHILE, NOT SURE WHAT THE HELL TO DO. ALL I'D EVER KNOWN WAS RISING SPIRIT... MISSIONS...KILLING.
I TRIED TO KEEP A LOW PROFILE. TRIED TO STAY OFF RISING SPIRIT'S RADAR UNTIL I FIGURED OUT WHAT TO DO WITH MYSELF.
I ENDED UP HERE. COLORADO. THE RED RIVER INN. A FLEABAG THAT GIVES FLEABAGS FLEAS.
VACANCY
TOOK THE NAME RAY GARRISON. JUST CAME OUT WHEN THE MOTEL OWNER ASKED MY NAME. IT WAS ONE OF THE FAKE "LIVES" RISING SPIRIT HAD GIVEN ME. I HATE HOW EASY THEIR LIES BECOME MINE.

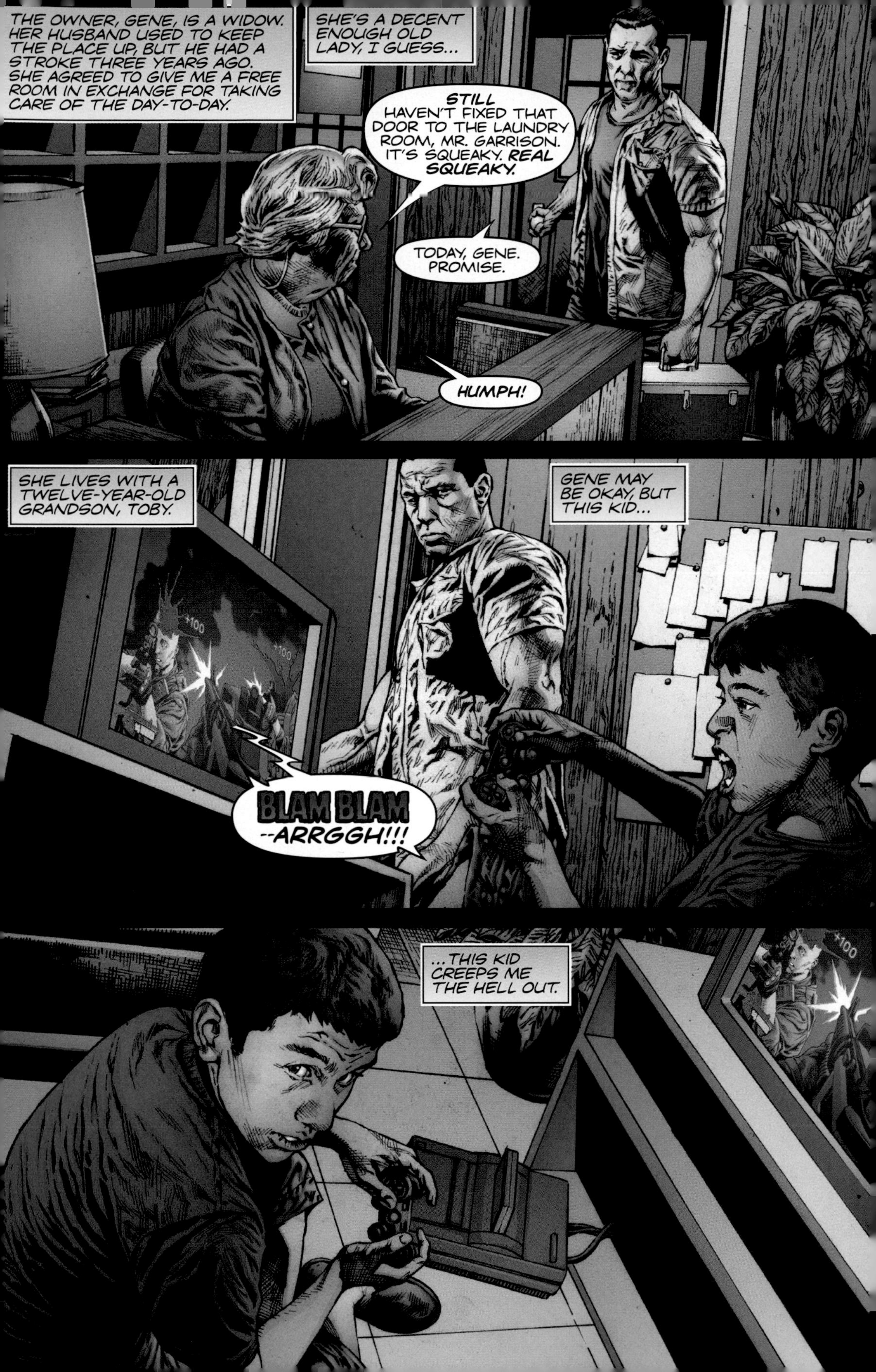
THE OWNER, GENE, IS A WIDOW. HER HUSBAND USED TO KEEP THE PLACE UP, BUT HE HAD A STROKE THREE YEARS AGO. SHE AGREED TO GIVE ME A FREE ROOM IN EXCHANGE FOR TAKING CARE OF THE DAY-TO-DAY.
SHE'S A DECENT ENOUGH OLD LADY, I GUESS...
STILL HAVEN'T FIXED THAT DOOR TO THE LAUNDRY ROOM, MR. GARRISON. IT'S SQUEAKY. REAL SQUEAKY.
TODAY, GENE. PROMISE.
HUMPH!
SHE LIVES WITH A TWELVE-YEAR-OLD GRANDSON, TOBY.
GENE MAY BE OKAY, BUT THIS KID...
BLAM BLAM --ARRGGH!!!
...THIS KID CREEPS ME THE HELL OUT.

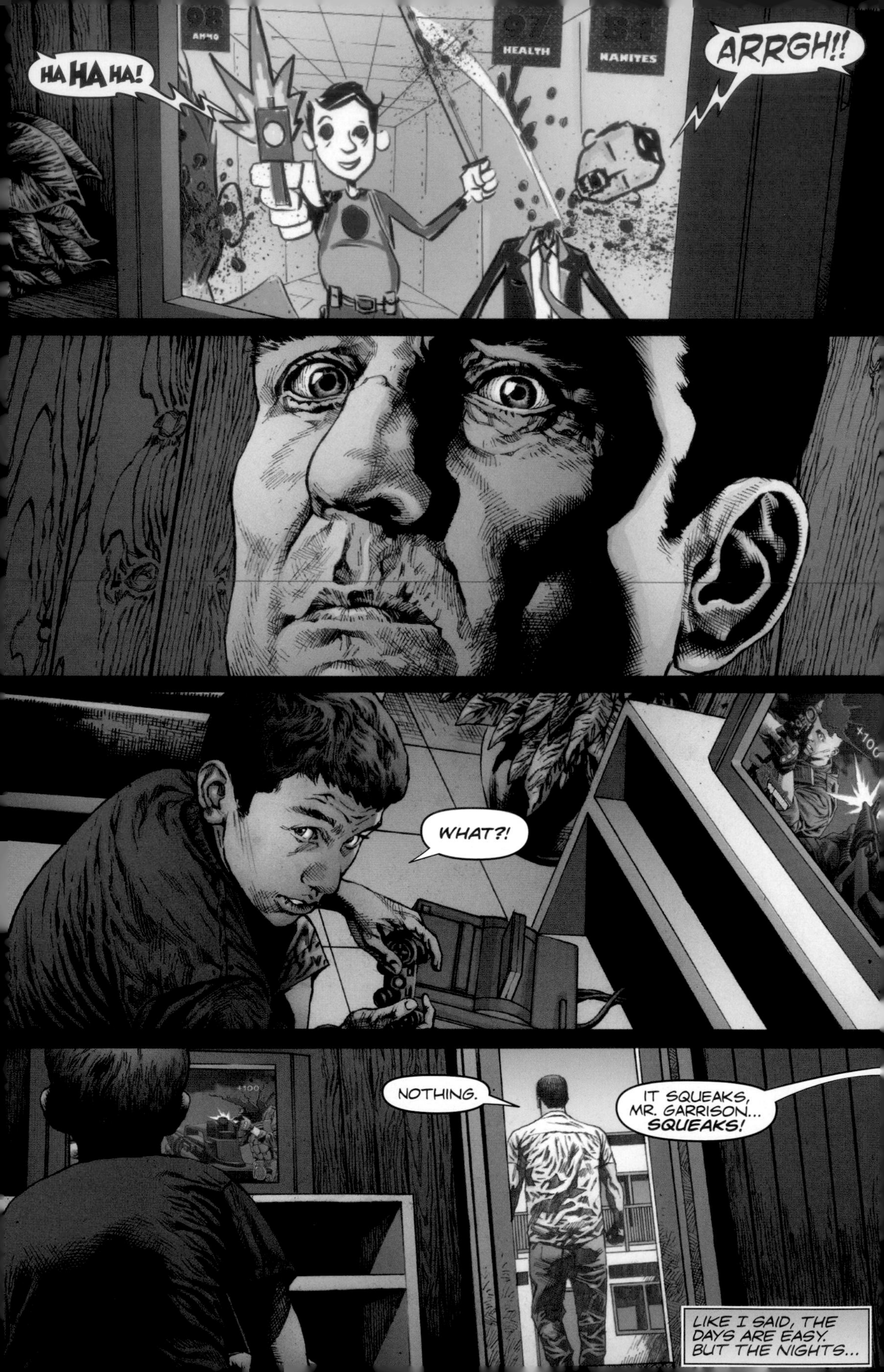
98
AMMO
97
HEALTH
NANITES
HA HA HA!
ARRGH!!
WHAT?!
NOTHING.
IT SQUEAKS, MR. GARRISON... SQUEAKS!
LIKE I SAID, THE DAYS ARE EASY. BUT THE NIGHTS...

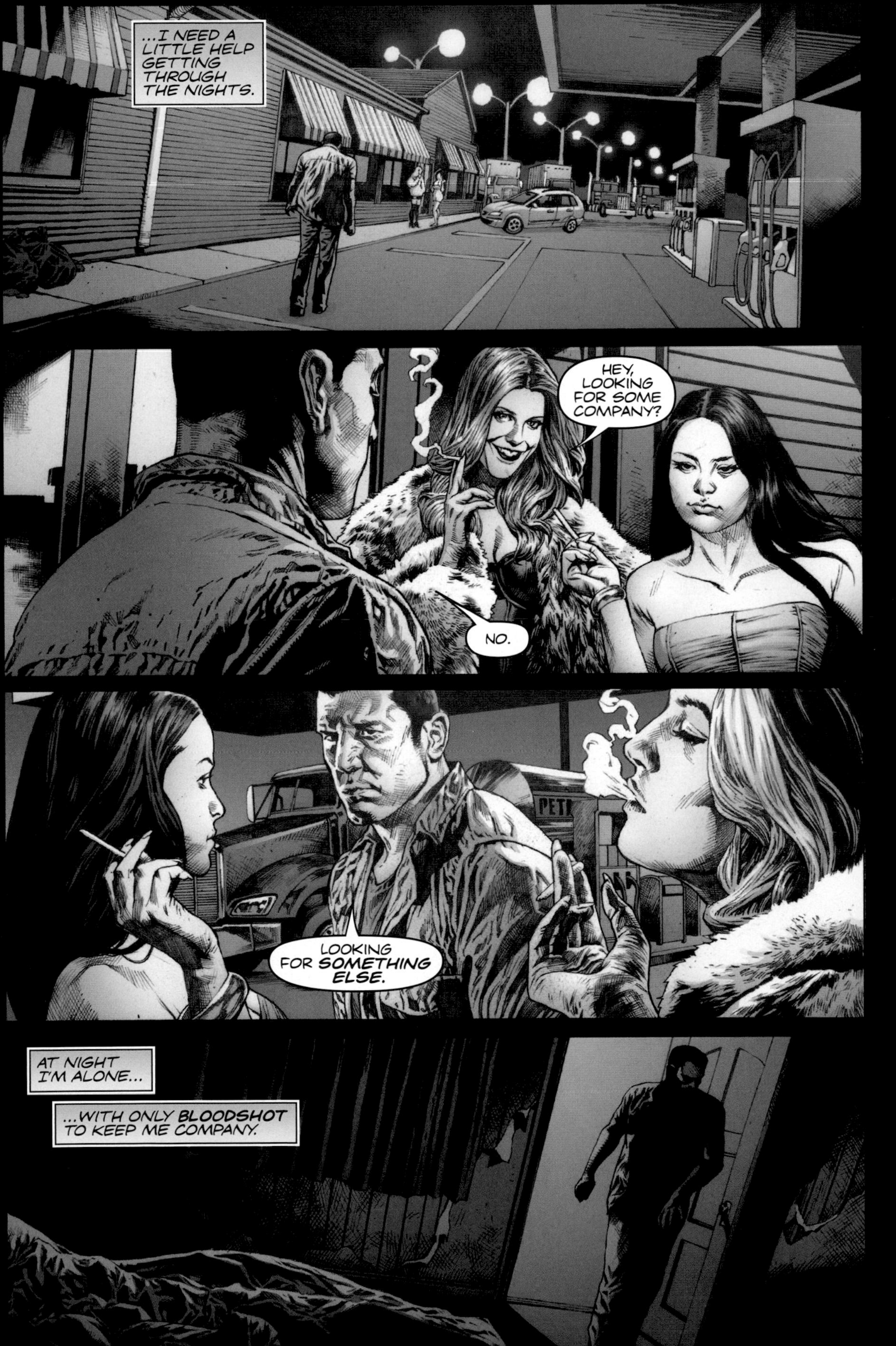
...I NEED A LITTLE HELP GETTING THROUGH THE NIGHTS.
HEY, LOOKING FOR SOME COMPANY?
NO.
LOOKING FOR **SOMETHING ELSE**.
AT NIGHT I'M ALONE...
...WITH ONLY **BLOODSHOT** TO KEEP ME COMPANY.

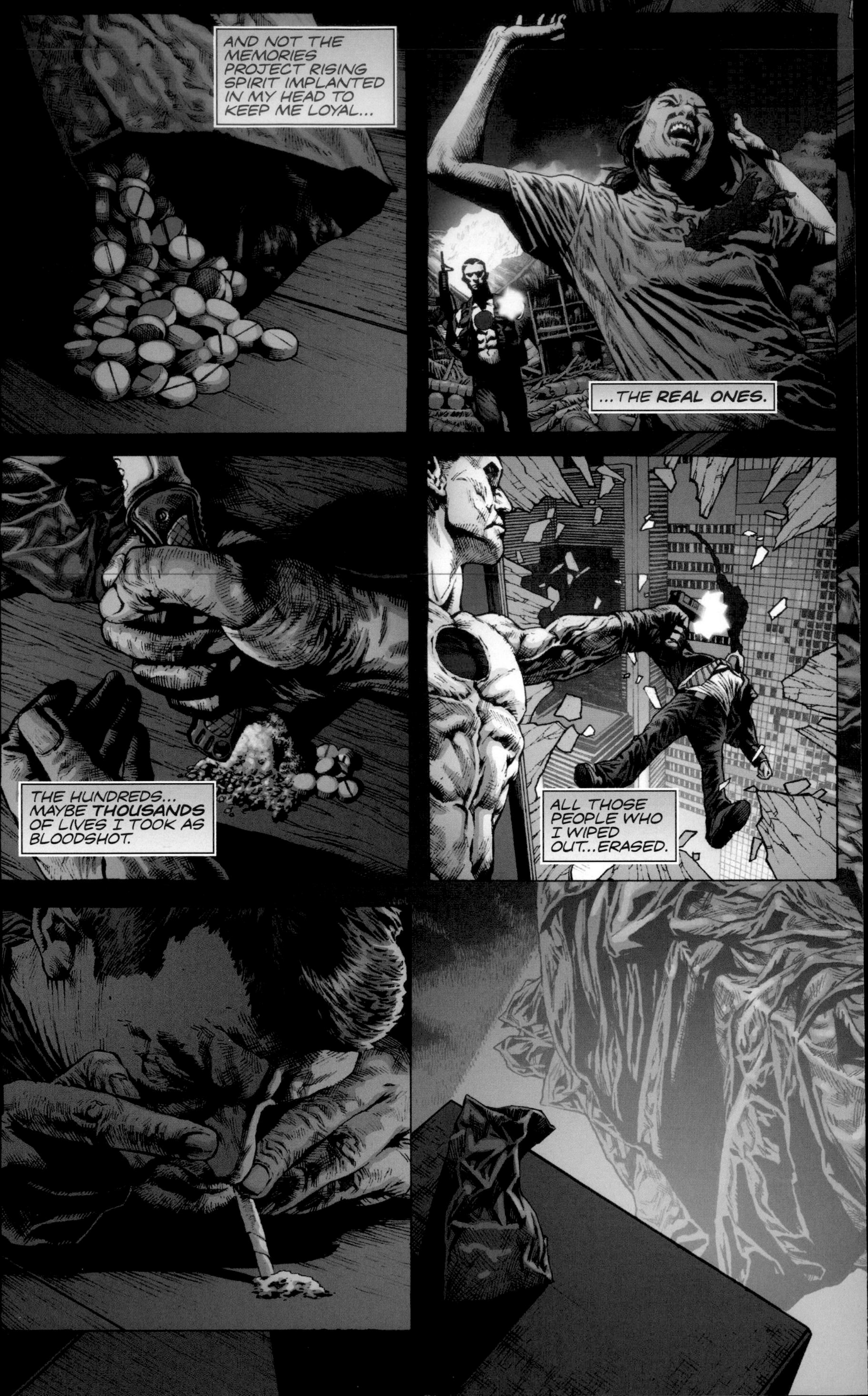
AND NOT THE MEMORIES PROJECT RISING SPIRIT IMPLANTED IN MY HEAD TO KEEP ME LOYAL...
...THE REAL ONES.
THE HUNDREDS... MAYBE THOUSANDS OF LIVES I TOOK AS BLOODSHOT.
ALL THOSE PEOPLE WHO I WIPED OUT...ERASED.

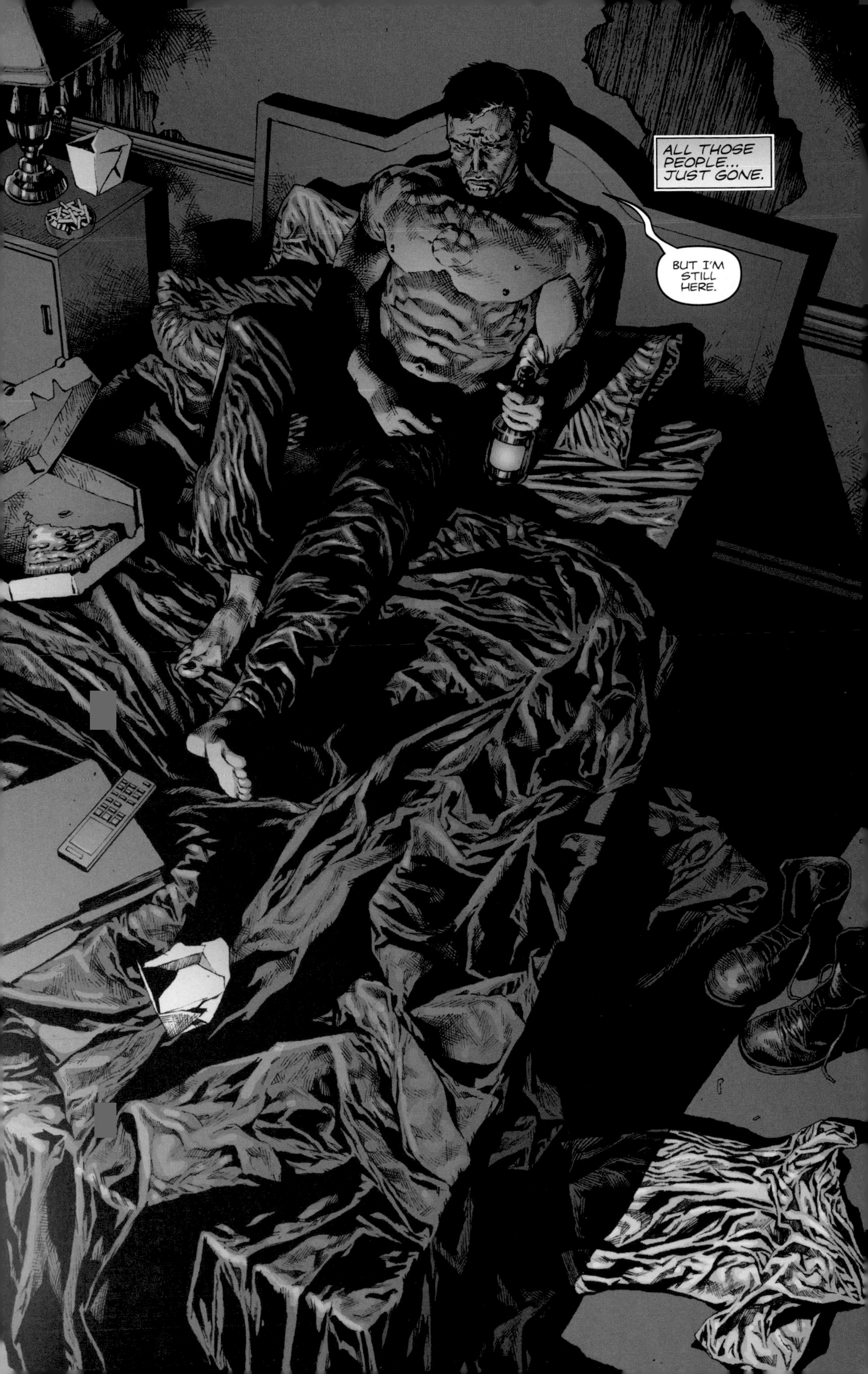
ALL THOSE PEOPLE... JUST GONE.
BUT I'M STILL HERE.

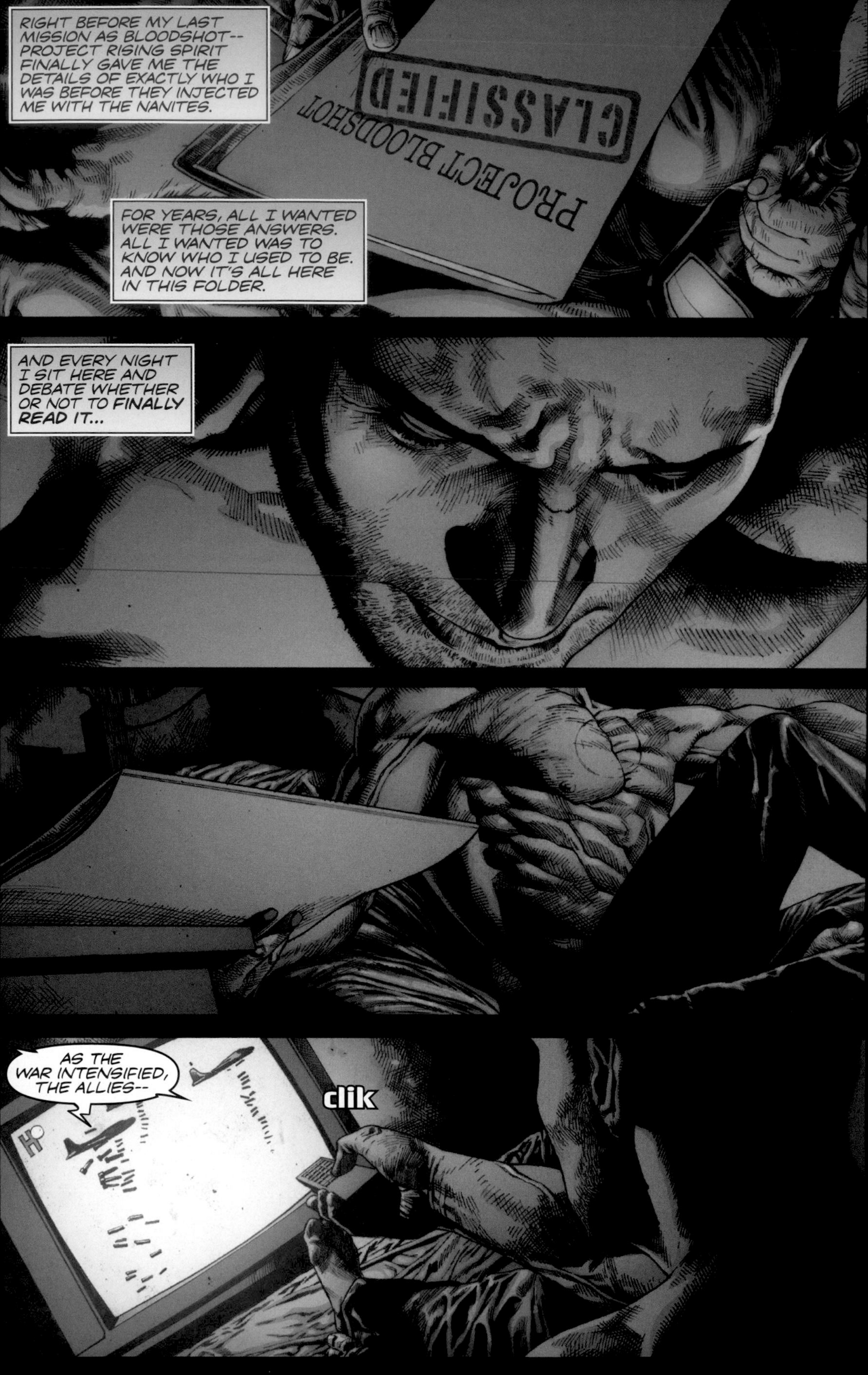
RIGHT BEFORE MY LAST MISSION AS BLOODSHOT-- PROJECT RISING SPIRIT FINALLY GAVE ME THE DETAILS OF EXACTLY WHO I WAS BEFORE THEY INJECTED ME WITH THE NANITES.
CLASSIFIED
PROJECT BLOODSHOT
FOR YEARS, ALL I WANTED WERE THOSE ANSWERS. ALL I WANTED WAS TO KNOW WHO I USED TO BE. AND NOW IT'S ALL HERE IN THIS FOLDER.
AND EVERY NIGHT I SIT HERE AND DEBATE WHETHER OR NOT TO FINALLY READ IT...
AS THE WAR INTENSIFIED, THE ALLIES--
clik

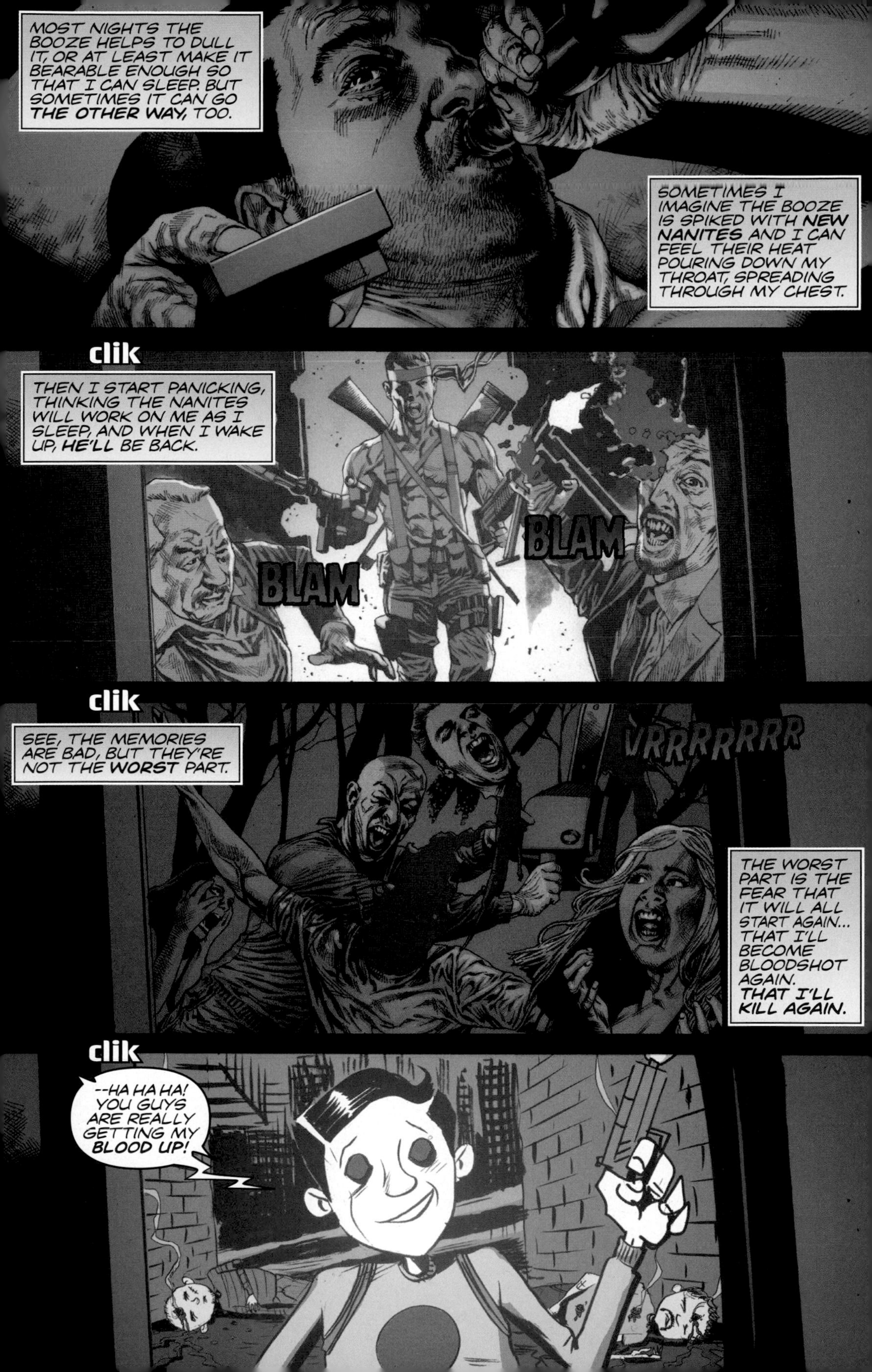

MOST NIGHTS THE BOOZE HELPS TO DULL IT, OR AT LEAST MAKE IT BEARABLE ENOUGH SO THAT I CAN SLEEP. BUT SOMETIMES IT CAN GO **THE OTHER WAY**, TOO.
SOMETIMES I IMAGINE THE BOOZE IS SPIKED WITH **NEW NANITES** AND I CAN FEEL THEIR HEAT POURING DOWN MY THROAT, SPREADING THROUGH MY CHEST.
clik
THEN I START PANICKING, THINKING THE NANITES WILL WORK ON ME AS I SLEEP, AND WHEN I WAKE UP, **HE'LL** BE BACK.
BLAM
BLAM
clik
SEE, THE MEMORIES ARE BAD, BUT THEY'RE NOT THE **WORST** PART.
VRRRRRRR
THE WORST PART IS THE FEAR THAT IT WILL ALL START AGAIN... THAT I'LL BECOME BLOODSHOT AGAIN. **THAT I'LL KILL AGAIN.**
clik
--HA HA HA! YOU GUYS ARE REALLY GETTING MY **BLOOD UP**!

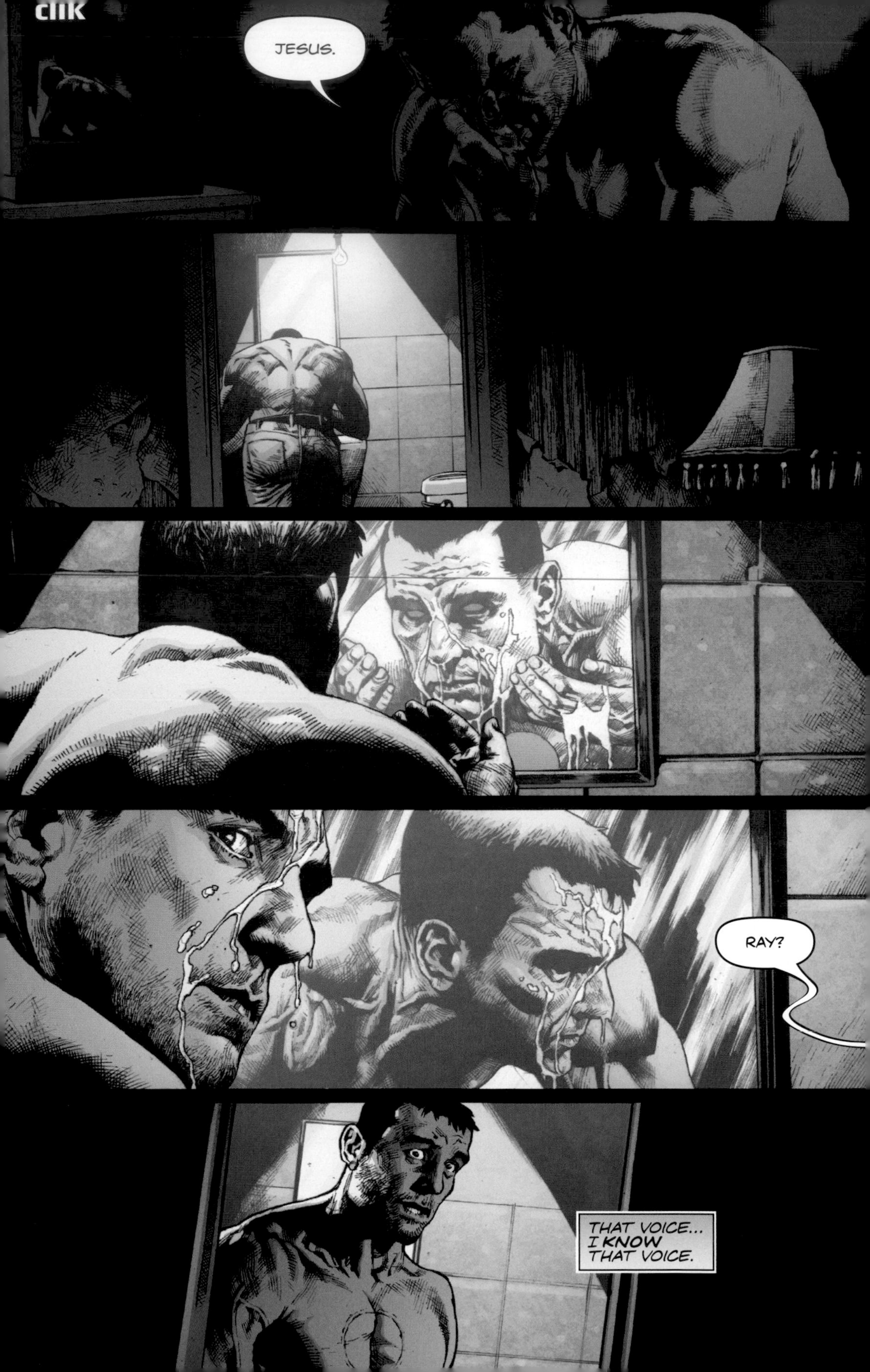
CLIK
JESUS.
RAY?
THAT VOICE... I KNOW THAT VOICE.

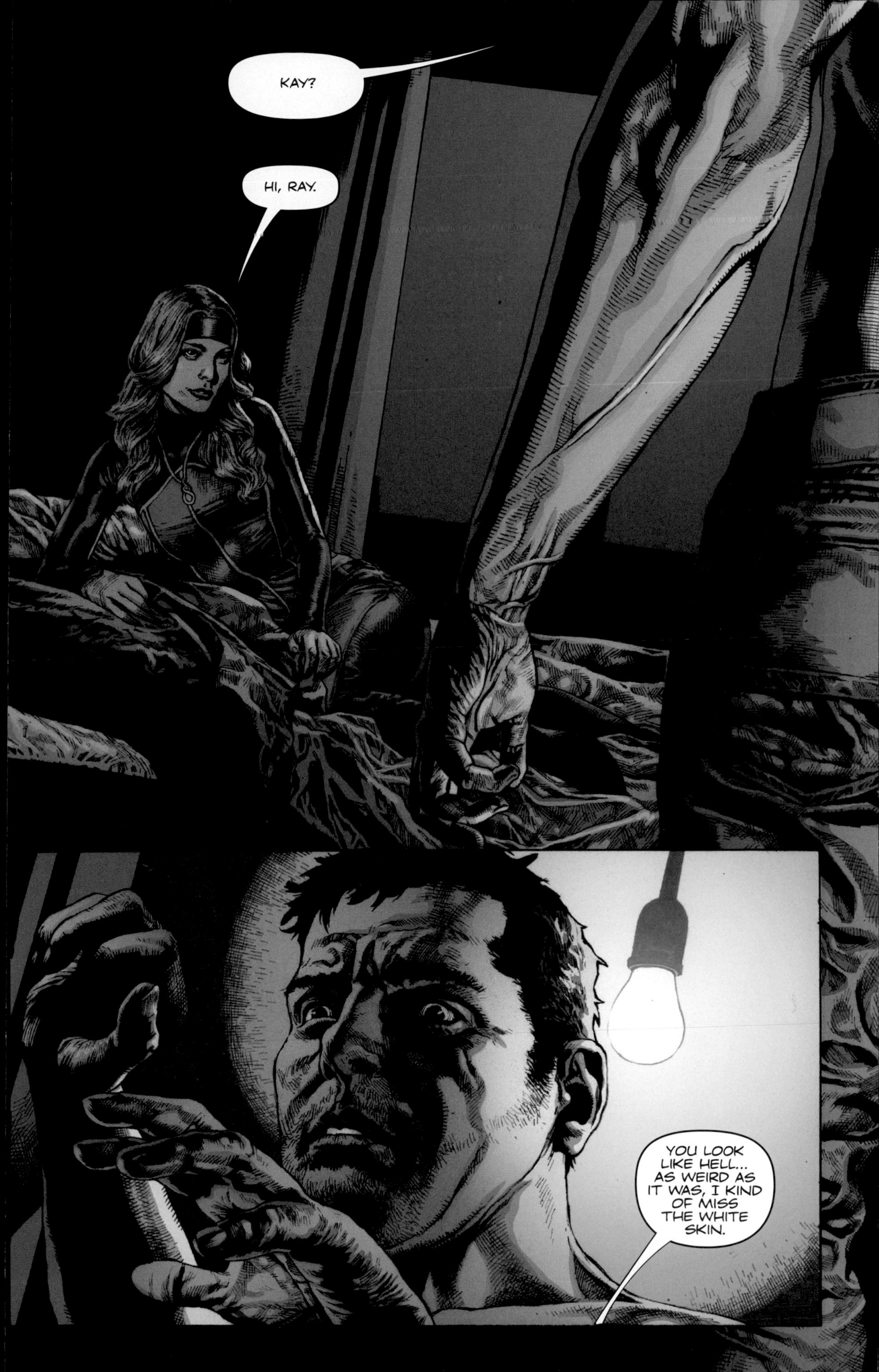
KAY?
HI, RAY.
YOU LOOK LIKE HELL... AS WEIRD AS IT WAS, I KIND OF MISS THE WHITE SKIN.

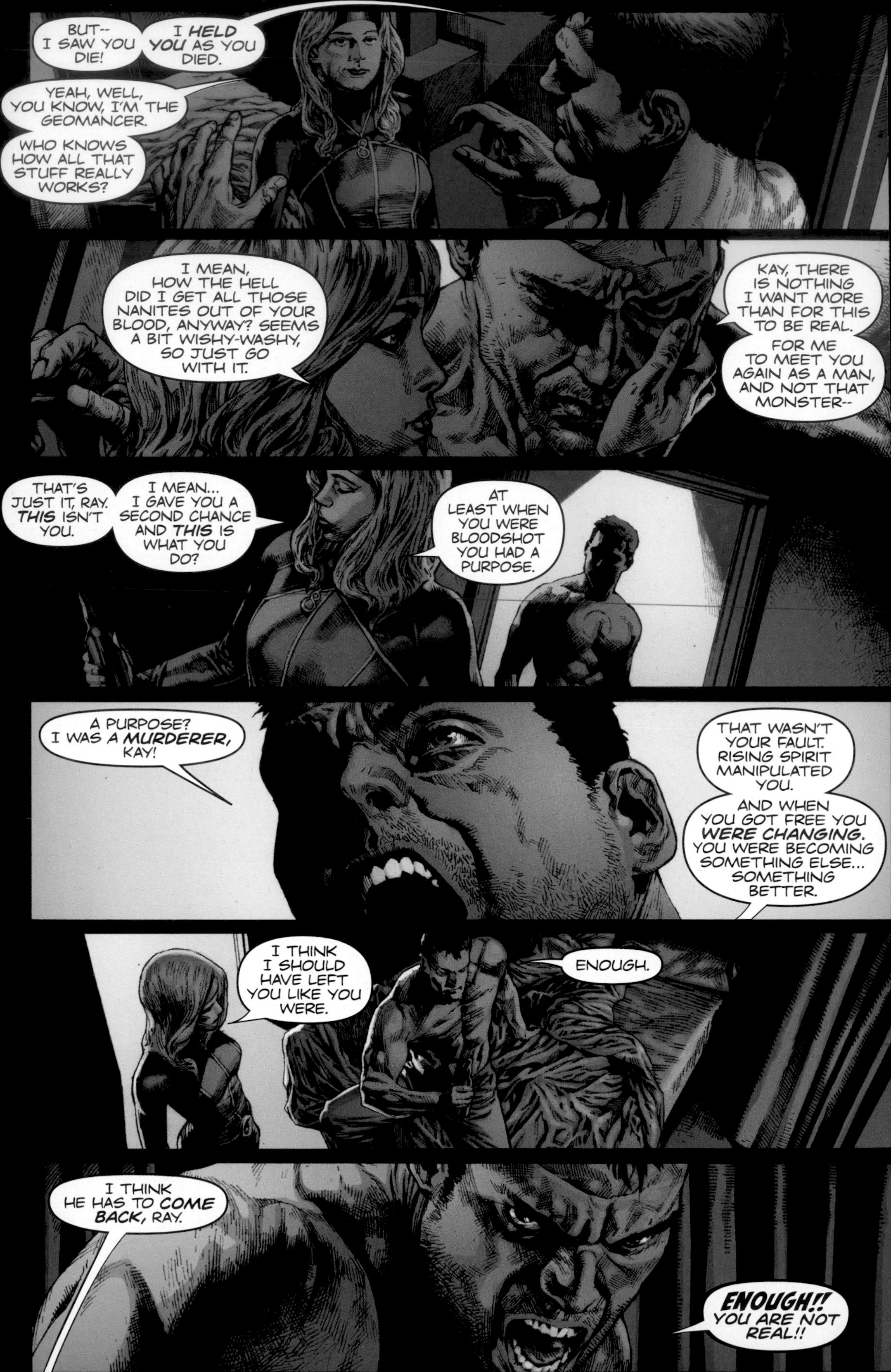
BUT-- I SAW YOU DIE!
I **HELD YOU** AS YOU DIED.
YEAH, WELL, YOU KNOW, I'M THE GEOMANCER.
WHO KNOWS HOW ALL THAT STUFF REALLY WORKS?
I MEAN, HOW THE HELL DID I GET ALL THOSE NANITES OUT OF YOUR BLOOD, ANYWAY? SEEMS A BIT WISHY-WASHY, SO JUST GO WITH IT.
KAY, THERE IS NOTHING I WANT MORE THAN FOR THIS TO BE REAL.
FOR ME TO MEET YOU AGAIN AS A MAN, AND NOT THAT MONSTER--
THAT'S JUST IT, RAY. **THIS** ISN'T YOU.
I MEAN... I GAVE YOU A SECOND CHANCE AND **THIS** IS WHAT YOU DO?
AT LEAST WHEN YOU WERE BLOODSHOT YOU HAD A PURPOSE.
A PURPOSE? I WAS A ***MURDERER,*** KAY!
THAT WASN'T YOUR FAULT. RISING SPIRIT MANIPULATED YOU.
AND WHEN YOU GOT FREE YOU **WERE CHANGING.** YOU WERE BECOMING SOMETHING ELSE... SOMETHING BETTER.
I THINK I SHOULD HAVE LEFT YOU LIKE YOU WERE.
ENOUGH.
I THINK HE HAS TO **COME BACK,** RAY.
ENOUGH!! YOU ARE NOT REAL!!

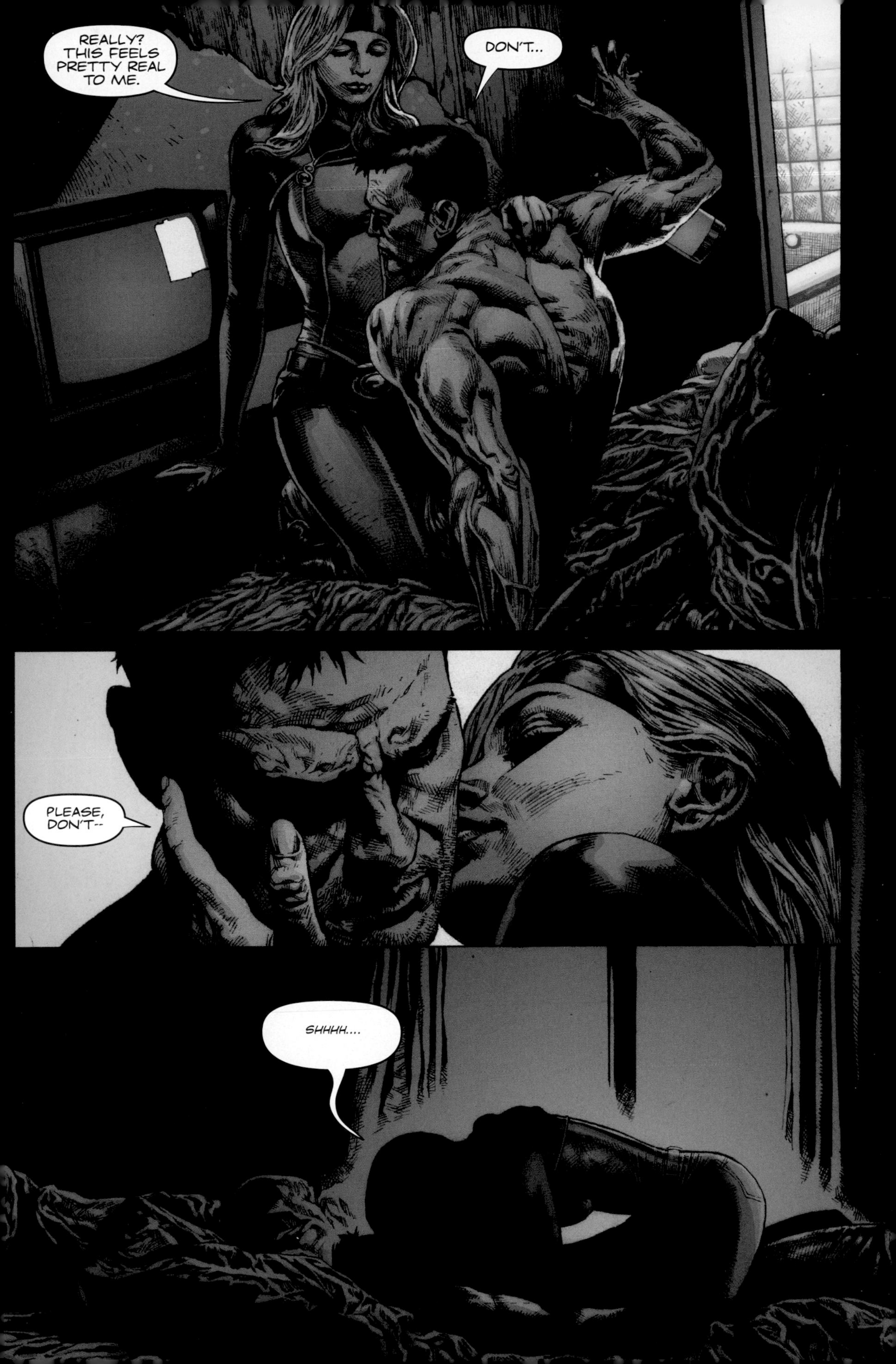
REALLY? THIS FEELS PRETTY REAL TO ME.
DON'T...
PLEASE, DON'T--
SHHHH....

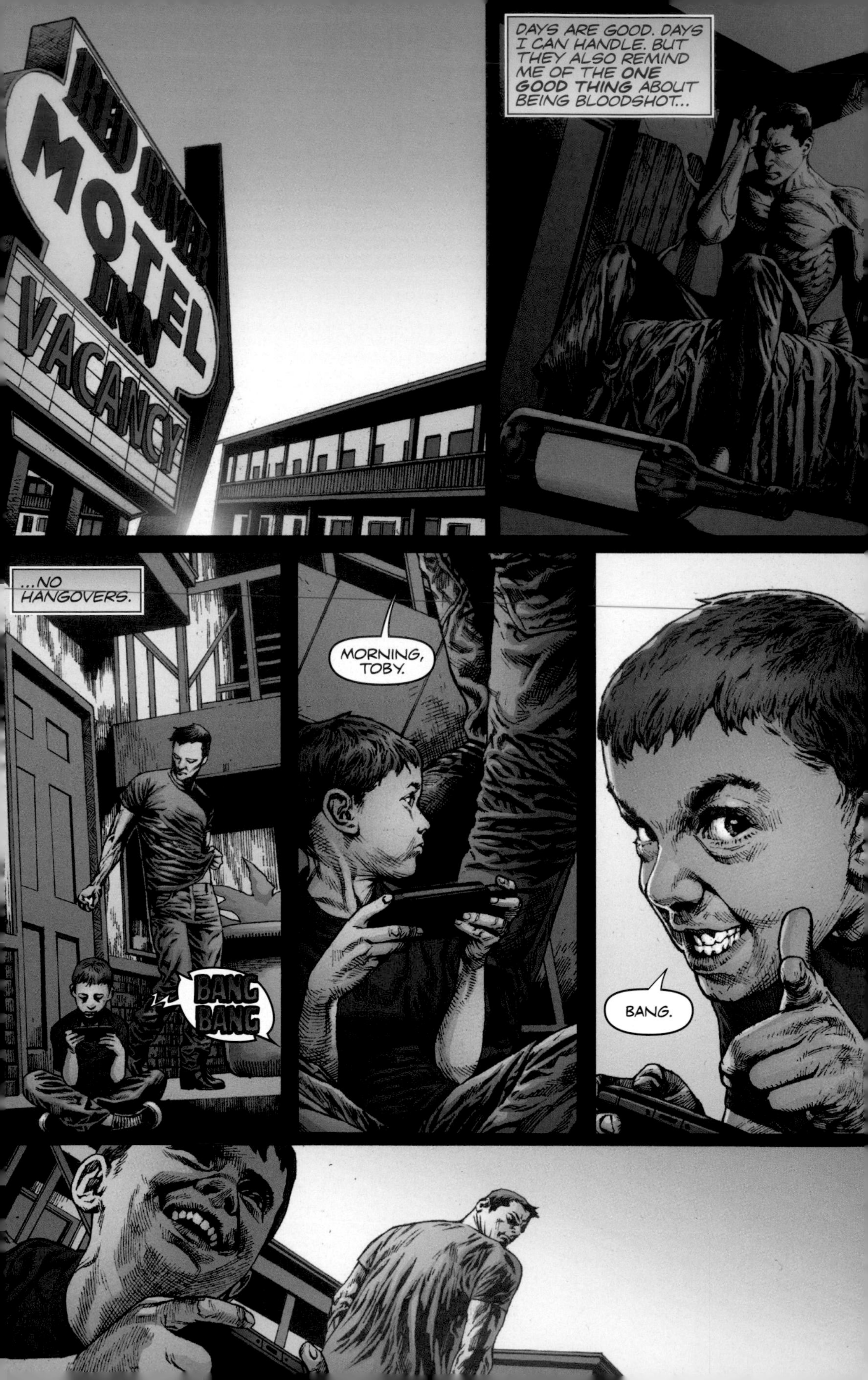
RED RIVER MOTEL INN
VACANCY
DAYS ARE GOOD. DAYS I CAN HANDLE. BUT THEY ALSO REMIND ME OF THE ONE GOOD THING ABOUT BEING BLOODSHOT...
...NO HANGOVERS.
BANG BANG
MORNING, TOBY.
BANG.

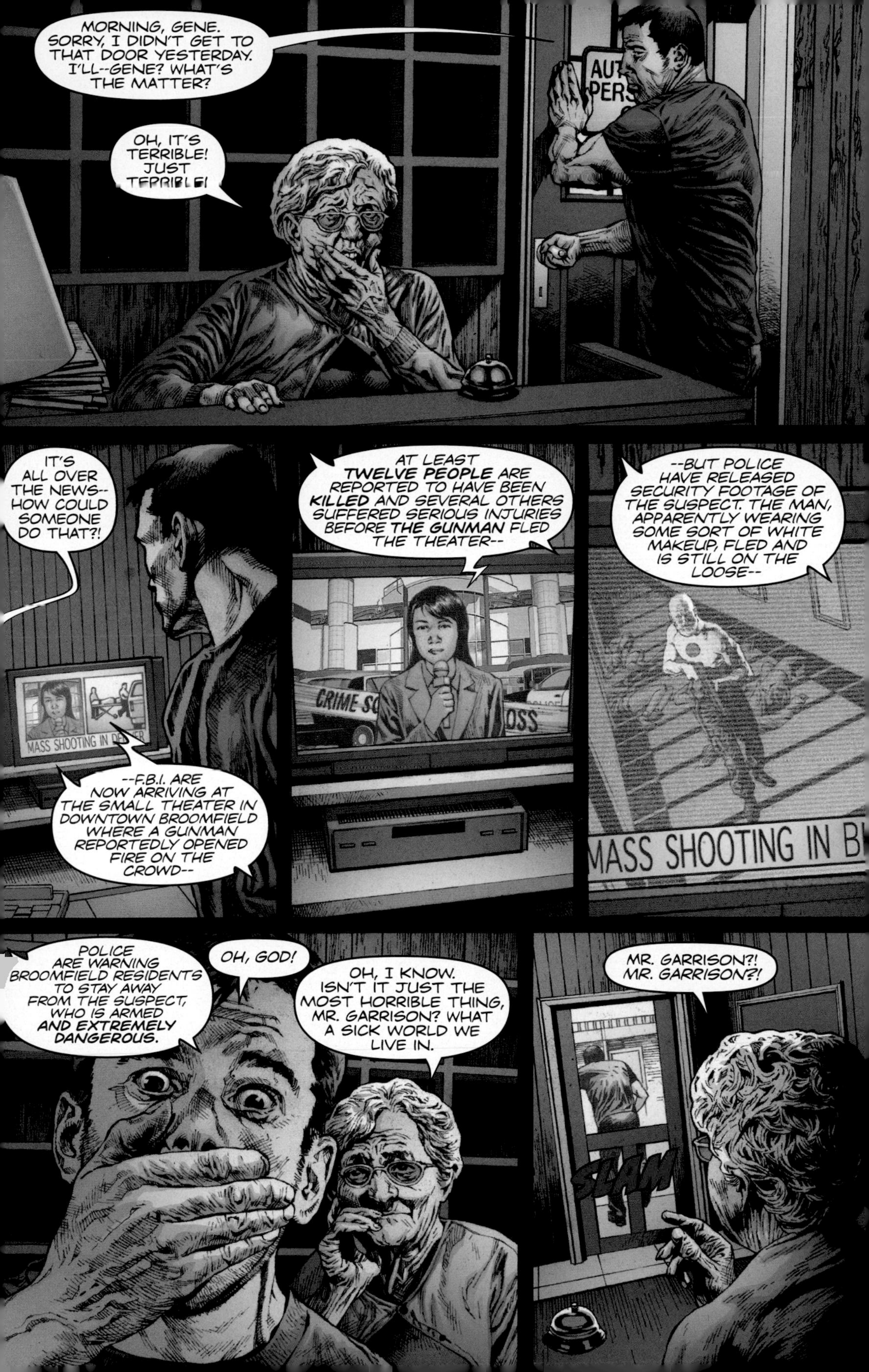
MORNING, GENE. SORRY, I DIDN'T GET TO THAT DOOR YESTERDAY. I'LL--GENE? WHAT'S THE MATTER?
OH, IT'S TERRIBLE! JUST TERRIBLE!
IT'S ALL OVER THE NEWS-- HOW COULD SOMEONE DO THAT?!
MASS SHOOTING IN DE
--F.B.I. ARE NOW ARRIVING AT THE SMALL THEATER IN DOWNTOWN BROOMFIELD WHERE A GUNMAN REPORTEDLY OPENED FIRE ON THE CROWD--
AT LEAST **TWELVE PEOPLE** ARE REPORTED TO HAVE BEEN **KILLED** AND SEVERAL OTHERS SUFFERED SERIOUS INJURIES BEFORE **THE GUNMAN** FLED THE THEATER--
--BUT POLICE HAVE RELEASED SECURITY FOOTAGE OF THE SUSPECT. THE MAN, APPARENTLY WEARING SOME SORT OF WHITE MAKEUP, FLED AND IS STILL ON THE LOOSE--
MASS SHOOTING IN B
POLICE ARE WARNING BROOMFIELD RESIDENTS TO STAY AWAY FROM THE SUSPECT, WHO IS ARMED **AND EXTREMELY DANGEROUS.**
OH, GOD!
OH, I KNOW. ISN'T IT JUST THE MOST HORRIBLE THING, MR. GARRISON? WHAT A SICK WORLD WE LIVE IN.
MR. GARRISON?! MR. GARRISON?!
SLAM

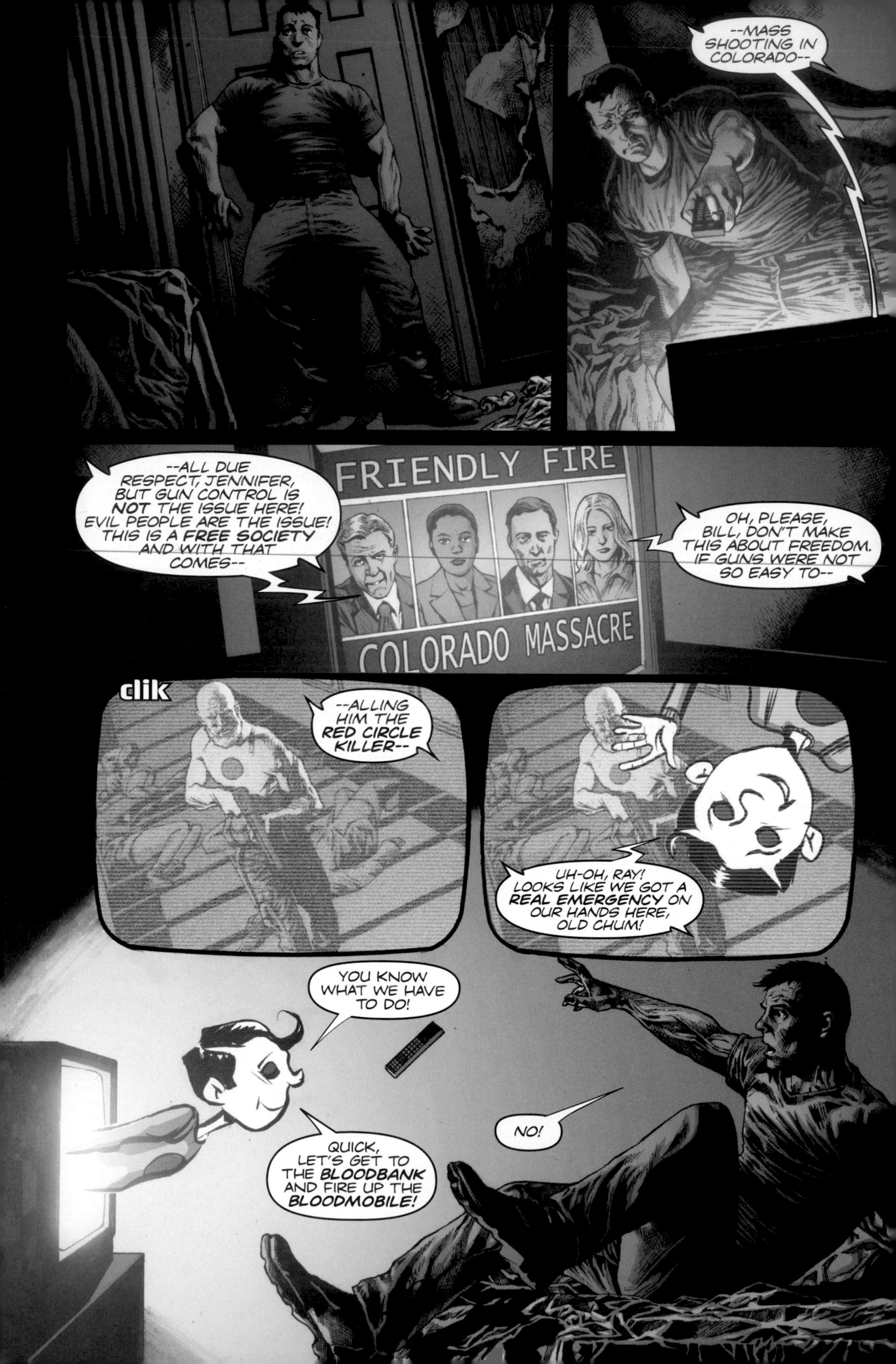

--MASS SHOOTING IN COLORADO--
--ALL DUE RESPECT, JENNIFER, BUT GUN CONTROL IS **NOT** THE ISSUE HERE! EVIL PEOPLE ARE THE ISSUE! THIS IS A **FREE SOCIETY** AND WITH THAT COMES--
FRIENDLY FIRE
COLORADO MASSACRE
OH, PLEASE, BILL, DON'T MAKE THIS ABOUT FREEDOM. IF GUNS WERE NOT SO EASY TO--
clik
--ALLING HIM THE **RED CIRCLE KILLER**--
UH-OH, RAY! LOOKS LIKE WE GOT A **REAL EMERGENCY** ON OUR HANDS HERE, OLD CHUM!
YOU KNOW WHAT WE HAVE TO DO!
QUICK, LET'S GET TO THE **BLOODBANK** AND FIRE UP THE **BLOODMOBILE!**
NO!

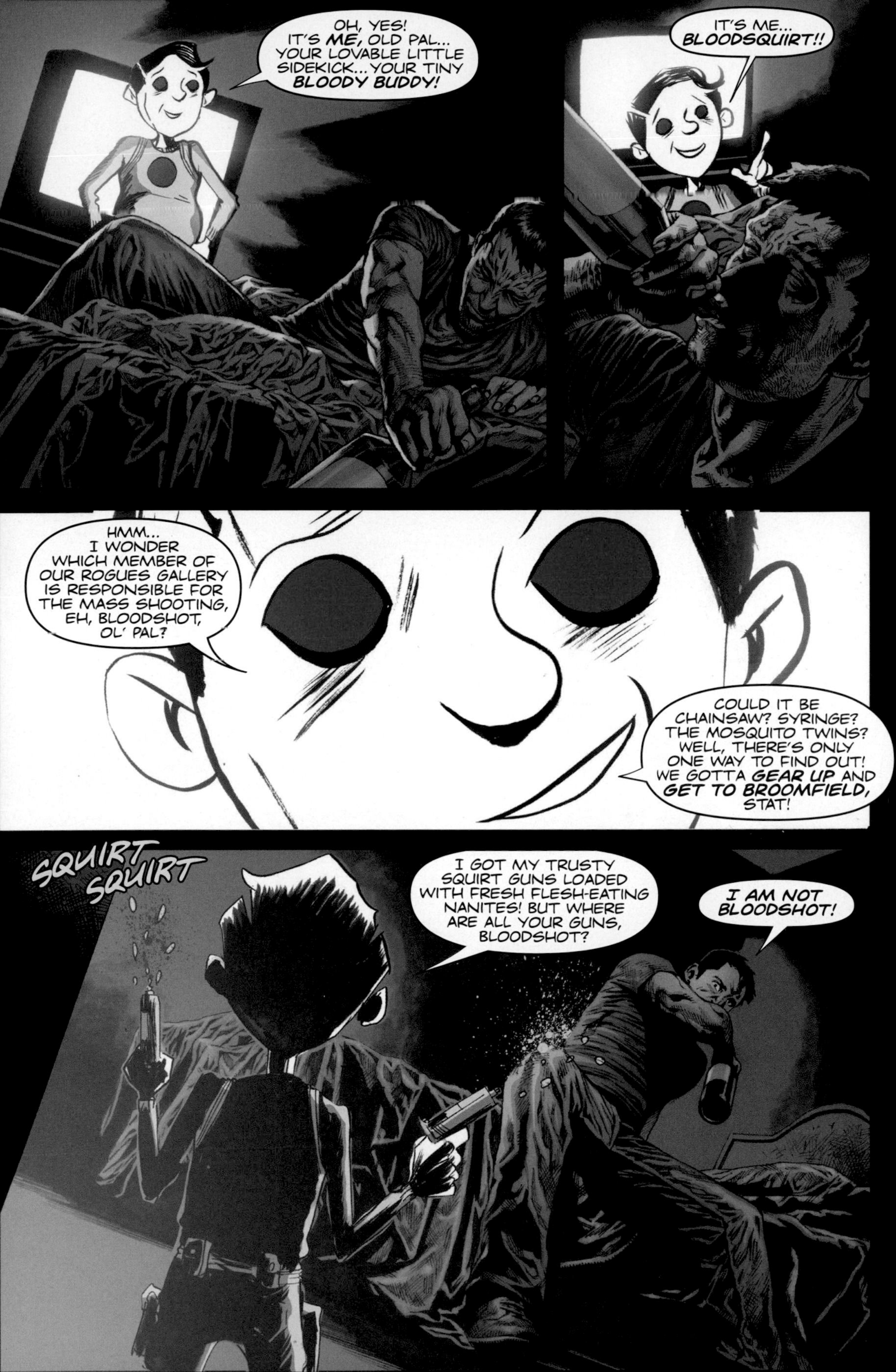
OH, YES! IT'S ME, OLD PAL... YOUR LOVABLE LITTLE SIDEKICK...YOUR TINY BLOODY BUDDY!
IT'S ME... BLOODSQUIRT!!
HMM... I WONDER WHICH MEMBER OF OUR ROGUES GALLERY IS RESPONSIBLE FOR THE MASS SHOOTING, EH, BLOODSHOT, OL' PAL?
COULD IT BE CHAINSAW? SYRINGE? THE MOSQUITO TWINS? WELL, THERE'S ONLY ONE WAY TO FIND OUT! WE GOTTA GEAR UP AND GET TO BROOMFIELD, STAT!
SQUIRT SQUIRT
I GOT MY TRUSTY SQUIRT GUNS LOADED WITH FRESH FLESH-EATING NANITES! BUT WHERE ARE ALL YOUR GUNS, BLOODSHOT?
I AM NOT BLOODSHOT!

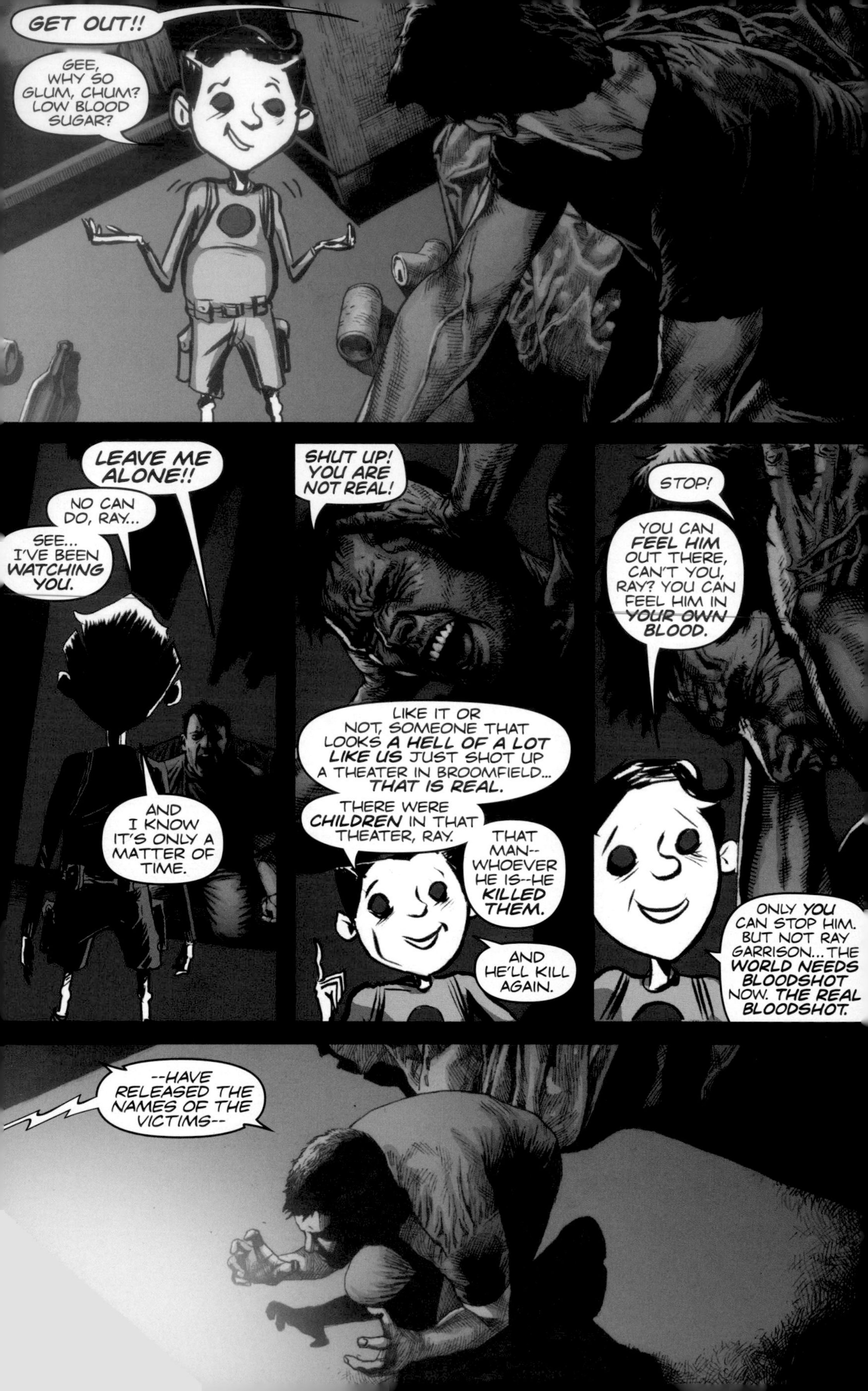
GET OUT!!
GEE, WHY SO GLUM, CHUM? LOW BLOOD SUGAR?
LEAVE ME ALONE!!
NO CAN DO, RAY...
SEE... I'VE BEEN WATCHING YOU.
AND I KNOW IT'S ONLY A MATTER OF TIME.
SHUT UP! YOU ARE NOT REAL!
LIKE IT OR NOT, SOMEONE THAT LOOKS A HELL OF A LOT LIKE US JUST SHOT UP A THEATER IN BROOMFIELD... THAT IS REAL.
THERE WERE CHILDREN IN THAT THEATER, RAY.
THAT MAN--WHOEVER HE IS--HE KILLED THEM.
AND HE'LL KILL AGAIN.
STOP!
YOU CAN FEEL HIM OUT THERE, CAN'T YOU, RAY? YOU CAN FEEL HIM IN YOUR OWN BLOOD.
ONLY YOU CAN STOP HIM. BUT NOT RAY GARRISON... THE WORLD NEEDS BLOODSHOT NOW. THE REAL BLOODSHOT.
--HAVE RELEASED THE NAMES OF THE VICTIMS--

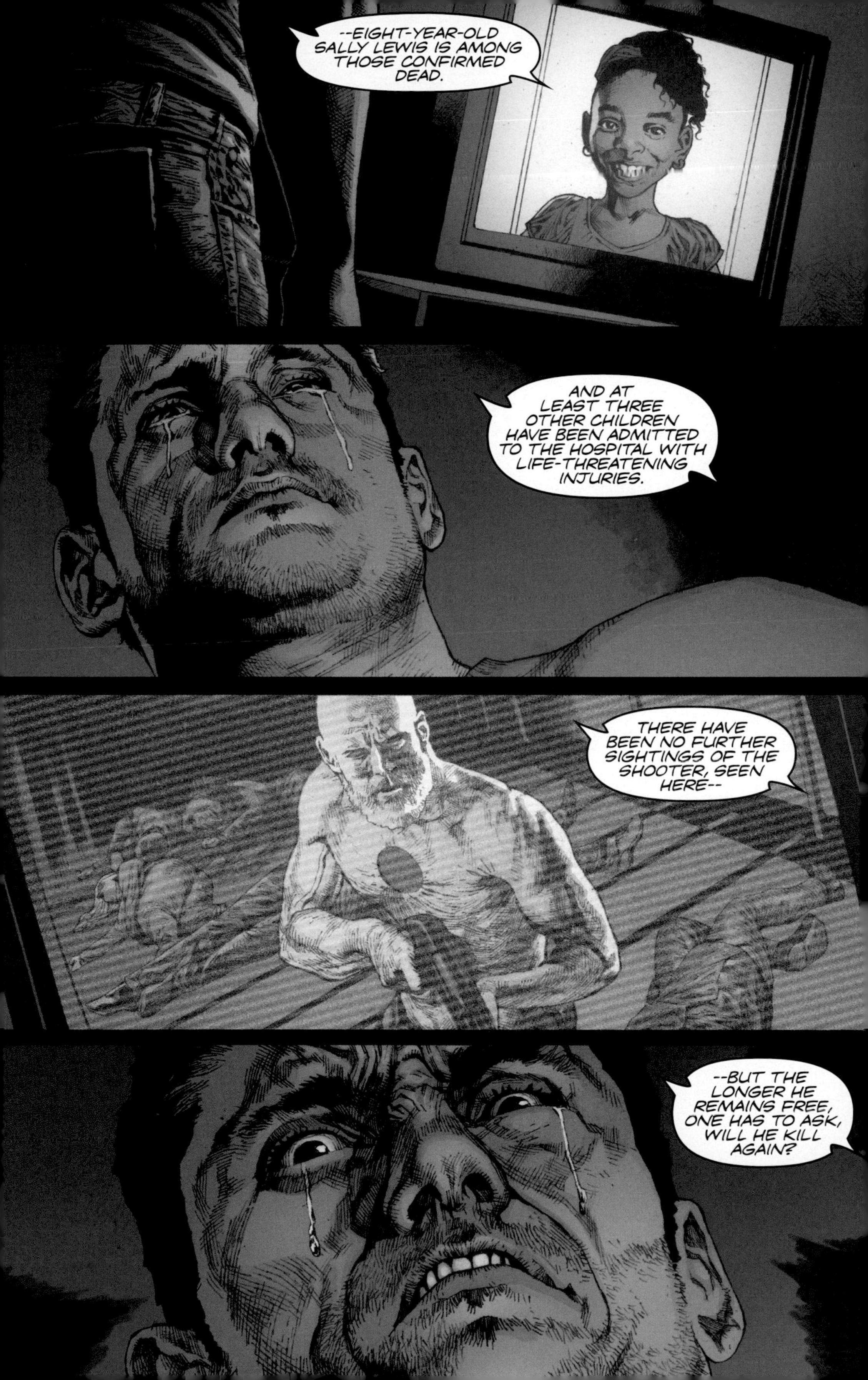
--EIGHT-YEAR-OLD SALLY LEWIS IS AMONG THOSE CONFIRMED DEAD.
AND AT LEAST THREE OTHER CHILDREN HAVE BEEN ADMITTED TO THE HOSPITAL WITH LIFE-THREATENING INJURIES.
THERE HAVE BEEN NO FURTHER SIGHTINGS OF THE SHOOTER, SEEN HERE--
--BUT THE LONGER HE REMAINS FREE, ONE HAS TO ASK, WILL HE KILL AGAIN?

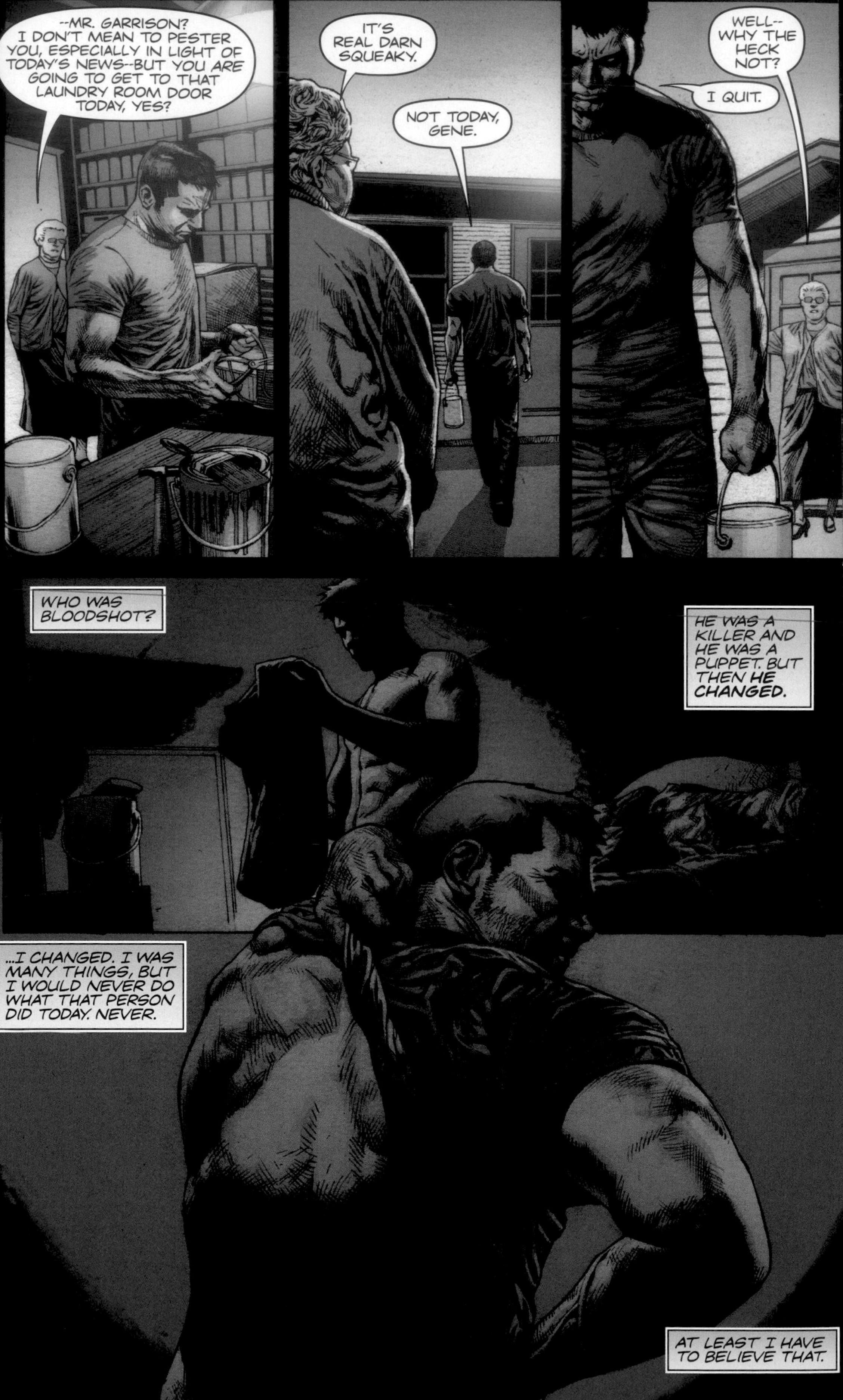
--MR. GARRISON? I DON'T MEAN TO PESTER YOU, ESPECIALLY IN LIGHT OF TODAY'S NEWS--BUT YOU ARE GOING TO GET TO THAT LAUNDRY ROOM DOOR TODAY, YES?
IT'S REAL DARN SQUEAKY.
NOT TODAY, GENE.
WELL-- WHY THE HECK NOT?
I QUIT.
WHO WAS BLOODSHOT?
HE WAS A KILLER AND HE WAS A PUPPET. BUT THEN HE CHANGED.
...I CHANGED. I WAS MANY THINGS, BUT I WOULD NEVER DO WHAT THAT PERSON DID TODAY. NEVER.
AT LEAST I HAVE TO BELIEVE THAT.

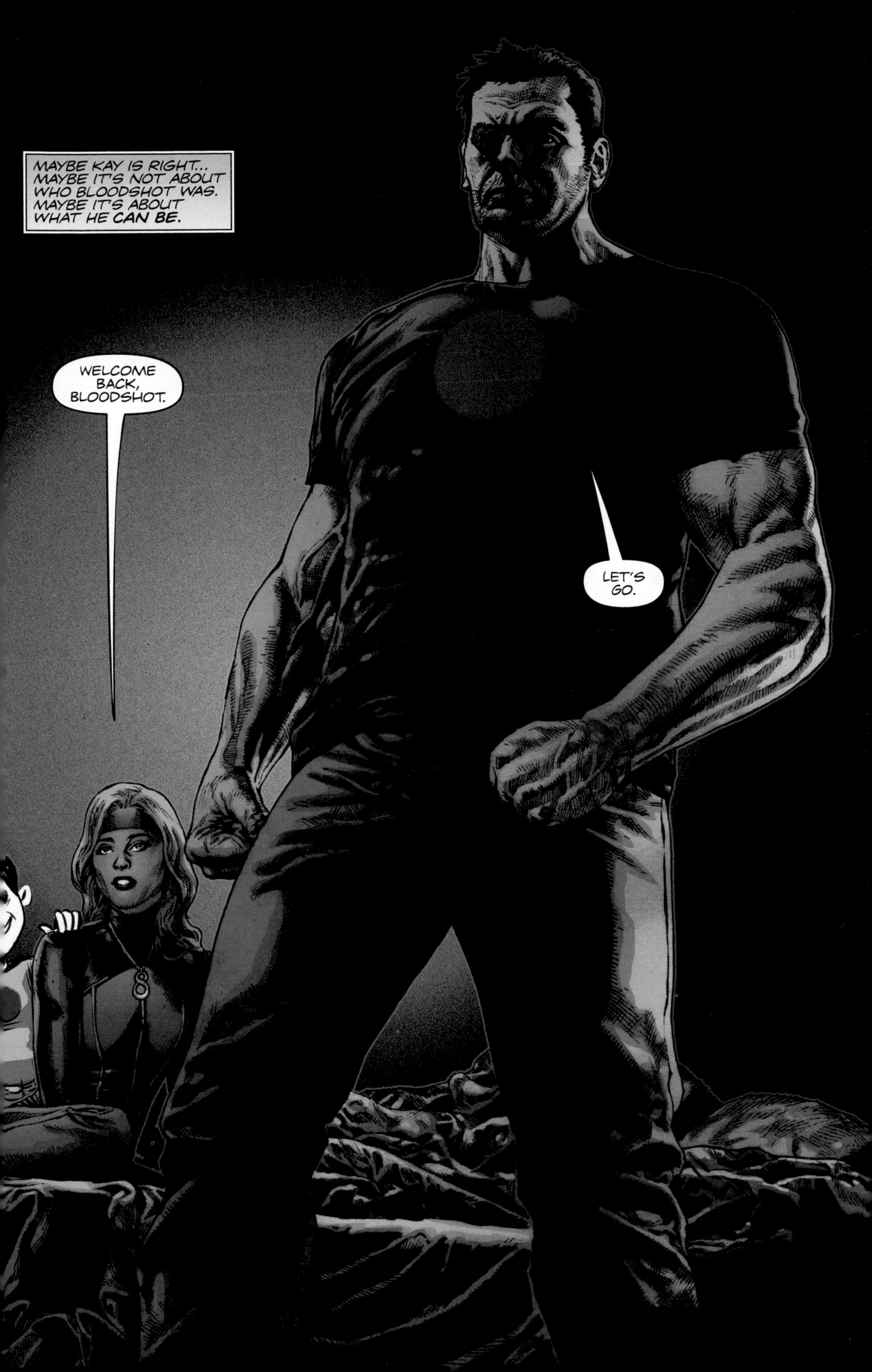
MAYBE KAY IS RIGHT... MAYBE IT'S NOT ABOUT WHO BLOODSHOT WAS. MAYBE IT'S ABOUT WHAT HE CAN BE.
WELCOME BACK, BLOODSHOT.
LET'S GO.

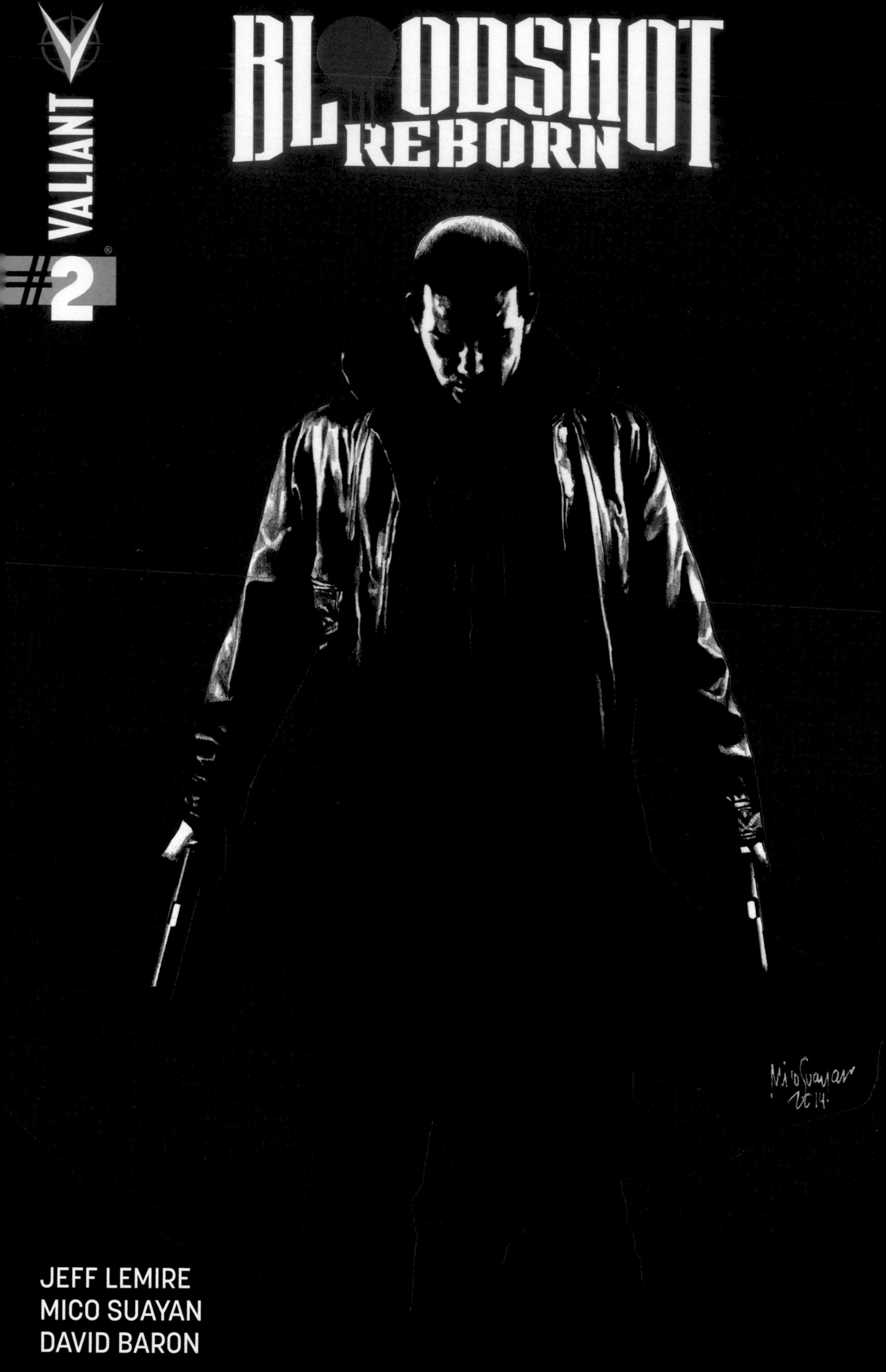
VALIANT
#2
BLOODSHOT
REBORN
JEFF LEMIRE
MICO SUAYAN
DAVID BARON

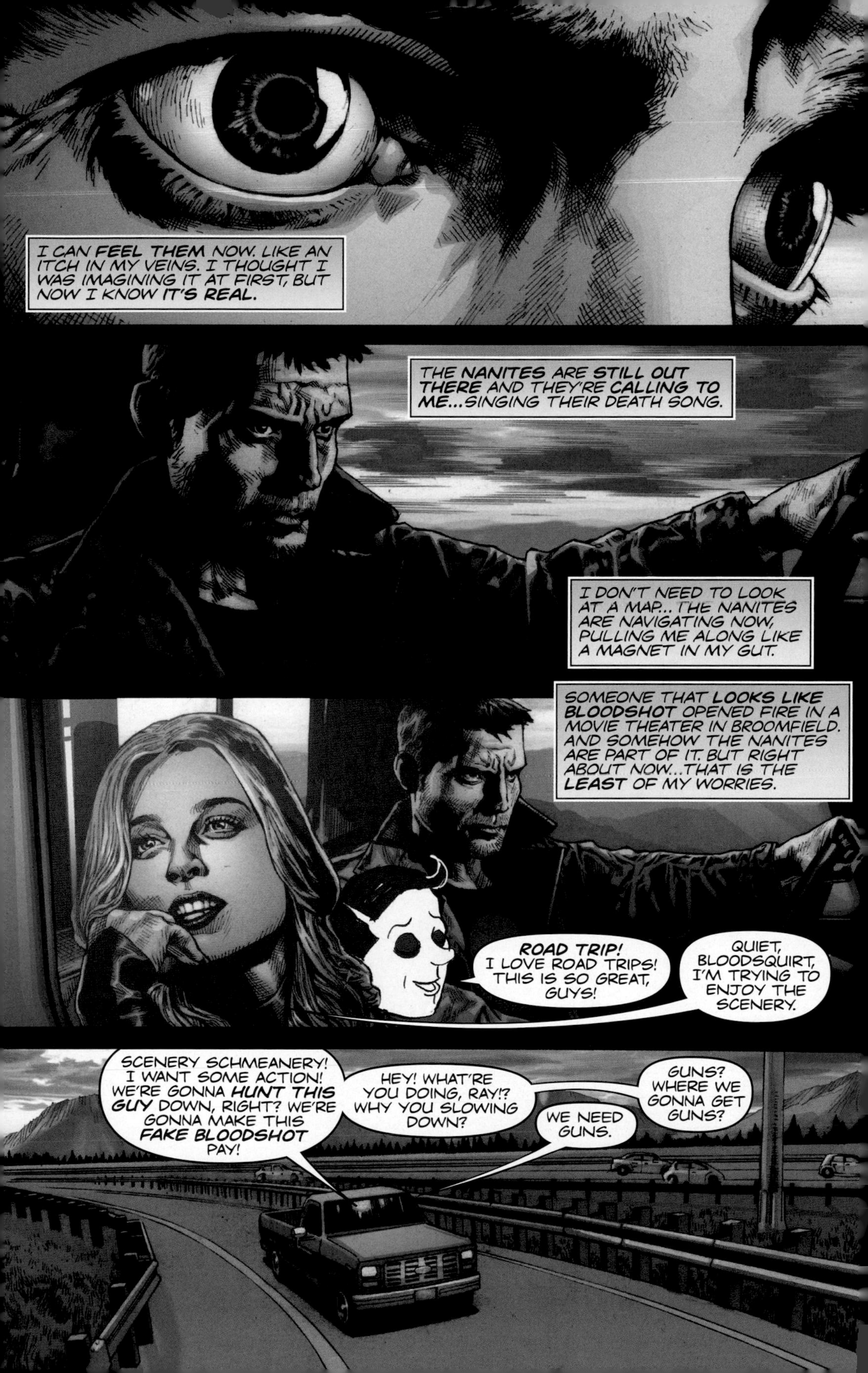
I CAN FEEL THEM NOW. LIKE AN ITCH IN MY VEINS. I THOUGHT I WAS IMAGINING IT AT FIRST, BUT NOW I KNOW IT'S REAL.
THE NANITES ARE STILL OUT THERE AND THEY'RE CALLING TO ME...SINGING THEIR DEATH SONG.
I DON'T NEED TO LOOK AT A MAP... THE NANITES ARE NAVIGATING NOW, PULLING ME ALONG LIKE A MAGNET IN MY GUT.
SOMEONE THAT LOOKS LIKE BLOODSHOT OPENED FIRE IN A MOVIE THEATER IN BROOMFIELD. AND SOMEHOW THE NANITES ARE PART OF IT. BUT RIGHT ABOUT NOW...THAT IS THE LEAST OF MY WORRIES.
ROAD TRIP! I LOVE ROAD TRIPS! THIS IS SO GREAT, GUYS!
QUIET, BLOODSQUIRT, I'M TRYING TO ENJOY THE SCENERY.
SCENERY SCHMEANERY! I WANT SOME ACTION! WE'RE GONNA HUNT THIS GUY DOWN, RIGHT? WE'RE GONNA MAKE THIS FAKE BLOODSHOT PAY!
HEY! WHAT'RE YOU DOING, RAY!? WHY YOU SLOWING DOWN?
WE NEED GUNS.
GUNS? WHERE WE GONNA GET GUNS?

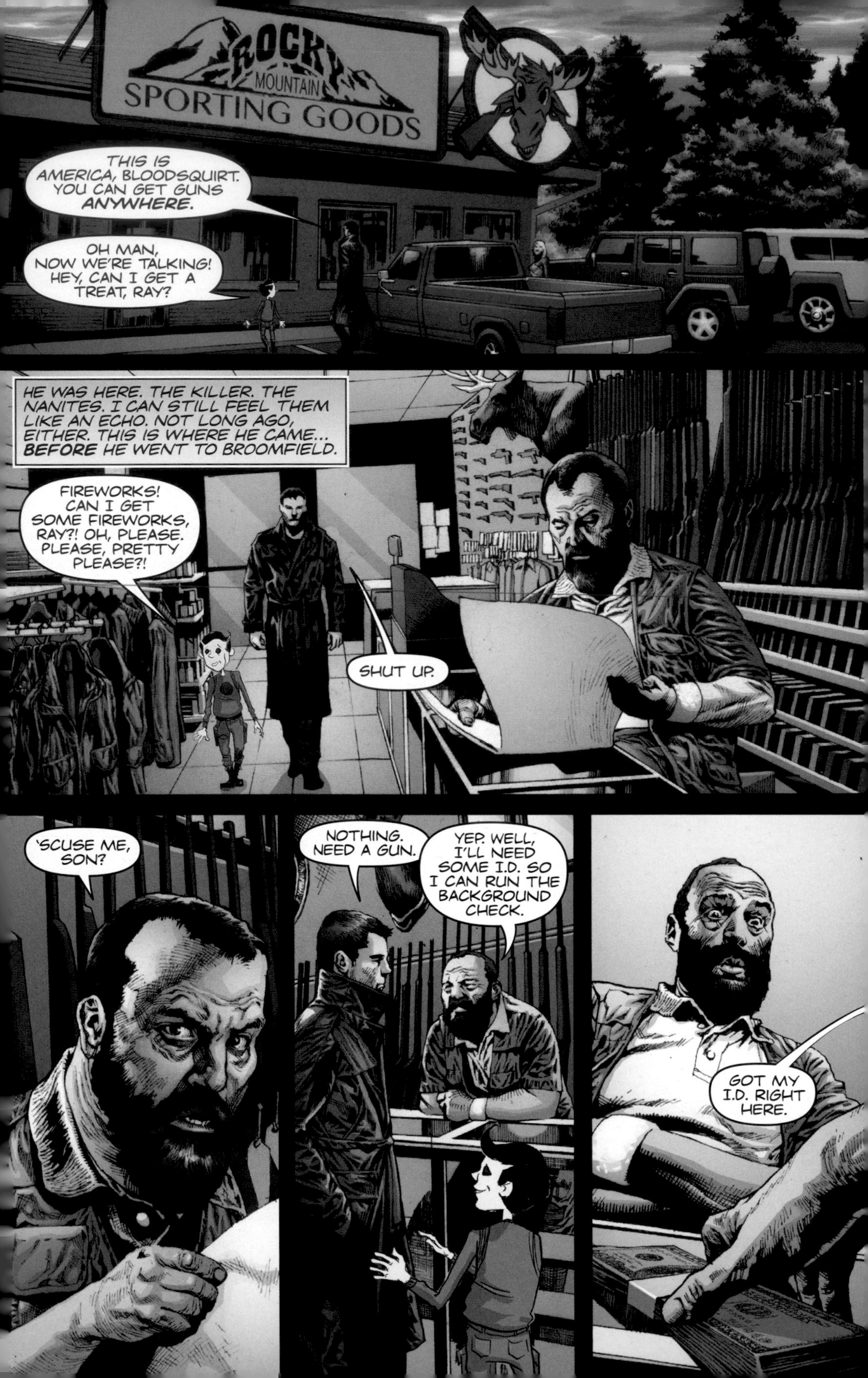
ROCKY MOUNTAIN SPORTING GOODS
THIS IS AMERICA, BLOODSQUIRT. YOU CAN GET GUNS ANYWHERE.
OH MAN, NOW WE'RE TALKING! HEY, CAN I GET A TREAT, RAY?
HE WAS HERE. THE KILLER. THE NANITES. I CAN STILL FEEL THEM LIKE AN ECHO. NOT LONG AGO, EITHER. THIS IS WHERE HE CAME... BEFORE HE WENT TO BROOMFIELD.
FIREWORKS! CAN I GET SOME FIREWORKS, RAY?! OH, PLEASE. PLEASE, PRETTY PLEASE?!
SHUT UP.
'SCUSE ME, SON?
NOTHING. NEED A GUN.
YEP. WELL, I'LL NEED SOME I.D. SO I CAN RUN THE BACKGROUND CHECK.
GOT MY I.D. RIGHT HERE.

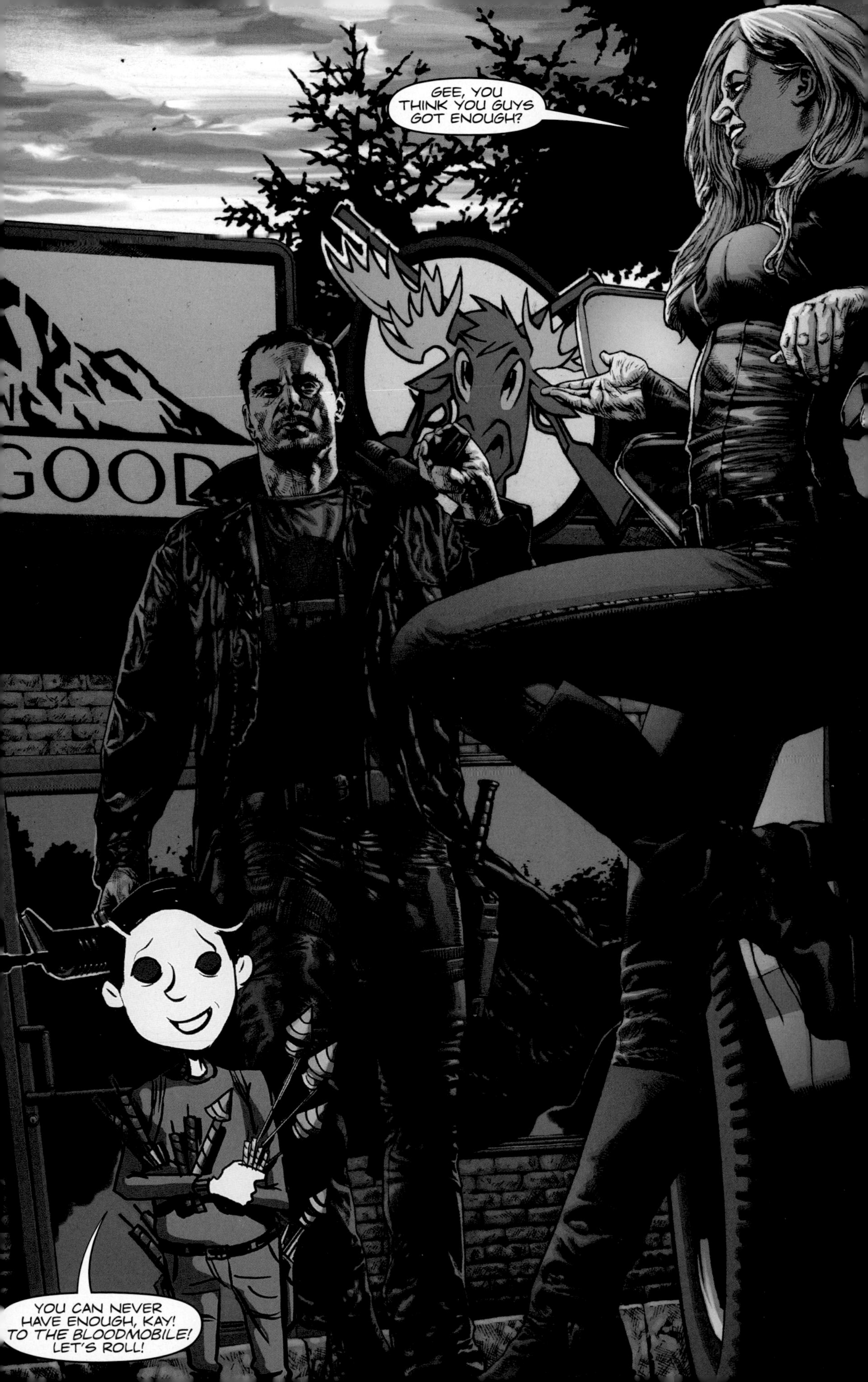
GOOD
GEE, YOU THINK YOU GUYS GOT ENOUGH?
YOU CAN NEVER HAVE ENOUGH, KAY! TO THE BLOODMOBILE! LET'S ROLL!

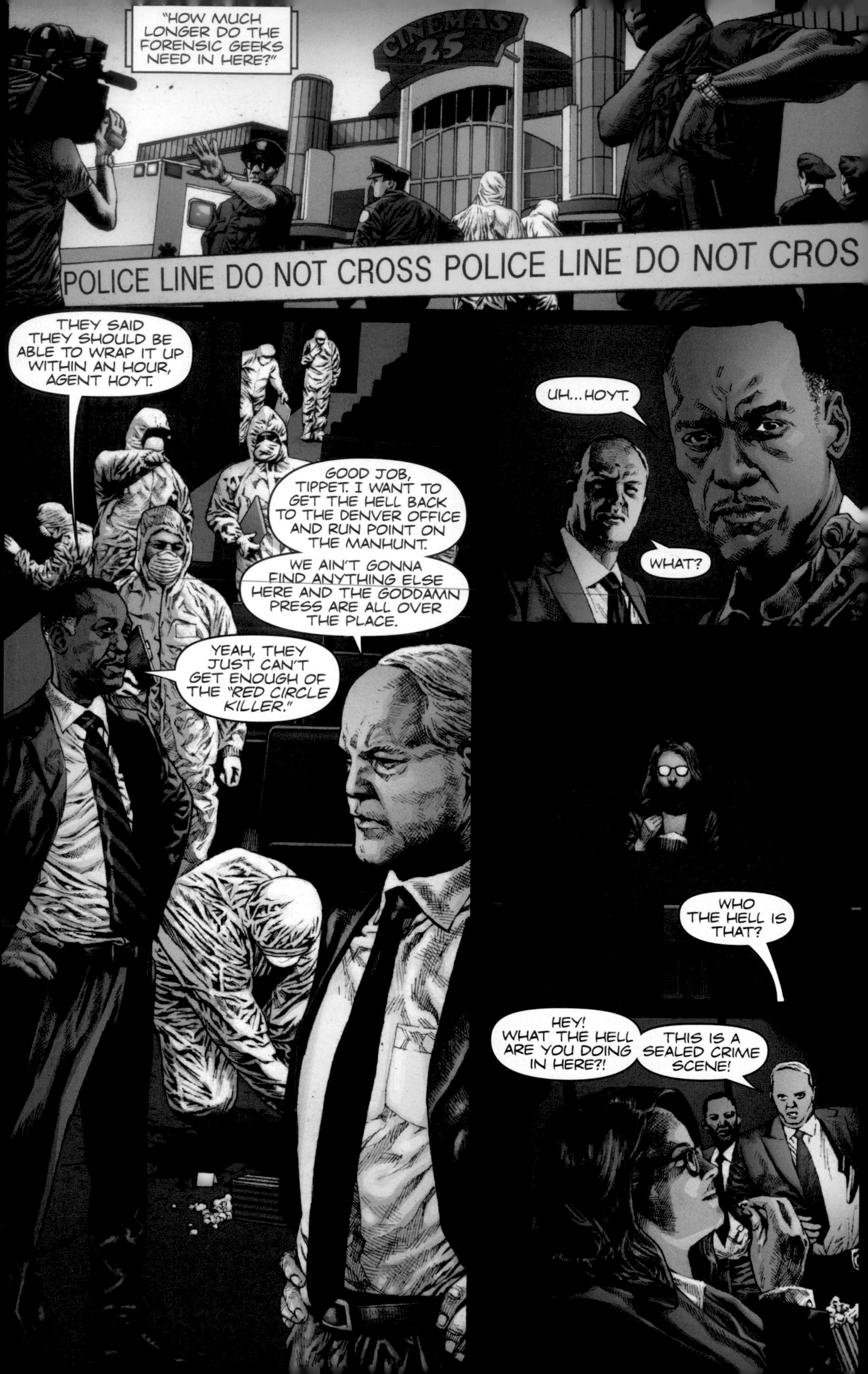
"HOW MUCH LONGER DO THE FORENSIC GEEKS NEED IN HERE?"
CINEMAS 25
POLICE LINE DO NOT CROSS POLICE LINE DO NOT CROS
THEY SAID THEY SHOULD BE ABLE TO WRAP IT UP WITHIN AN HOUR, AGENT HOYT.
GOOD JOB, TIPPET. I WANT TO GET THE HELL BACK TO THE DENVER OFFICE AND RUN POINT ON THE MANHUNT.
WE AIN'T GONNA FIND ANYTHING ELSE HERE AND THE GODDAMN PRESS ARE ALL OVER THE PLACE.
YEAH, THEY JUST CAN'T GET ENOUGH OF THE "RED CIRCLE KILLER."
UH...HOYT.
WHAT?
WHO THE HELL IS THAT?
HEY! WHAT THE HELL ARE YOU DOING IN HERE?!
THIS IS A SEALED CRIME SCENE!

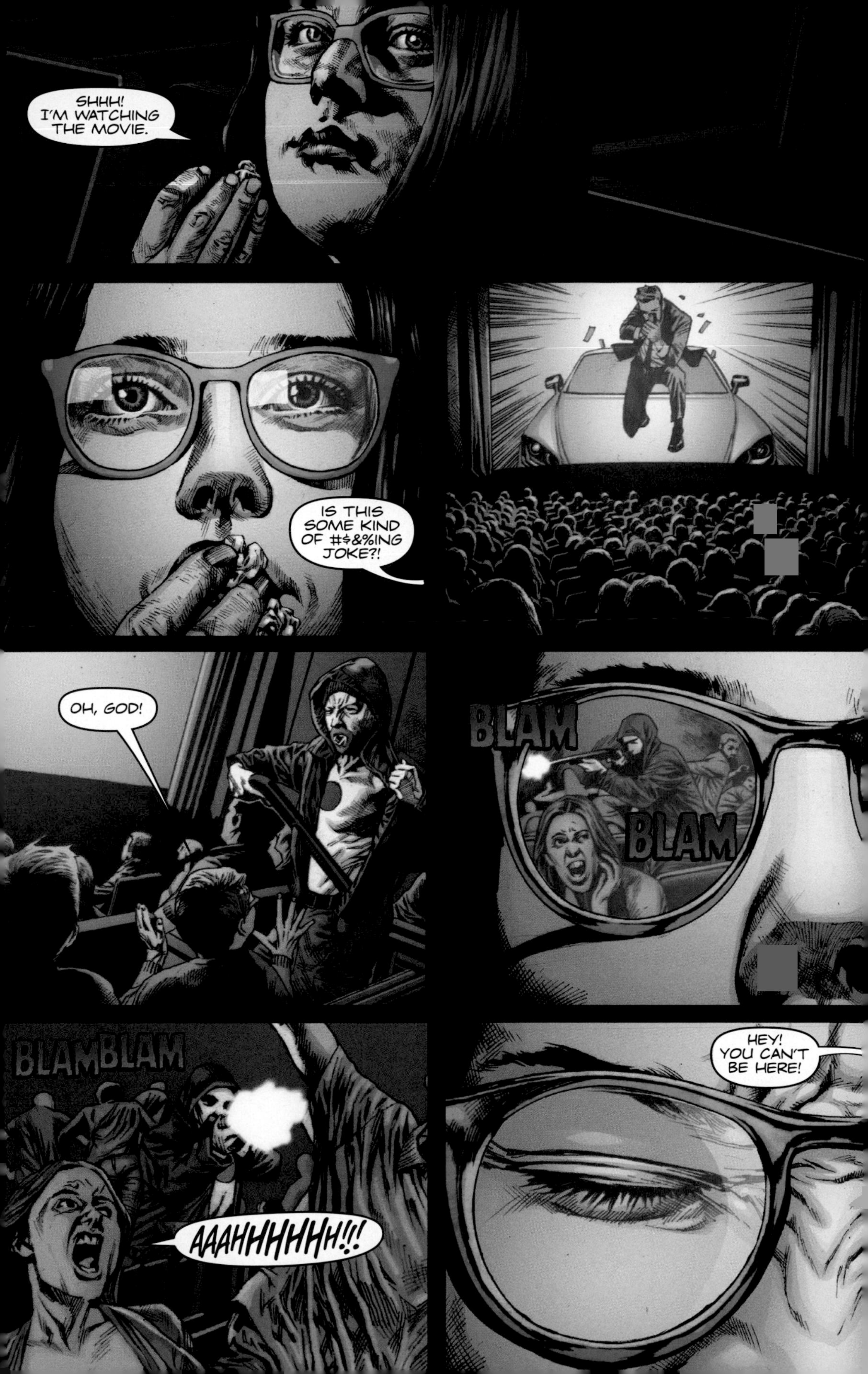
SHHH! I'M WATCHING THE MOVIE.
IS THIS SOME KIND OF #$&%ING JOKE?!
OH, GOD!
BLAM
BLAM
BLAMBLAM
AAAHHHHHH!!!
HEY! YOU CAN'T BE HERE!

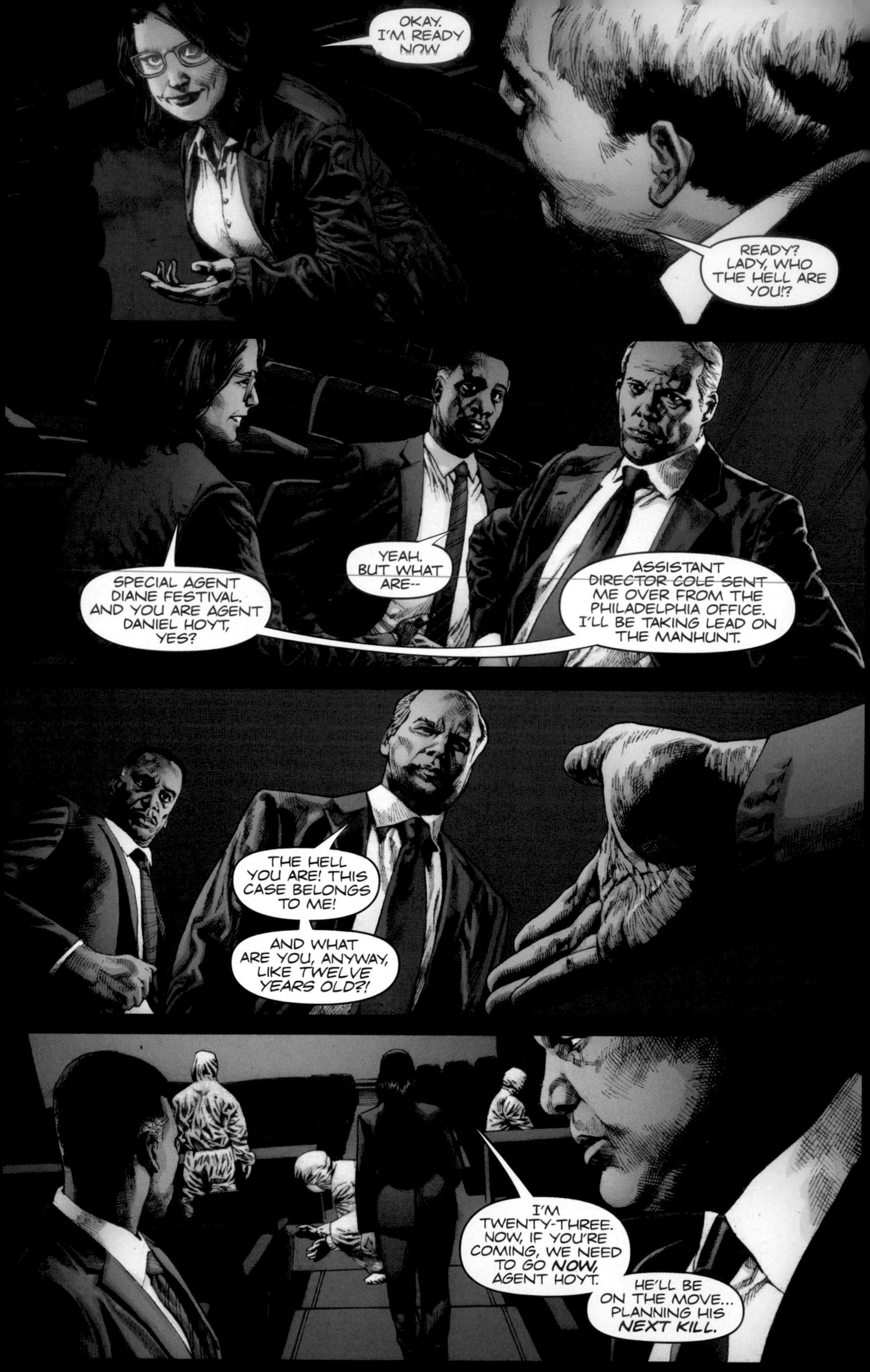
OKAY. I'M READY NOW
READY? LADY, WHO THE HELL ARE YOU!?
SPECIAL AGENT DIANE FESTIVAL. AND YOU ARE AGENT DANIEL HOYT, YES?
YEAH. BUT WHAT ARE--
ASSISTANT DIRECTOR COLE SENT ME OVER FROM THE PHILADELPHIA OFFICE. I'LL BE TAKING LEAD ON THE MANHUNT.
THE HELL YOU ARE! THIS CASE BELONGS TO ME!
AND WHAT ARE YOU, ANYWAY, LIKE TWELVE YEARS OLD?!
I'M TWENTY-THREE. NOW, IF YOU'RE COMING, WE NEED TO GO NOW, AGENT HOYT.
HE'LL BE ON THE MOVE... PLANNING HIS NEXT KILL.

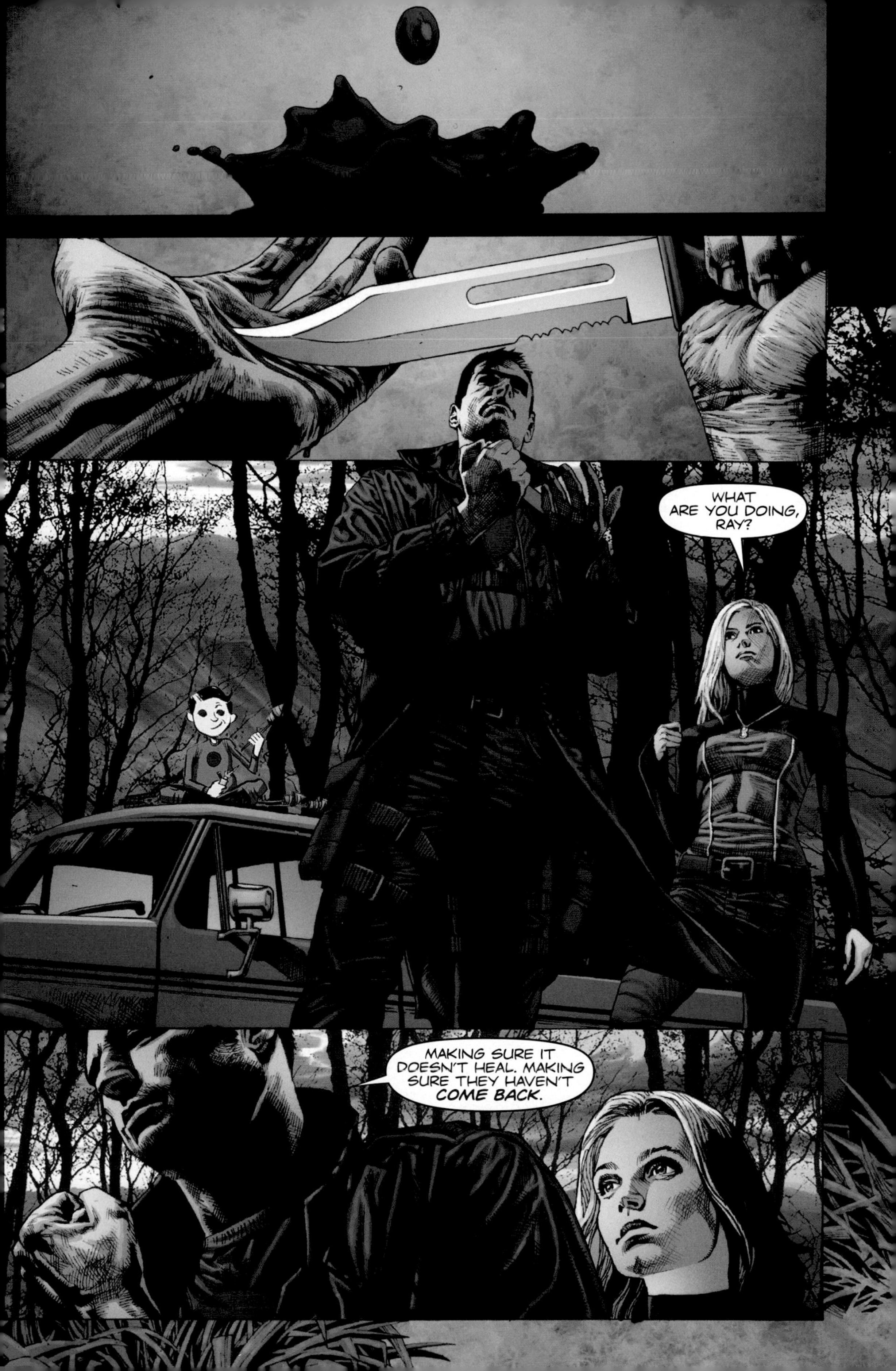
WHAT ARE YOU DOING, RAY?
MAKING SURE IT DOESN'T HEAL. MAKING SURE THEY HAVEN'T COME BACK.

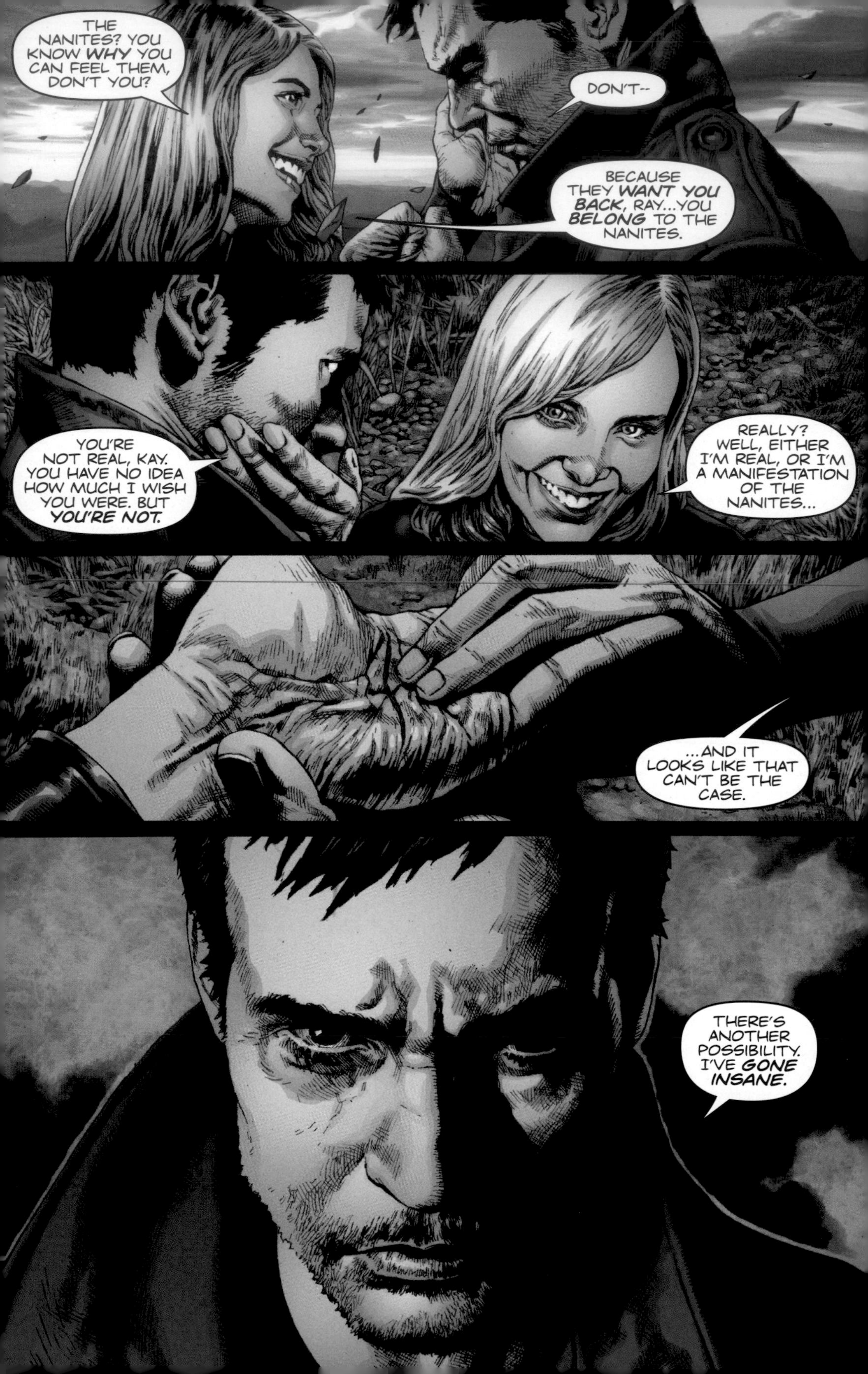
THE NANITES? YOU KNOW WHY YOU CAN FEEL THEM, DON'T YOU?
DON'T--
BECAUSE THEY WANT YOU BACK, RAY...YOU BELONG TO THE NANITES.
YOU'RE NOT REAL, KAY. YOU HAVE NO IDEA HOW MUCH I WISH YOU WERE. BUT YOU'RE NOT.
REALLY? WELL, EITHER I'M REAL, OR I'M A MANIFESTATION OF THE NANITES...
...AND IT LOOKS LIKE THAT CAN'T BE THE CASE.
THERE'S ANOTHER POSSIBILITY. I'VE GONE INSANE.

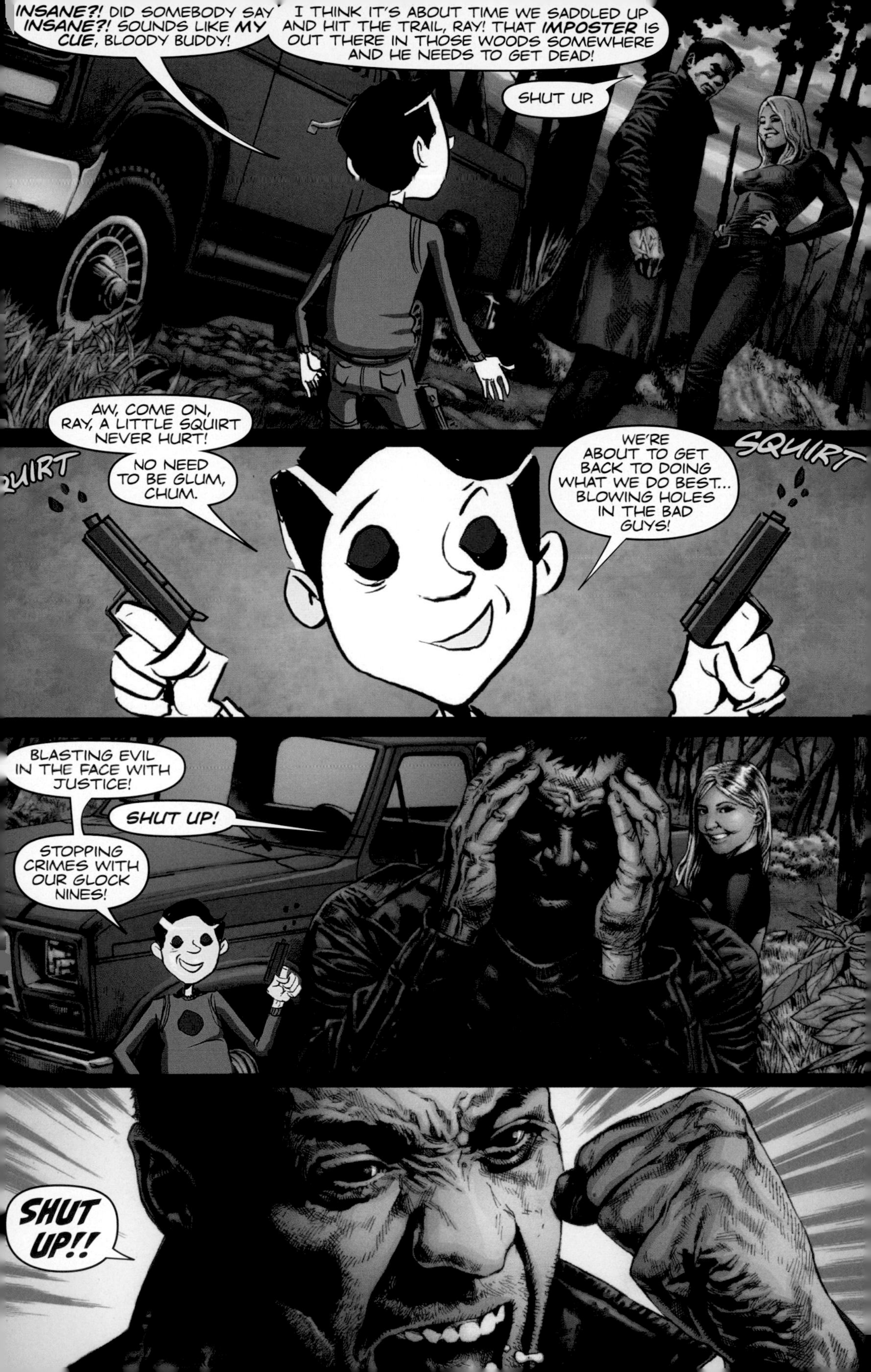

INSANE?! DID SOMEBODY SAY INSANE?! SOUNDS LIKE MY CUE, BLOODY BUDDY!
I THINK IT'S ABOUT TIME WE SADDLED UP AND HIT THE TRAIL, RAY! THAT IMPOSTER IS OUT THERE IN THOSE WOODS SOMEWHERE AND HE NEEDS TO GET DEAD!
SHUT UP.
AW, COME ON, RAY, A LITTLE SQUIRT NEVER HURT!
NO NEED TO BE GLUM, CHUM.
WE'RE ABOUT TO GET BACK TO DOING WHAT WE DO BEST... BLOWING HOLES IN THE BAD GUYS!
SQUIRT
BLASTING EVIL IN THE FACE WITH JUSTICE!
SHUT UP!
STOPPING CRIMES WITH OUR GLOCK NINES!
SHUT UP!!

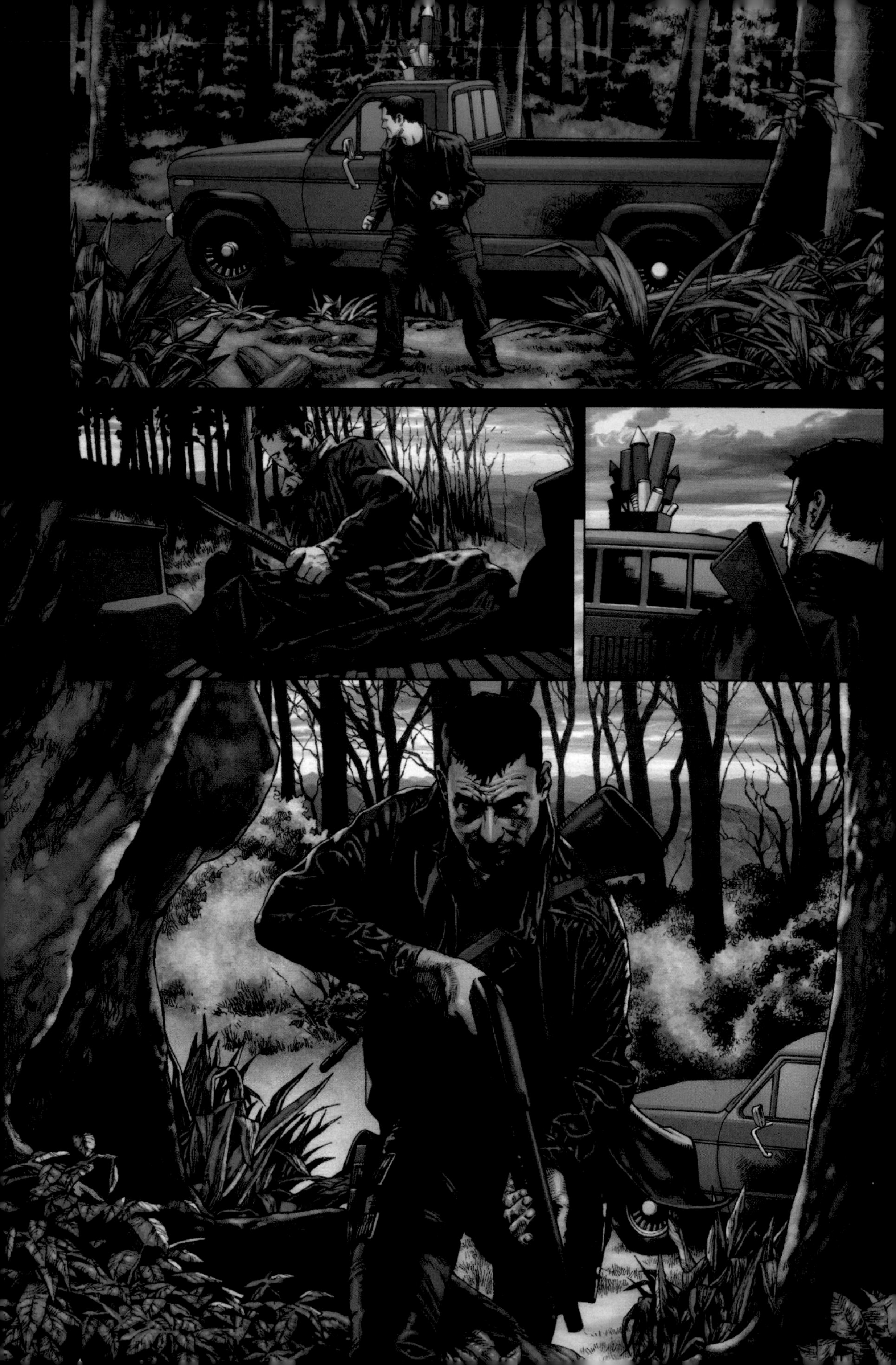

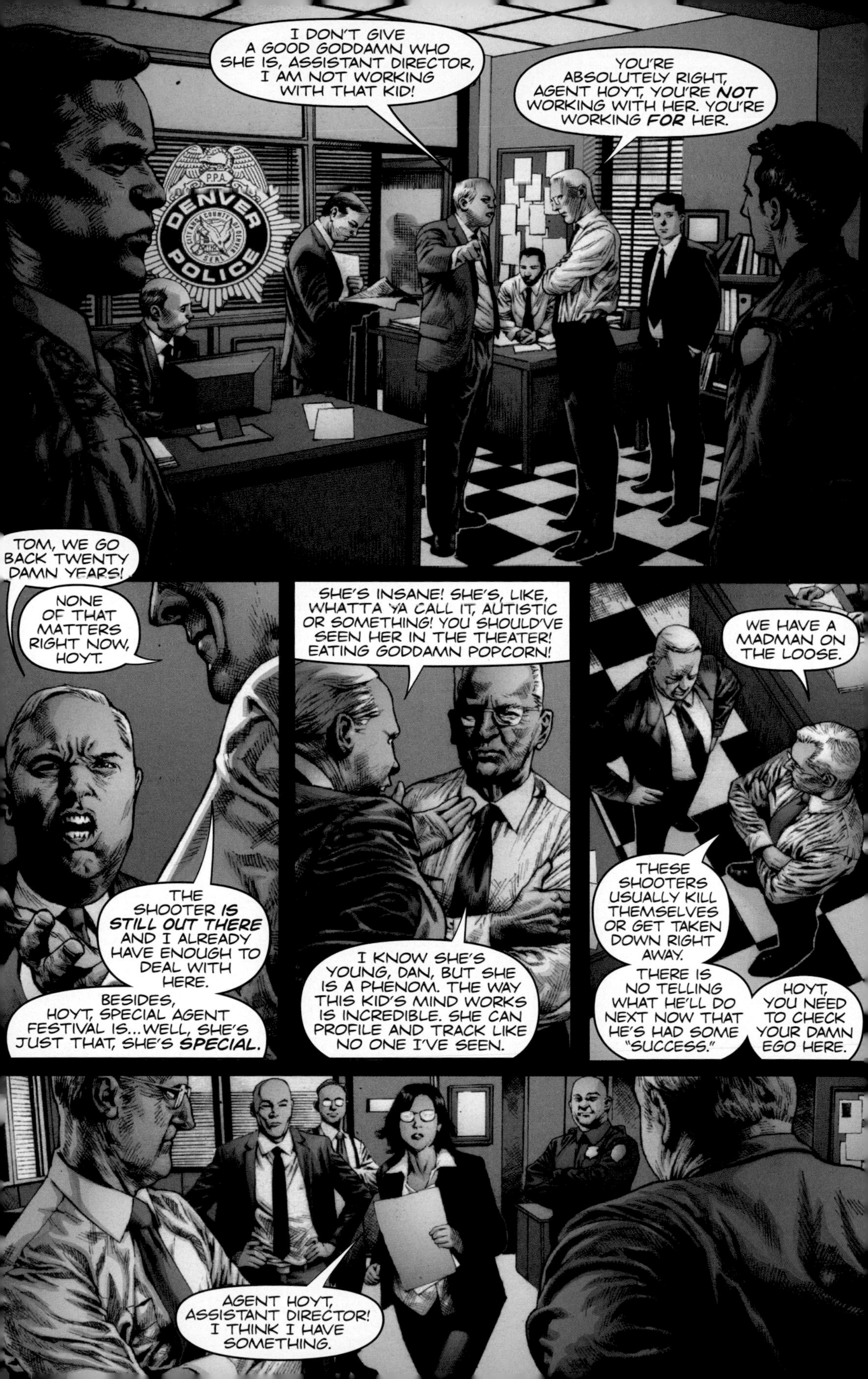

DENVER POLICE
P.P.A.
CITY AND COUNTY OF DENVER SEAL
I DON'T GIVE A GOOD GODDAMN WHO SHE IS, ASSISTANT DIRECTOR, I AM NOT WORKING WITH THAT KID!
YOU'RE ABSOLUTELY RIGHT, AGENT HOYT, YOU'RE **NOT** WORKING WITH HER. YOU'RE WORKING **FOR** HER.
TOM, WE GO BACK TWENTY DAMN YEARS!
NONE OF THAT MATTERS RIGHT NOW, HOYT.
THE SHOOTER **IS STILL OUT THERE** AND I ALREADY HAVE ENOUGH TO DEAL WITH HERE.
BESIDES, HOYT, SPECIAL AGENT FESTIVAL IS...WELL, SHE'S JUST THAT, SHE'S **SPECIAL**.
SHE'S INSANE! SHE'S, LIKE, WHATTA YA CALL IT, AUTISTIC OR SOMETHING! YOU SHOULD'VE SEEN HER IN THE THEATER! EATING GODDAMN POPCORN!
I KNOW SHE'S YOUNG, DAN, BUT SHE IS A PHENOM. THE WAY THIS KID'S MIND WORKS IS INCREDIBLE. SHE CAN PROFILE AND TRACK LIKE NO ONE I'VE SEEN.
WE HAVE A MADMAN ON THE LOOSE.
THESE SHOOTERS USUALLY KILL THEMSELVES OR GET TAKEN DOWN RIGHT AWAY.
THERE IS NO TELLING WHAT HE'LL DO NEXT NOW THAT HE'S HAD SOME "SUCCESS."
HOYT, YOU NEED TO CHECK YOUR DAMN EGO HERE.
AGENT HOYT, ASSISTANT DIRECTOR! I THINK I HAVE SOMETHING.

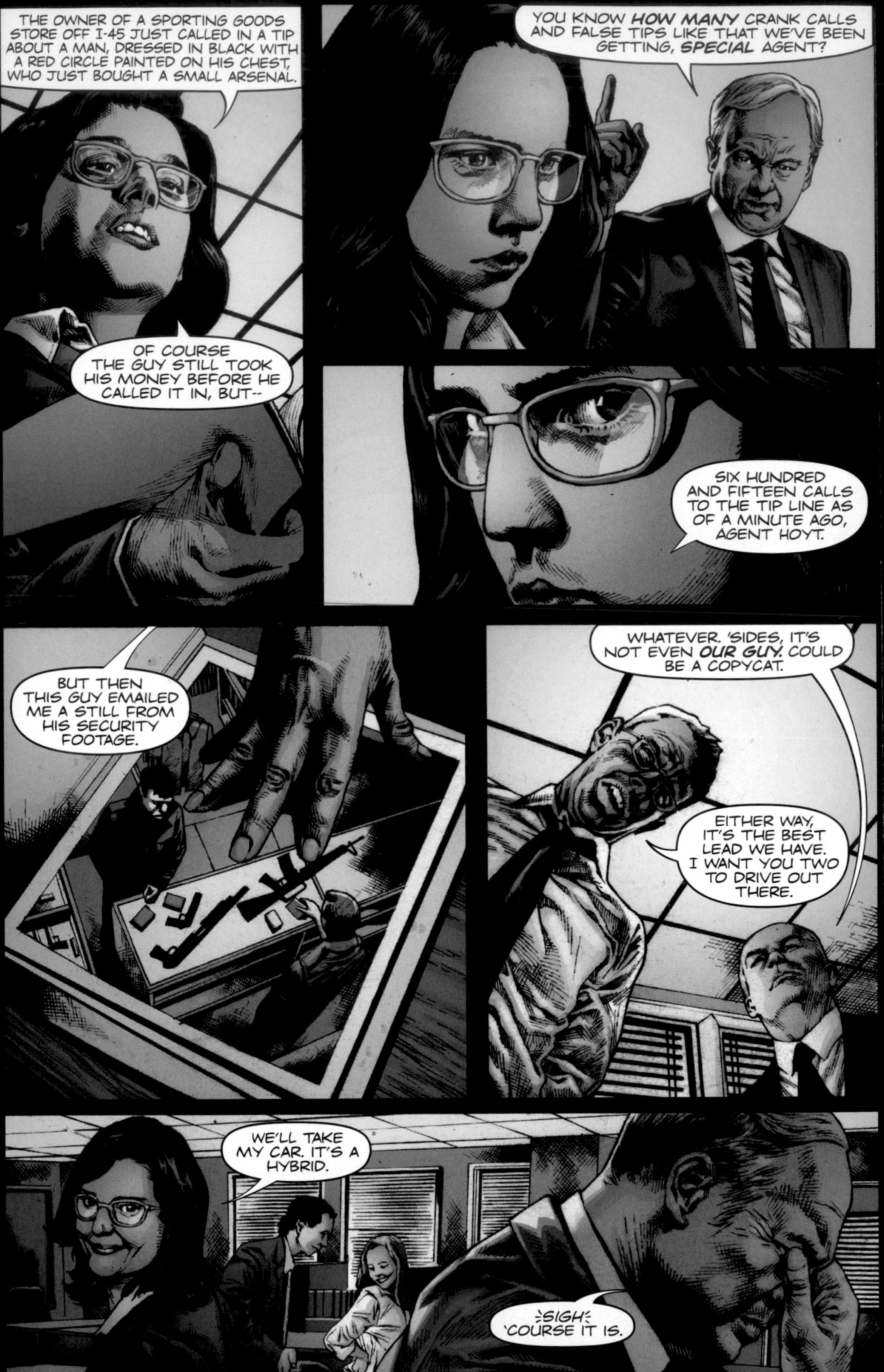
THE OWNER OF A SPORTING GOODS STORE OFF I-45 JUST CALLED IN A TIP ABOUT A MAN, DRESSED IN BLACK WITH A RED CIRCLE PAINTED ON HIS CHEST, WHO JUST BOUGHT A SMALL ARSENAL.
YOU KNOW **HOW MANY** CRANK CALLS AND FALSE TIPS LIKE THAT WE'VE BEEN GETTING, **SPECIAL** AGENT?
OF COURSE THE GUY STILL TOOK HIS MONEY BEFORE HE CALLED IT IN, BUT--
SIX HUNDRED AND FIFTEEN CALLS TO THE TIP LINE AS OF A MINUTE AGO, AGENT HOYT.
BUT THEN THIS GUY EMAILED ME A STILL FROM HIS SECURITY FOOTAGE.
WHATEVER. 'SIDES, IT'S NOT EVEN **OUR GUY.** COULD BE A COPYCAT.
EITHER WAY, IT'S THE BEST LEAD WE HAVE. I WANT YOU TWO TO DRIVE OUT THERE.
WE'LL TAKE MY CAR. IT'S A HYBRID.
SIGH 'COURSE IT IS.

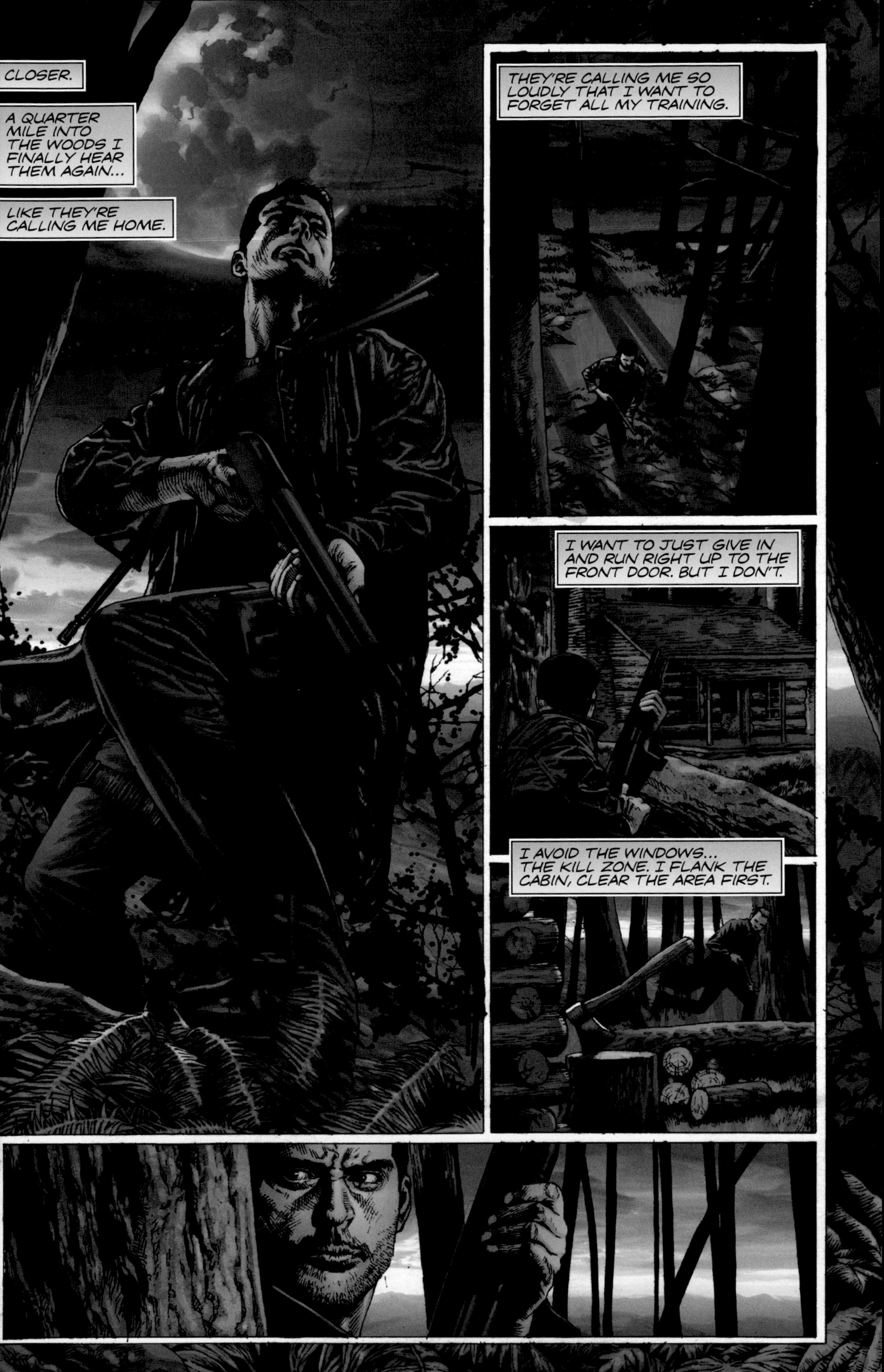
CLOSER.
A QUARTER MILE INTO THE WOODS I FINALLY HEAR THEM AGAIN...
LIKE THEY'RE CALLING ME HOME.
THEY'RE CALLING ME SO LOUDLY THAT I WANT TO FORGET ALL MY TRAINING.
I WANT TO JUST GIVE IN AND RUN RIGHT UP TO THE FRONT DOOR. BUT I DON'T.
I AVOID THE WINDOWS... THE KILL ZONE. I FLANK THE CABIN, CLEAR THE AREA FIRST.

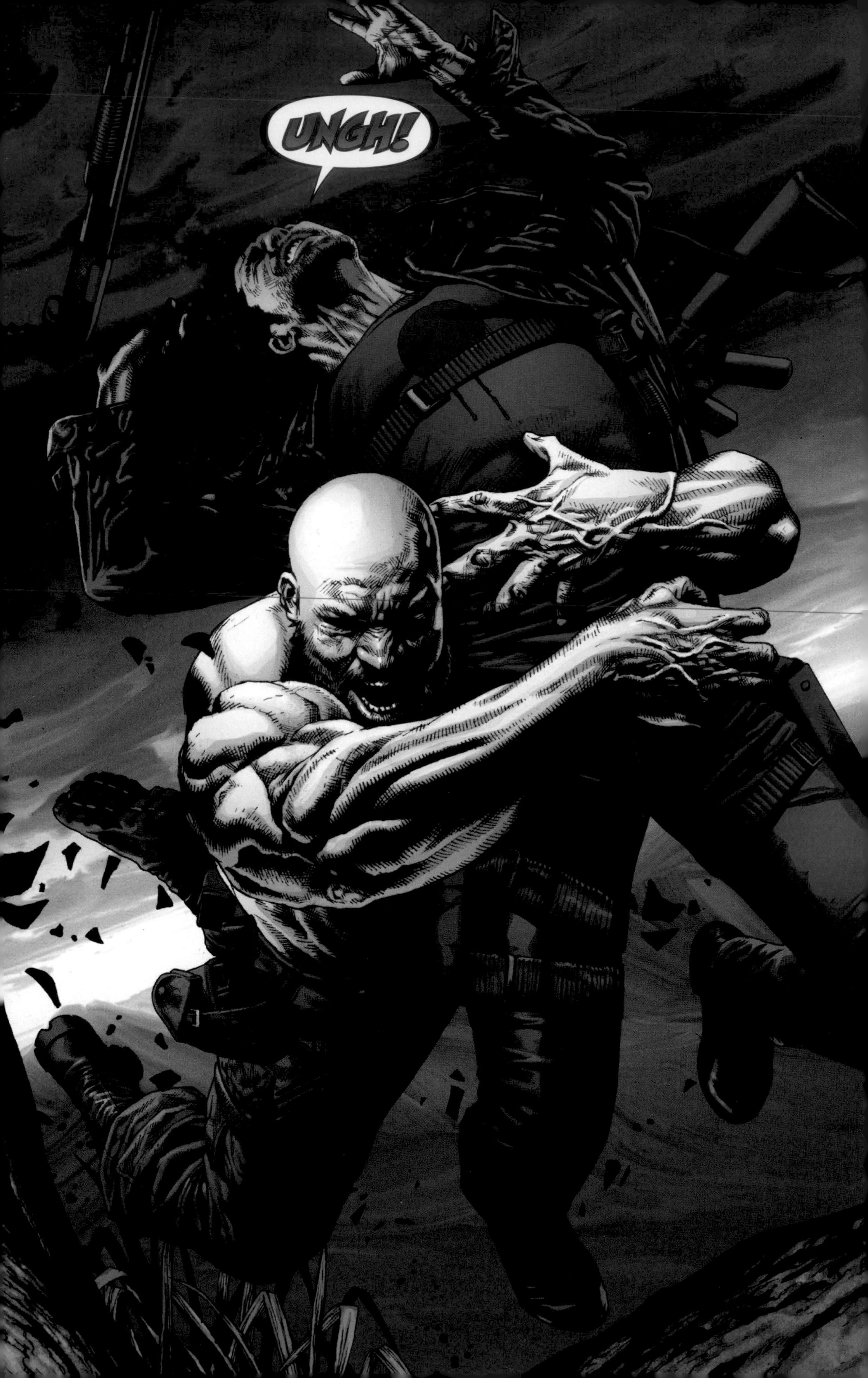
UNGH!

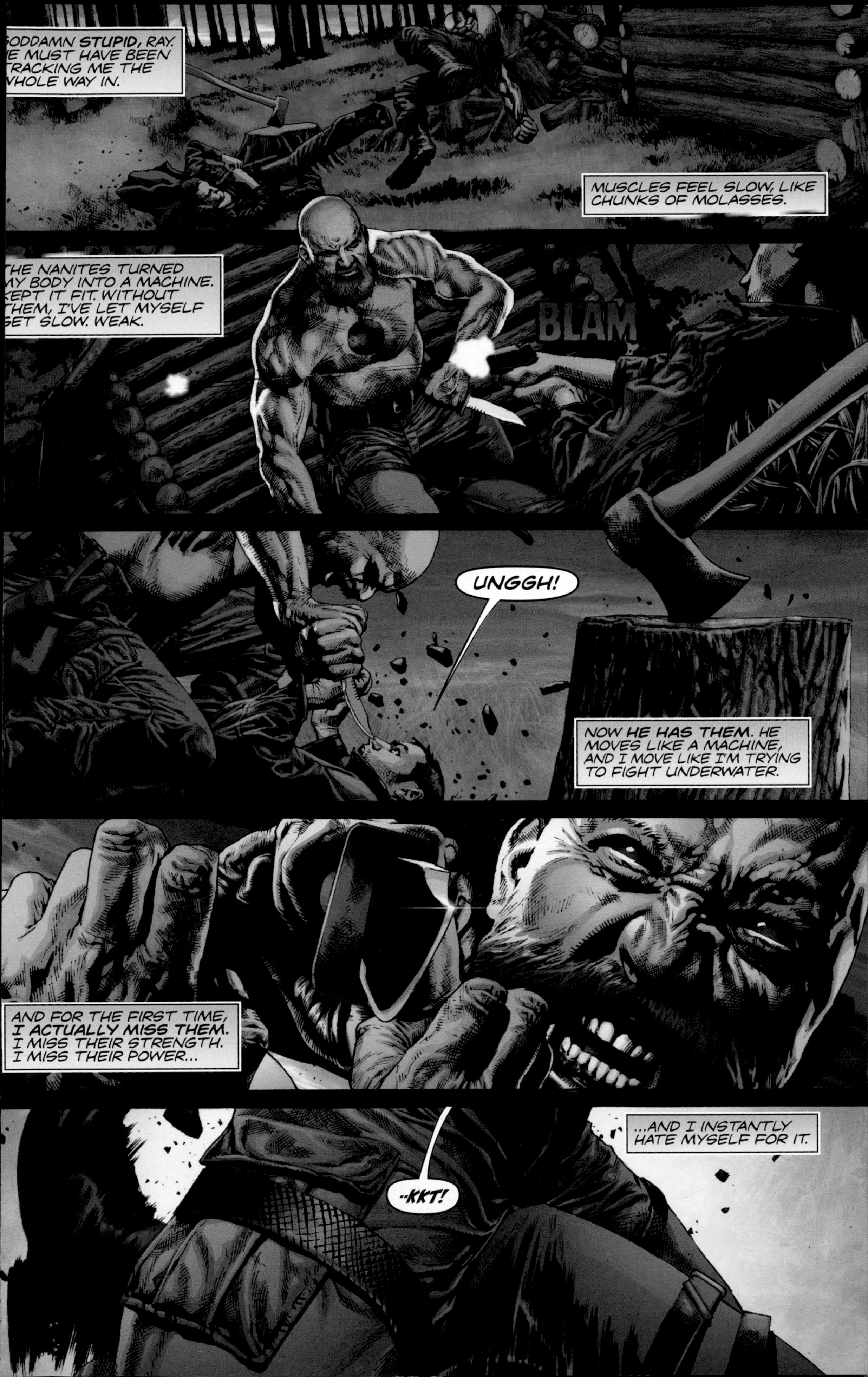
GODDAMN STUPID, RAY. HE MUST HAVE BEEN TRACKING ME THE WHOLE WAY IN.
MUSCLES FEEL SLOW, LIKE CHUNKS OF MOLASSES.
THE NANITES TURNED MY BODY INTO A MACHINE. KEPT IT FIT. WITHOUT THEM, I'VE LET MYSELF GET SLOW. WEAK.
BLAM
UNGGH!
NOW HE HAS THEM. HE MOVES LIKE A MACHINE, AND I MOVE LIKE I'M TRYING TO FIGHT UNDERWATER.
AND FOR THE FIRST TIME, I ACTUALLY MISS THEM. I MISS THEIR STRENGTH. I MISS THEIR POWER...
...AND I INSTANTLY HATE MYSELF FOR IT.
--KKT!

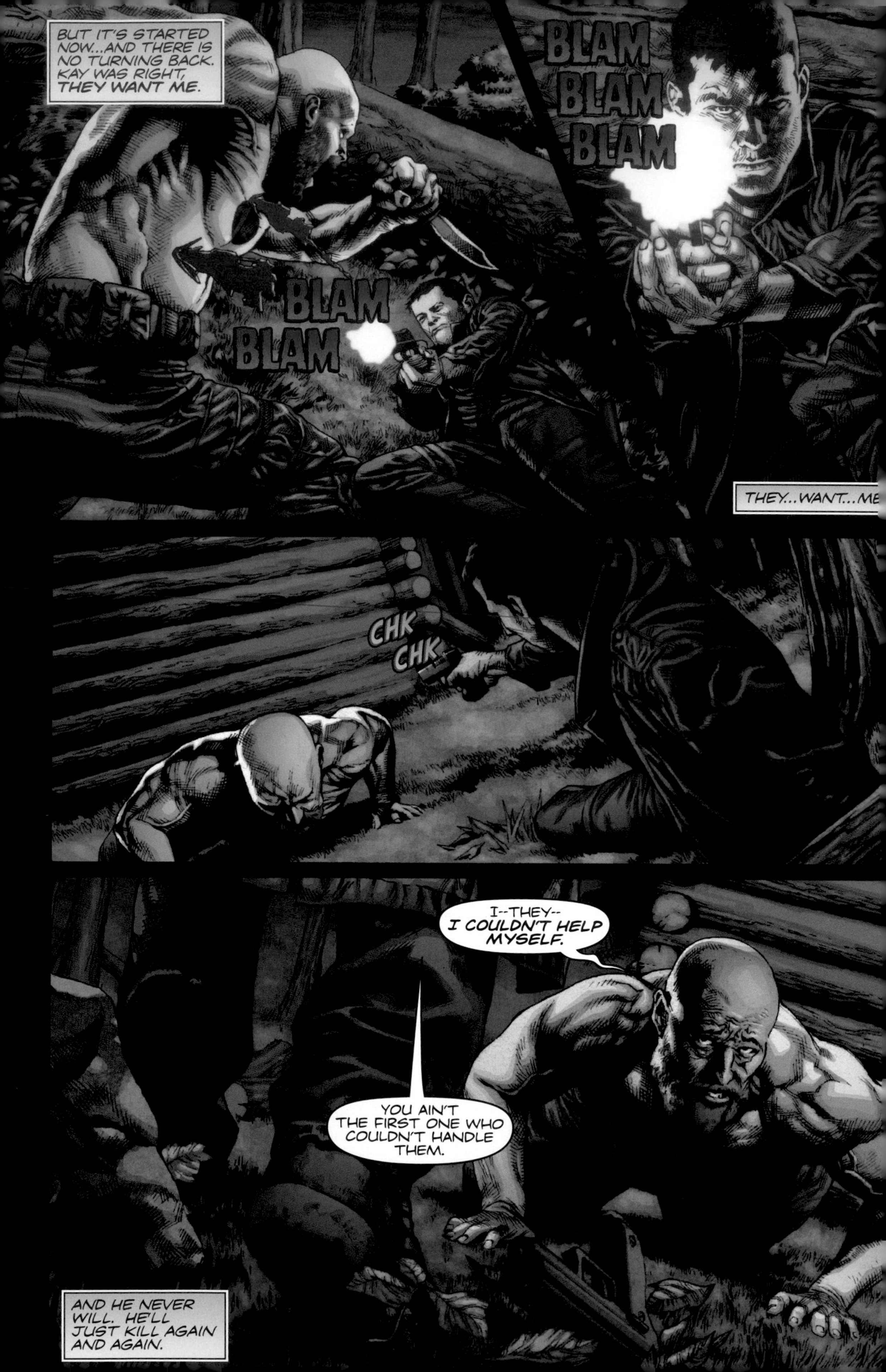
BUT IT'S STARTED NOW...AND THERE IS NO TURNING BACK. KAY WAS RIGHT, THEY WANT ME.
BLAM BLAM
BLAM BLAM BLAM
THEY...WANT...ME
CHK CHK
I--THEY-- I COULDN'T HELP MYSELF.
YOU AIN'T THE FIRST ONE WHO COULDN'T HANDLE THEM.
AND HE NEVER WILL. HE'LL JUST KILL AGAIN AND AGAIN.

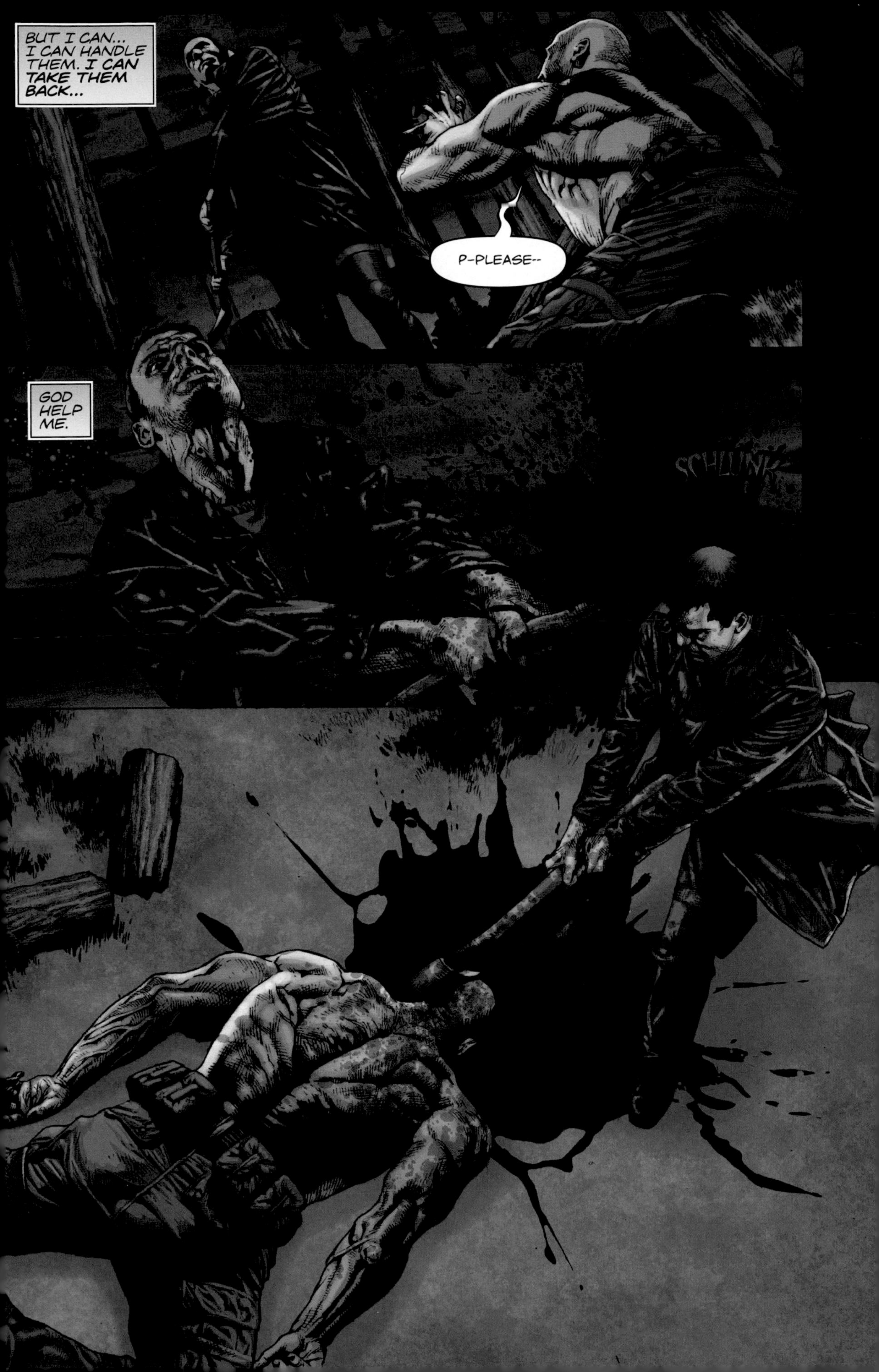
BUT I CAN... I CAN HANDLE THEM. I CAN TAKE THEM BACK...
P-PLEASE--
GOD HELP ME.
SCHLUNK

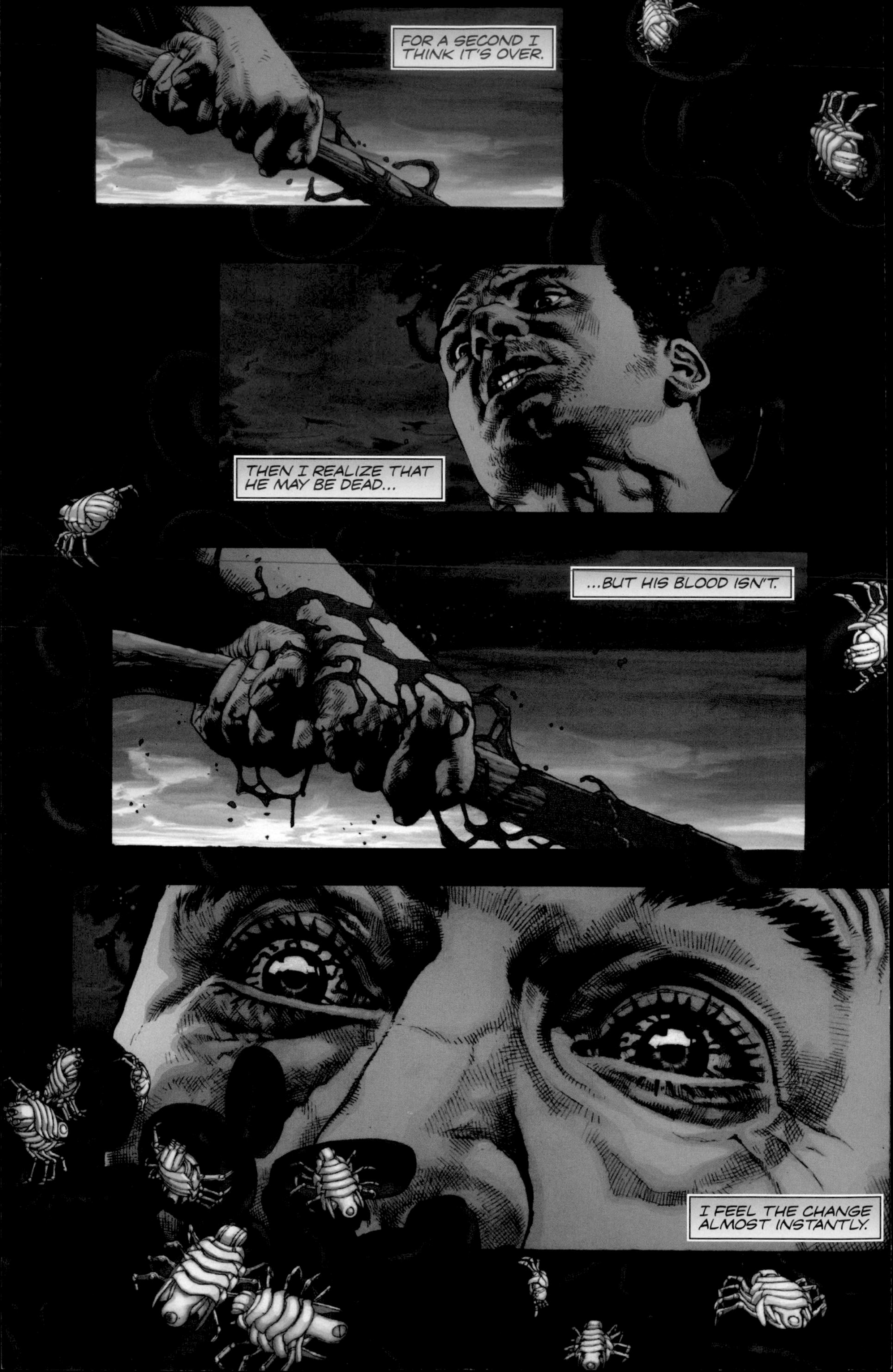
FOR A SECOND I THINK IT'S OVER.
THEN I REALIZE THAT HE MAY BE DEAD...
...BUT HIS BLOOD ISN'T.
I FEEL THE CHANGE ALMOST INSTANTLY.

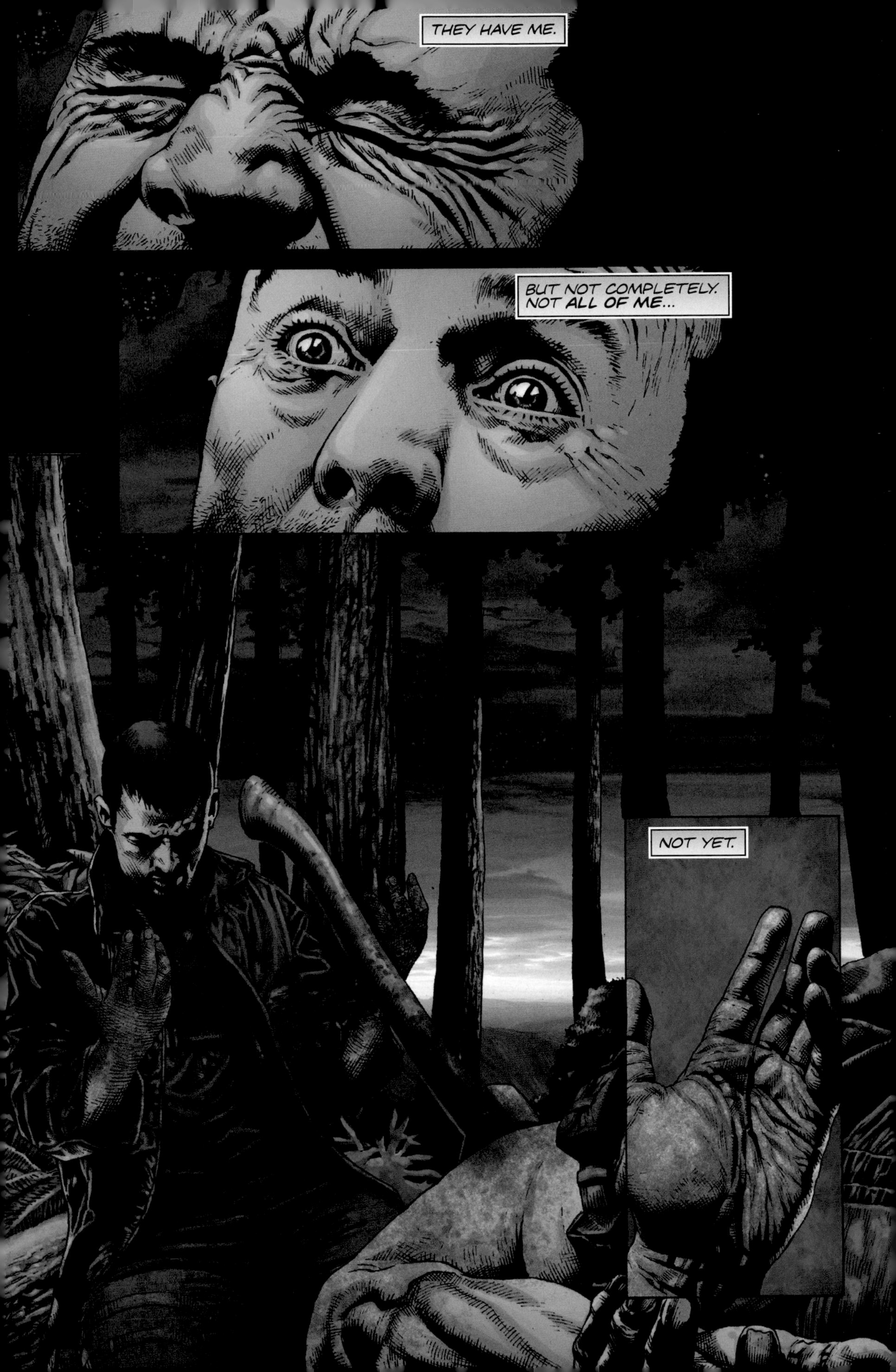
THEY HAVE ME.
BUT NOT COMPLETELY. NOT ALL OF ME...
NOT YET.

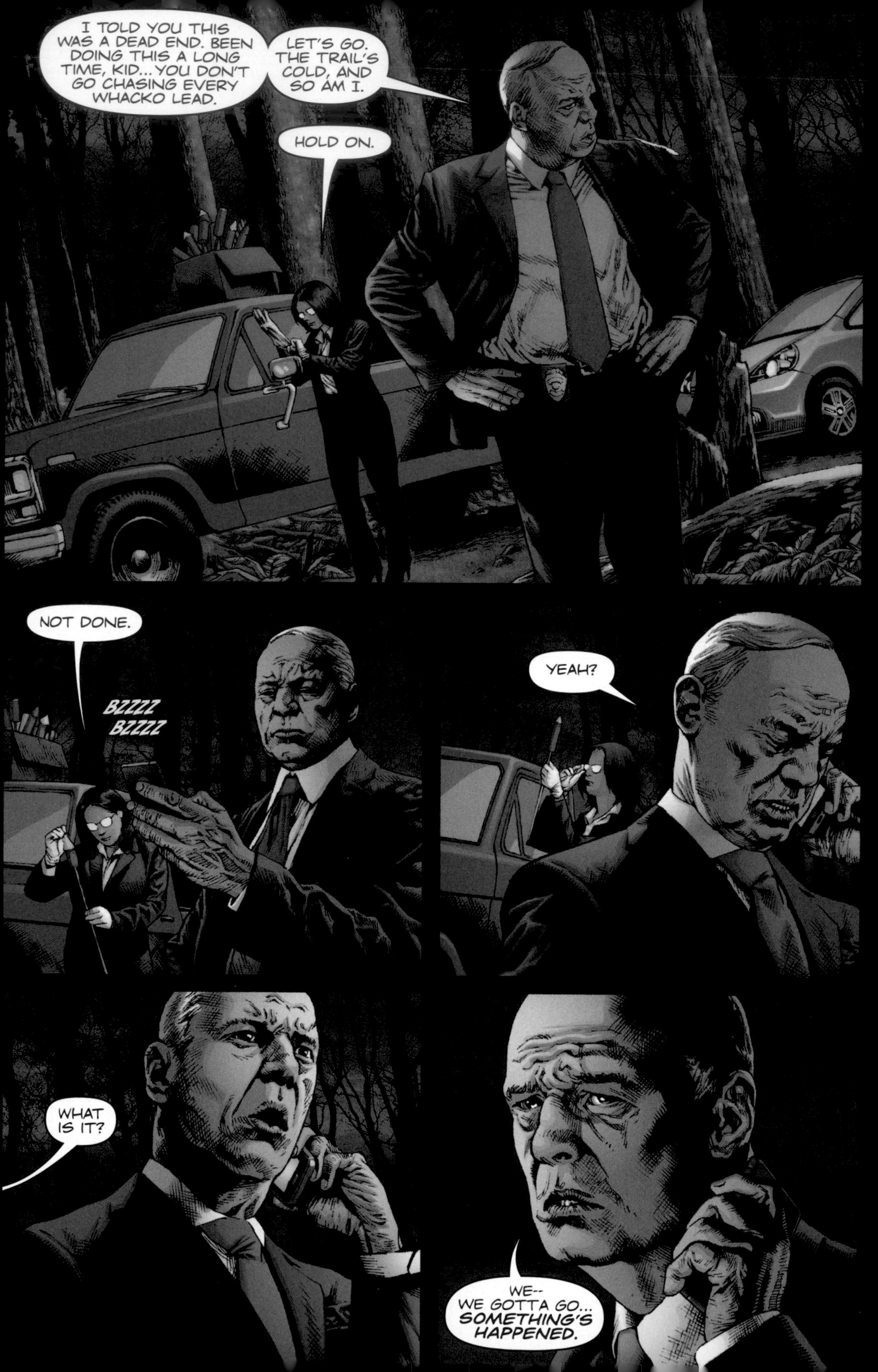
I TOLD YOU THIS WAS A DEAD END. BEEN DOING THIS A LONG TIME, KID... YOU DON'T GO CHASING EVERY WHACKO LEAD.
LET'S GO. THE TRAIL'S COLD, AND SO AM I.
HOLD ON.
NOT DONE.
BZZZZ
BZZZZ
YEAH?
WHAT IS IT?
WE--
WE GOTTA GO...
SOMETHING'S HAPPENED.

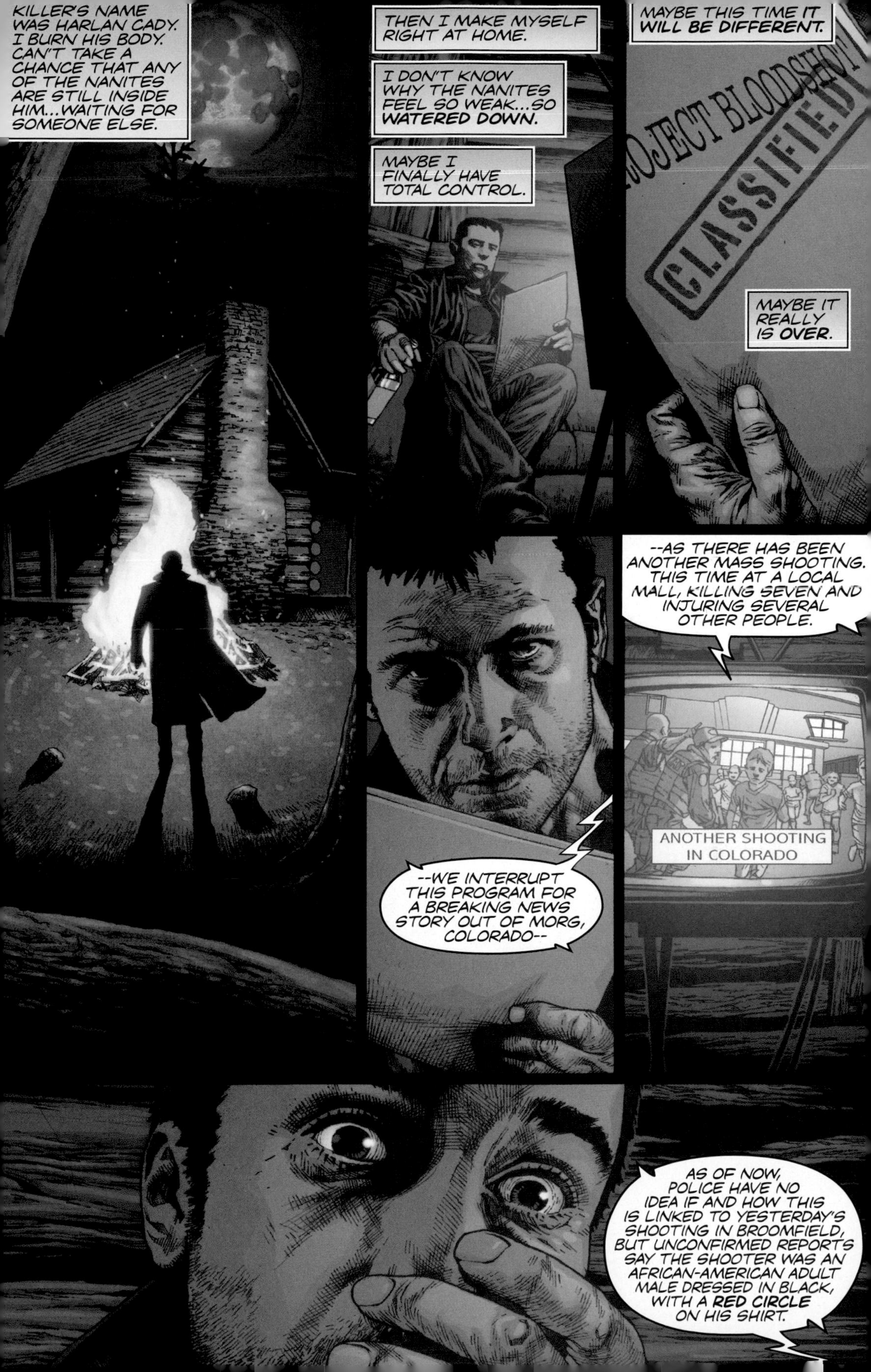
KILLER'S NAME WAS HARLAN CADY. I BURN HIS BODY. CAN'T TAKE A CHANCE THAT ANY OF THE NANITES ARE STILL INSIDE HIM...WAITING FOR SOMEONE ELSE.
THEN I MAKE MYSELF RIGHT AT HOME.
I DON'T KNOW WHY THE NANITES FEEL SO WEAK...SO WATERED DOWN.
MAYBE I FINALLY HAVE TOTAL CONTROL.
MAYBE THIS TIME IT WILL BE DIFFERENT.
PROJECT BLOODSHOT
CLASSIFIED
MAYBE IT REALLY IS OVER.
--WE INTERRUPT THIS PROGRAM FOR A BREAKING NEWS STORY OUT OF MORG, COLORADO--
--AS THERE HAS BEEN ANOTHER MASS SHOOTING. THIS TIME AT A LOCAL MALL, KILLING SEVEN AND INJURING SEVERAL OTHER PEOPLE.
ANOTHER SHOOTING IN COLORADO
AS OF NOW, POLICE HAVE NO IDEA IF AND HOW THIS IS LINKED TO YESTERDAY'S SHOOTING IN BROOMFIELD, BUT UNCONFIRMED REPORTS SAY THE SHOOTER WAS AN AFRICAN-AMERICAN ADULT MALE DRESSED IN BLACK, WITH A RED CIRCLE ON HIS SHIRT.

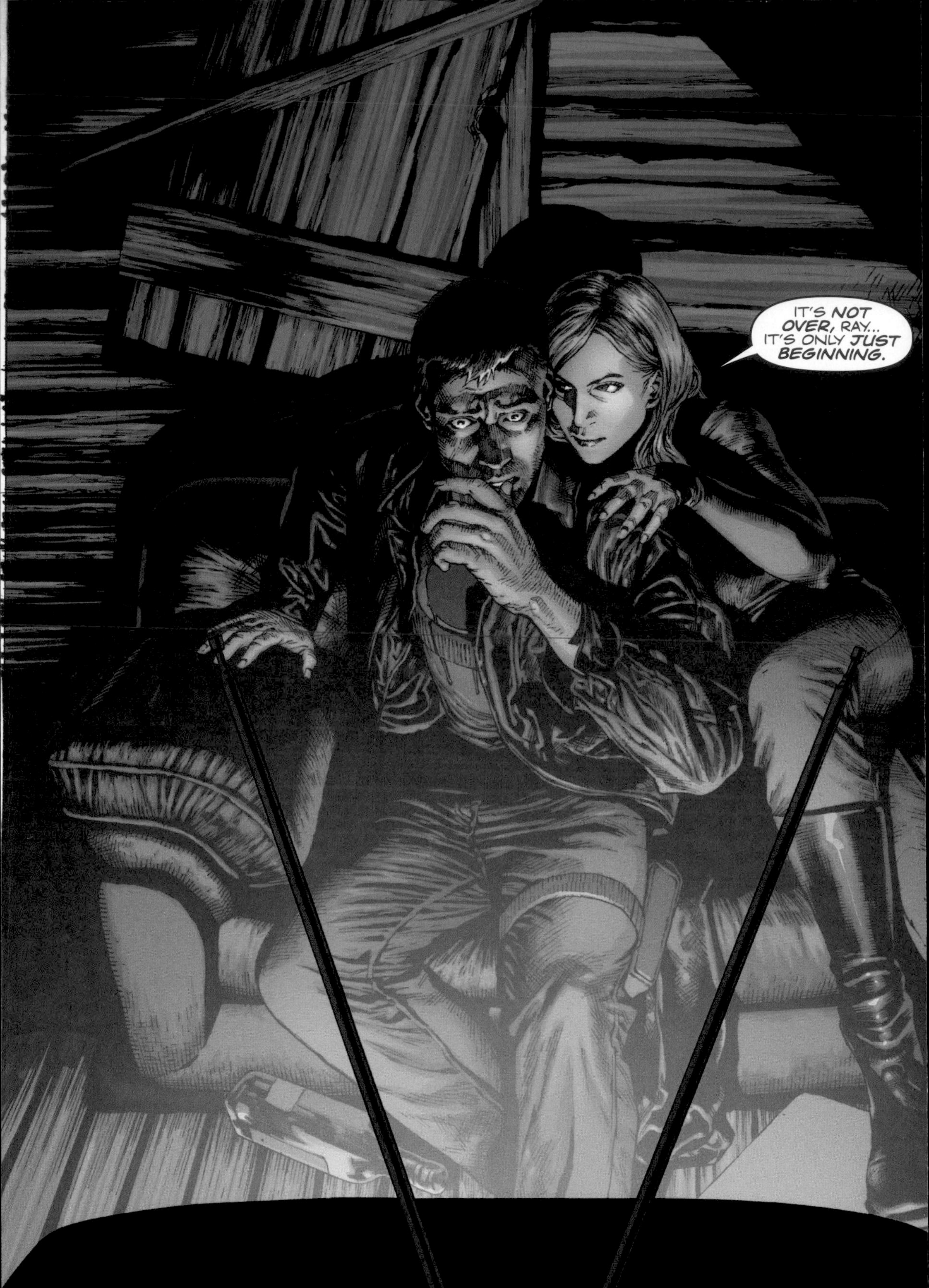
IT'S NOT OVER, RAY... IT'S ONLY JUST BEGINNING.

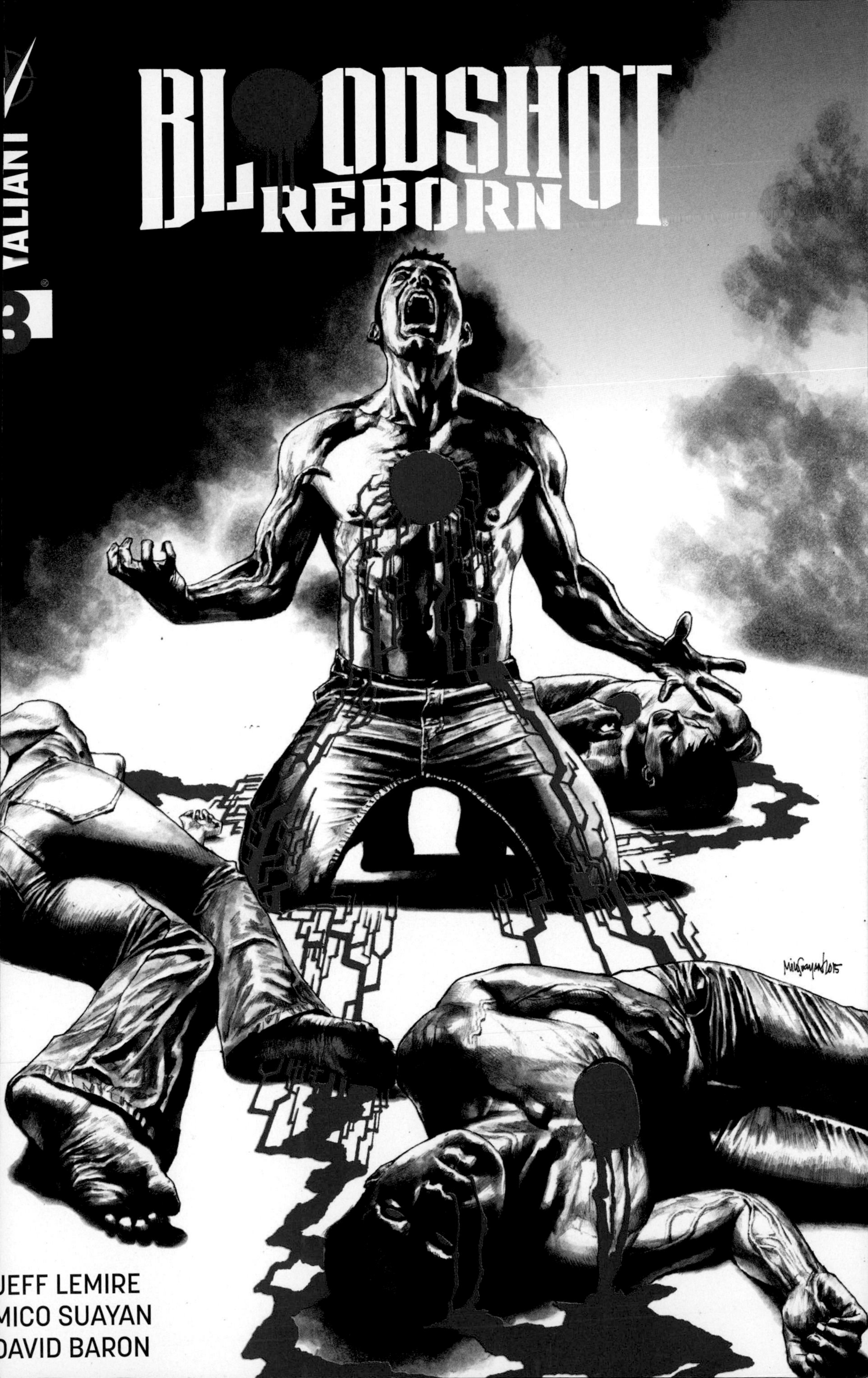
VALIANT
3
BLOODSHOT
REBORN
JEFF LEMIRE
MICO SUAYAN
DAVID BARON

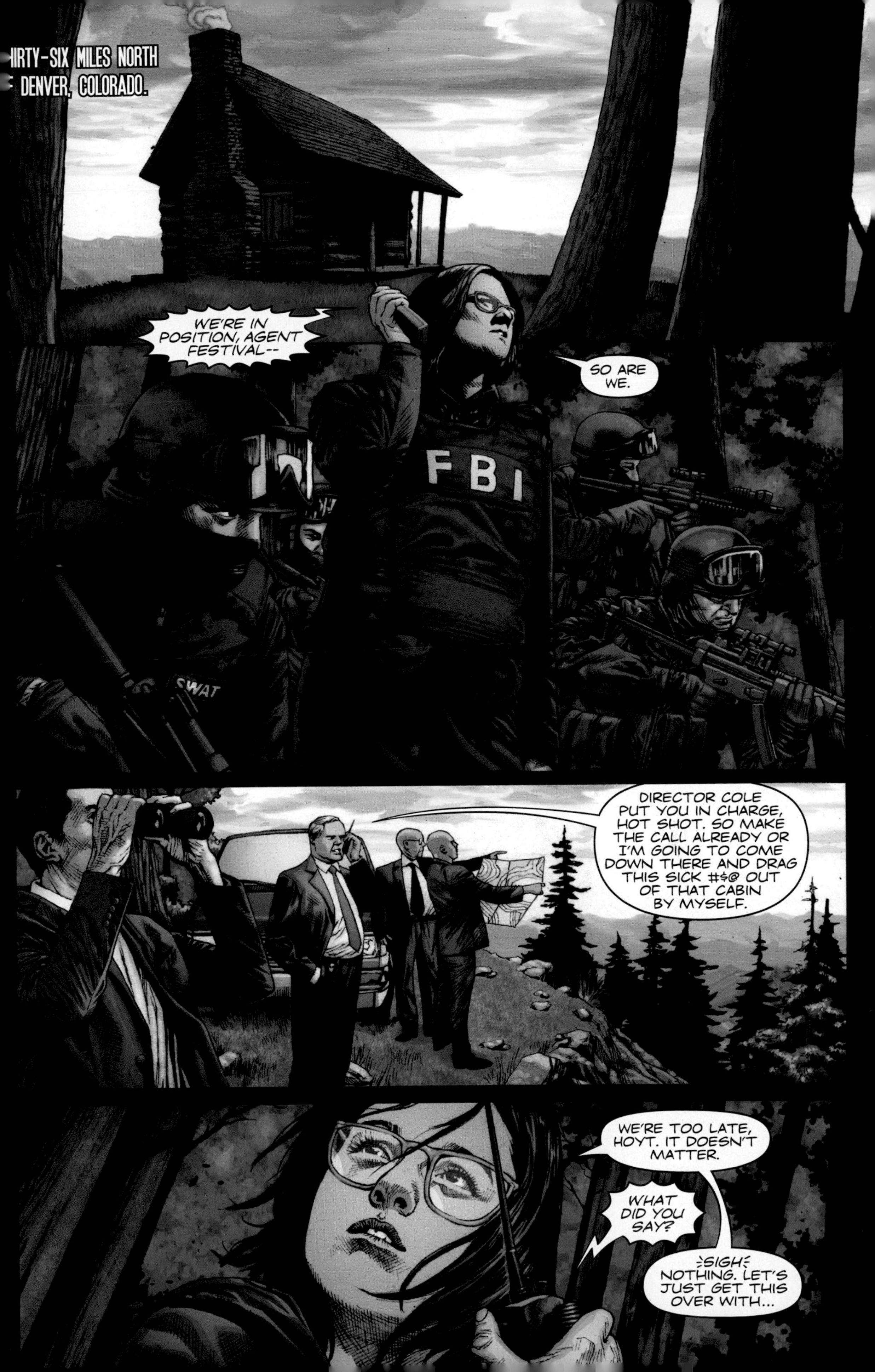
HIRTY-SIX MILES NORTH
F DENVER, COLORADO.
WE'RE IN POSITION, AGENT FESTIVAL--
SO ARE WE.
FBI
SWAT
DIRECTOR COLE PUT YOU IN CHARGE, HOT SHOT. SO MAKE THE CALL ALREADY OR I'M GOING TO COME DOWN THERE AND DRAG THIS SICK #$@ OUT OF THAT CABIN BY MYSELF.
WE'RE TOO LATE, HOYT. IT DOESN'T MATTER.
WHAT DID YOU SAY?
SIGH
NOTHING. LET'S JUST GET THIS OVER WITH...

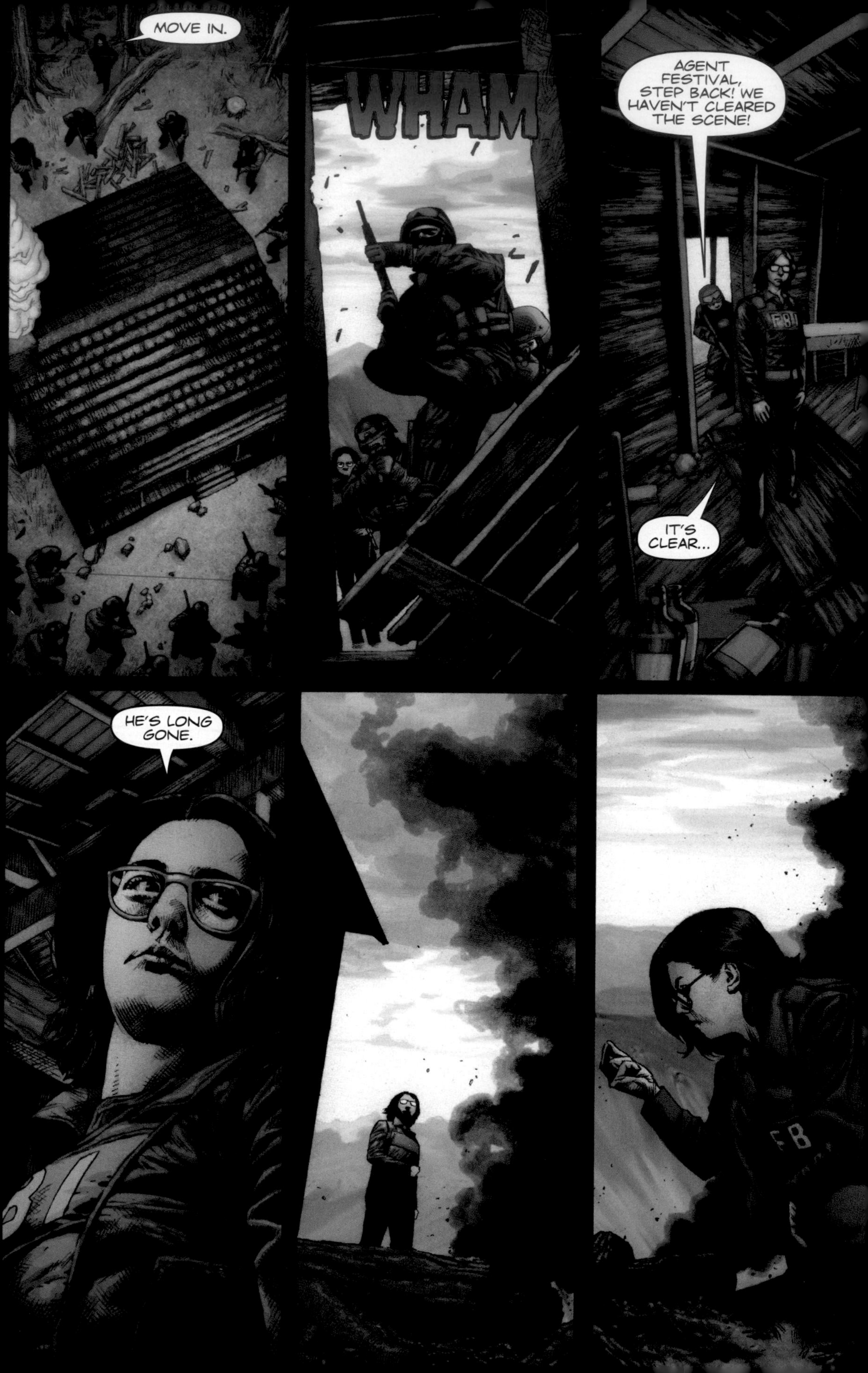
MOVE IN.
WHAM
AGENT FESTIVAL, STEP BACK! WE HAVEN'T CLEARED THE SCENE!
IT'S CLEAR...
HE'S LONG GONE.

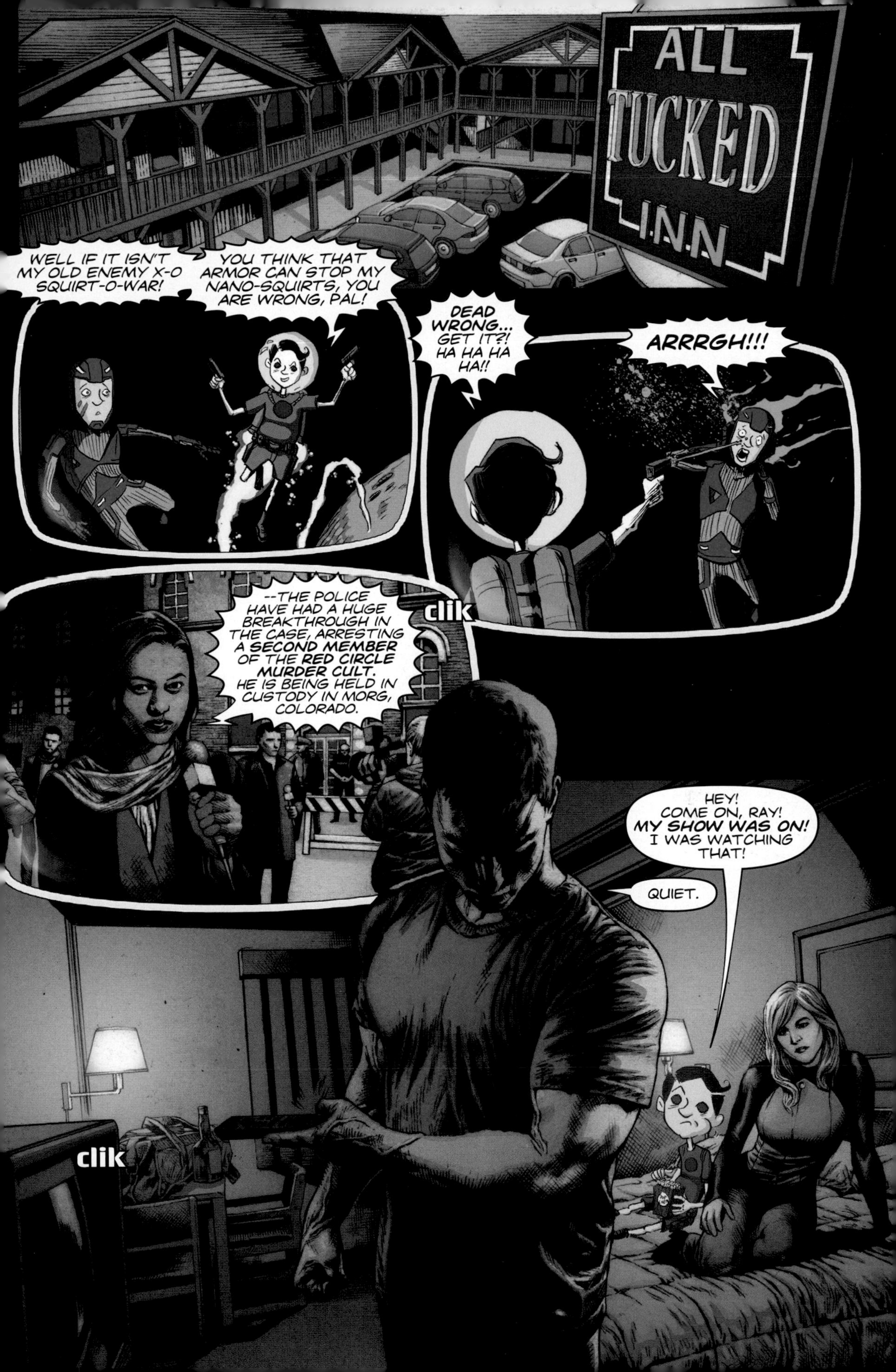
ALL TUCKED I.N.N
WELL IF IT ISN'T MY OLD ENEMY X-O SQUIRT-O-WAR!
YOU THINK THAT ARMOR CAN STOP MY NANO-SQUIRTS, YOU ARE WRONG, PAL!
DEAD WRONG... GET IT?! HA HA HA HA!!
ARRRGH!!!
clik
--THE POLICE HAVE HAD A HUGE BREAKTHROUGH IN THE CASE, ARRESTING A SECOND MEMBER OF THE RED CIRCLE MURDER CULT. HE IS BEING HELD IN CUSTODY IN MORG, COLORADO.
HEY! COME ON, RAY! MY SHOW WAS ON! I WAS WATCHING THAT!
QUIET.
clik

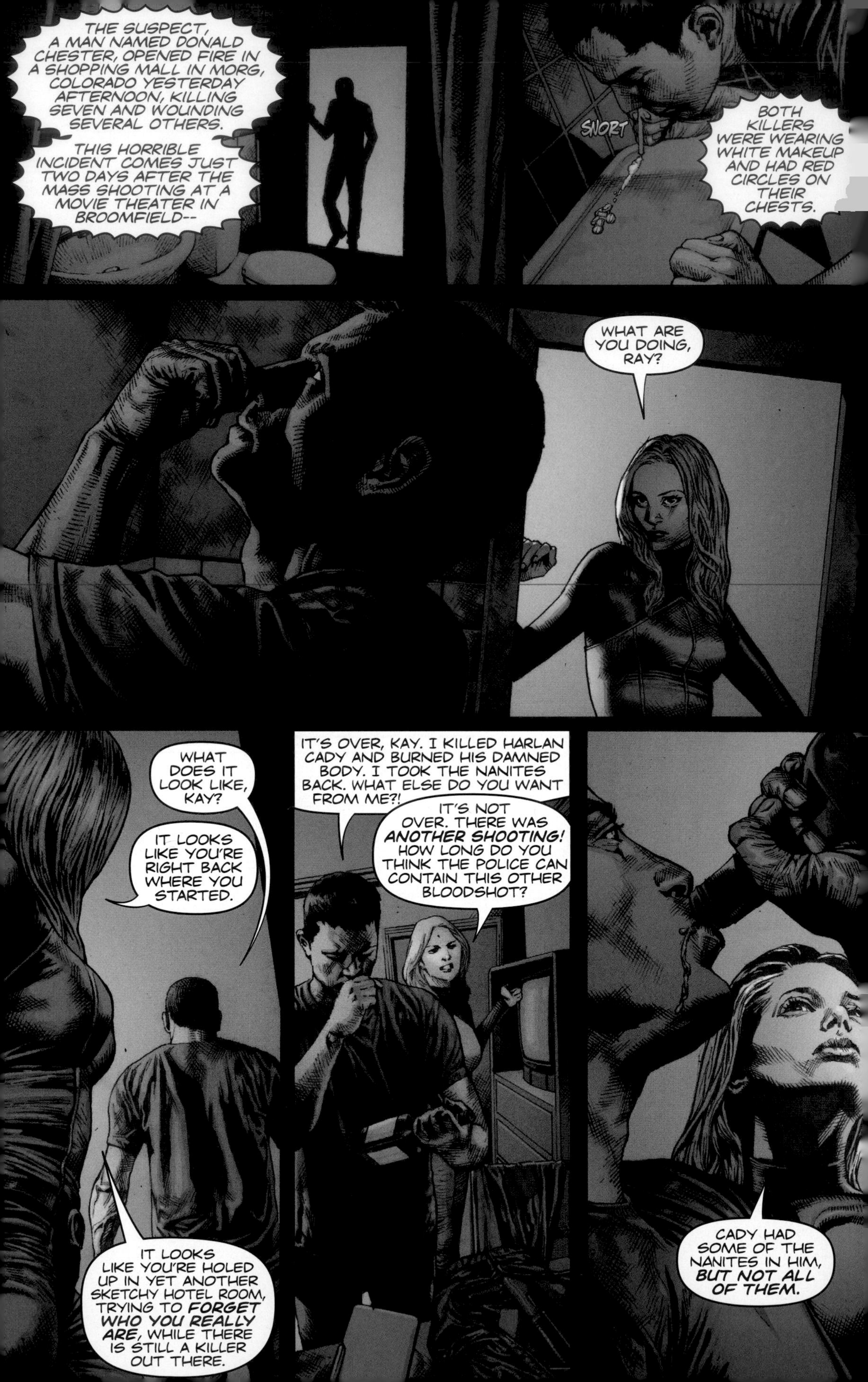
THE SUSPECT, A MAN NAMED DONALD CHESTER, OPENED FIRE IN A SHOPPING MALL IN MORG, COLORADO YESTERDAY AFTERNOON, KILLING SEVEN AND WOUNDING SEVERAL OTHERS.
THIS HORRIBLE INCIDENT COMES JUST TWO DAYS AFTER THE MASS SHOOTING AT A MOVIE THEATER IN BROOMFIELD--
SNORT
BOTH KILLERS WERE WEARING WHITE MAKEUP AND HAD RED CIRCLES ON THEIR CHESTS.
WHAT ARE YOU DOING, RAY?
WHAT DOES IT LOOK LIKE, KAY?
IT LOOKS LIKE YOU'RE RIGHT BACK WHERE YOU STARTED.
IT LOOKS LIKE YOU'RE HOLED UP IN YET ANOTHER SKETCHY HOTEL ROOM, TRYING TO FORGET WHO YOU REALLY ARE, WHILE THERE IS STILL A KILLER OUT THERE.
IT'S OVER, KAY. I KILLED HARLAN CADY AND BURNED HIS DAMNED BODY. I TOOK THE NANITES BACK. WHAT ELSE DO YOU WANT FROM ME?!
IT'S NOT OVER. THERE WAS ANOTHER SHOOTING! HOW LONG DO YOU THINK THE POLICE CAN CONTAIN THIS OTHER BLOODSHOT?
CADY HAD SOME OF THE NANITES IN HIM, BUT NOT ALL OF THEM.

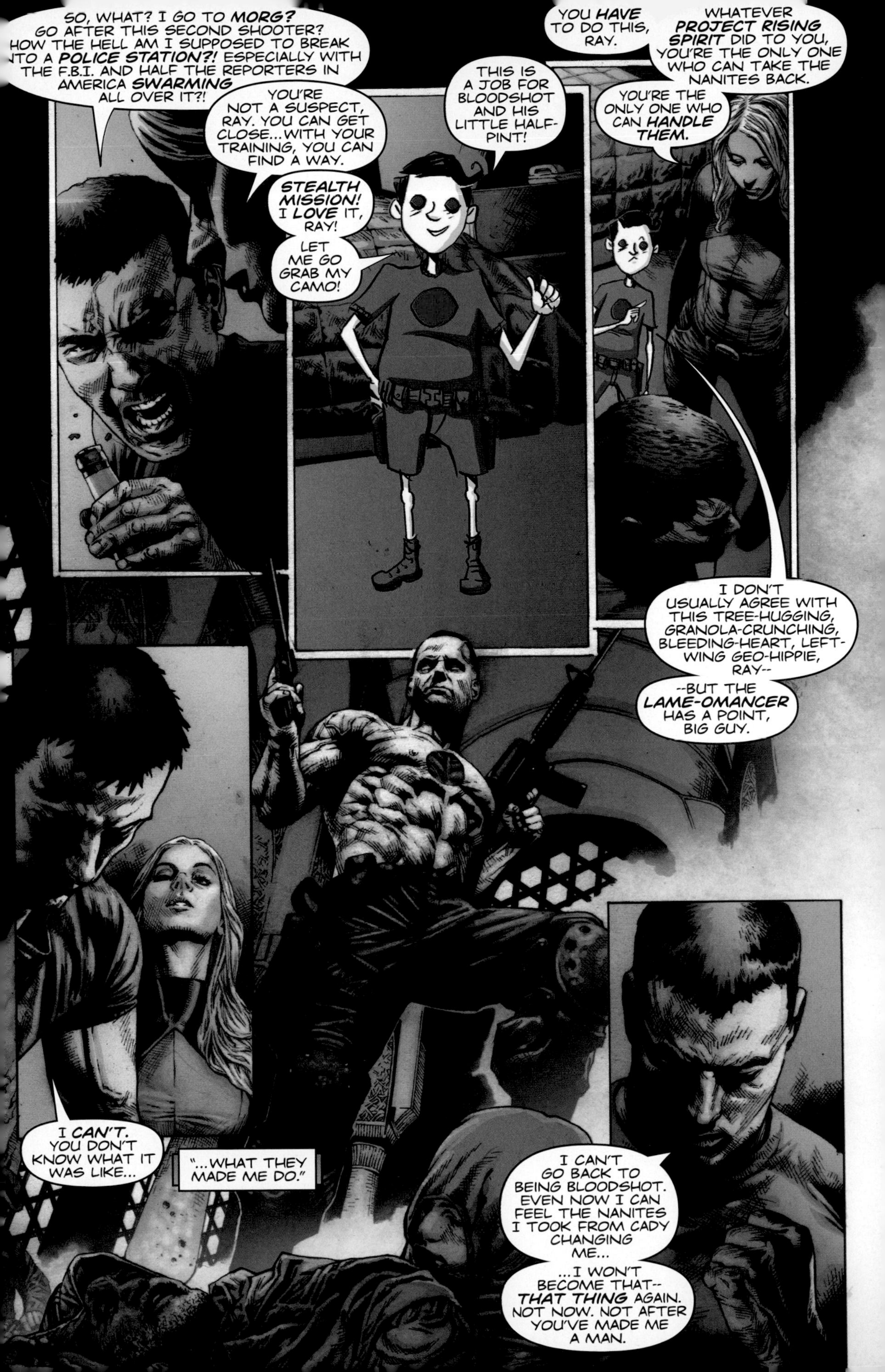

SO, WHAT? I GO TO **MORG?** GO AFTER THIS SECOND SHOOTER? HOW THE HELL AM I SUPPOSED TO BREAK INTO A **POLICE STATION?!** ESPECIALLY WITH THE F.B.I. AND HALF THE REPORTERS IN AMERICA **SWARMING** ALL OVER IT?!
YOU'RE NOT A SUSPECT, RAY. YOU CAN GET CLOSE...WITH YOUR TRAINING, YOU CAN FIND A WAY.
THIS IS A JOB FOR BLOODSHOT AND HIS LITTLE HALF-PINT!
STEALTH MISSION! I **LOVE** IT, RAY!
LET ME GO GRAB MY CAMO!
YOU **HAVE** TO DO THIS, RAY.
WHATEVER **PROJECT RISING SPIRIT** DID TO YOU, YOU'RE THE ONLY ONE WHO CAN TAKE THE NANITES BACK.
YOU'RE THE ONLY ONE WHO CAN **HANDLE THEM.**
I DON'T USUALLY AGREE WITH THIS TREE-HUGGING, GRANOLA-CRUNCHING, BLEEDING-HEART, LEFT-WING GEO-HIPPIE, RAY--
--BUT THE **LAME-OMANCER** HAS A POINT, BIG GUY.
I **CAN'T.** YOU DON'T KNOW WHAT IT WAS LIKE...
"...WHAT THEY MADE ME DO."
I CAN'T GO BACK TO BEING BLOODSHOT. EVEN NOW I CAN FEEL THE NANITES I TOOK FROM CADY CHANGING ME...
...I WON'T BECOME THAT-- **THAT THING** AGAIN. NOT NOW. NOT AFTER YOU'VE MADE ME A MAN.

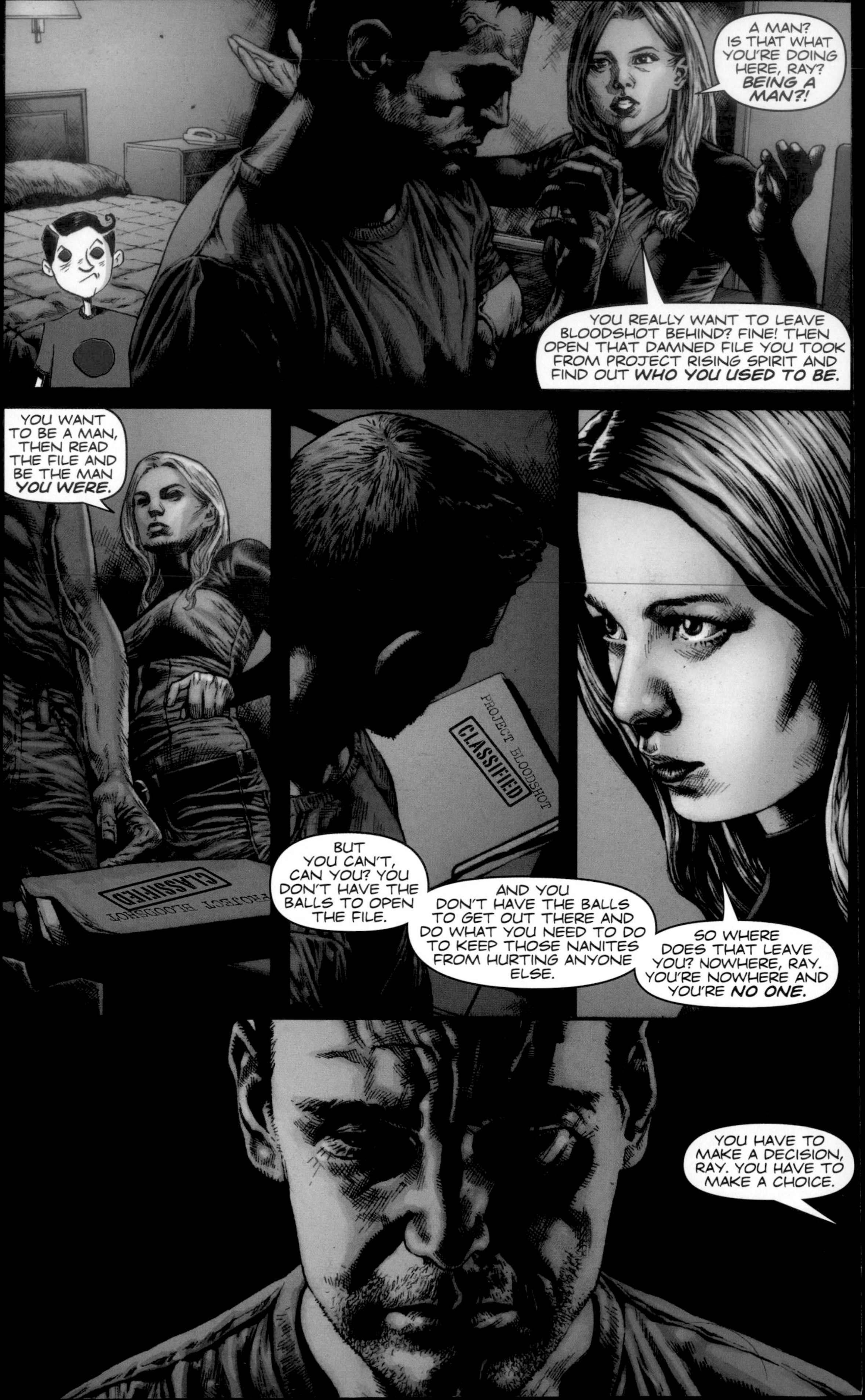

A MAN? IS THAT WHAT YOU'RE DOING HERE, RAY? *BEING A MAN?!*
YOU REALLY WANT TO LEAVE BLOODSHOT BEHIND? FINE! THEN OPEN THAT DAMNED FILE YOU TOOK FROM PROJECT RISING SPIRIT AND FIND OUT *WHO YOU USED TO BE.*
YOU WANT TO BE A MAN, THEN READ THE FILE AND BE THE MAN *YOU WERE.*
CLASSIFIED
PROJECT BLOODSHOT
PROJECT BLOODSHOT
CLASSIFIED
BUT YOU CAN'T, CAN YOU? YOU DON'T HAVE THE BALLS TO OPEN THE FILE.
AND YOU DON'T HAVE THE BALLS TO GET OUT THERE AND DO WHAT YOU NEED TO DO TO KEEP THOSE NANITES FROM HURTING ANYONE ELSE.
SO WHERE DOES THAT LEAVE YOU? NOWHERE, RAY. YOU'RE NOWHERE AND YOU'RE *NO ONE.*
YOU HAVE TO MAKE A DECISION, RAY. YOU HAVE TO MAKE A CHOICE.

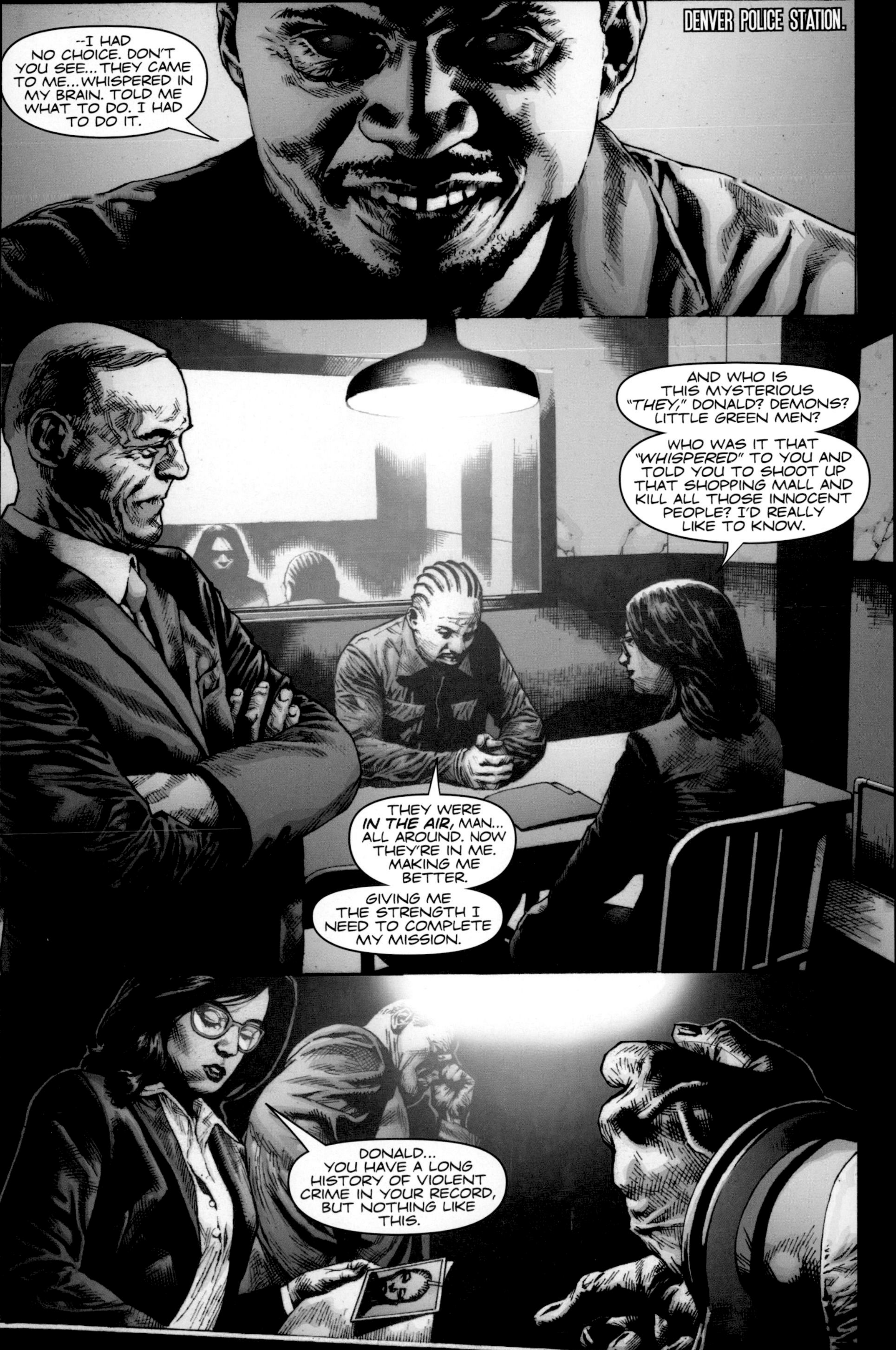
DENVER POLICE STATION.
--I HAD NO CHOICE. DON'T YOU SEE...THEY CAME TO ME...WHISPERED IN MY BRAIN. TOLD ME WHAT TO DO. I HAD TO DO IT.
AND WHO IS THIS MYSTERIOUS "THEY," DONALD? DEMONS? LITTLE GREEN MEN?
WHO WAS IT THAT "WHISPERED" TO YOU AND TOLD YOU TO SHOOT UP THAT SHOPPING MALL AND KILL ALL THOSE INNOCENT PEOPLE? I'D REALLY LIKE TO KNOW.
THEY WERE IN THE AIR, MAN... ALL AROUND. NOW THEY'RE IN ME. MAKING ME BETTER.
GIVING ME THE STRENGTH I NEED TO COMPLETE MY MISSION.
DONALD... YOU HAVE A LONG HISTORY OF VIOLENT CRIME IN YOUR RECORD, BUT NOTHING LIKE THIS.

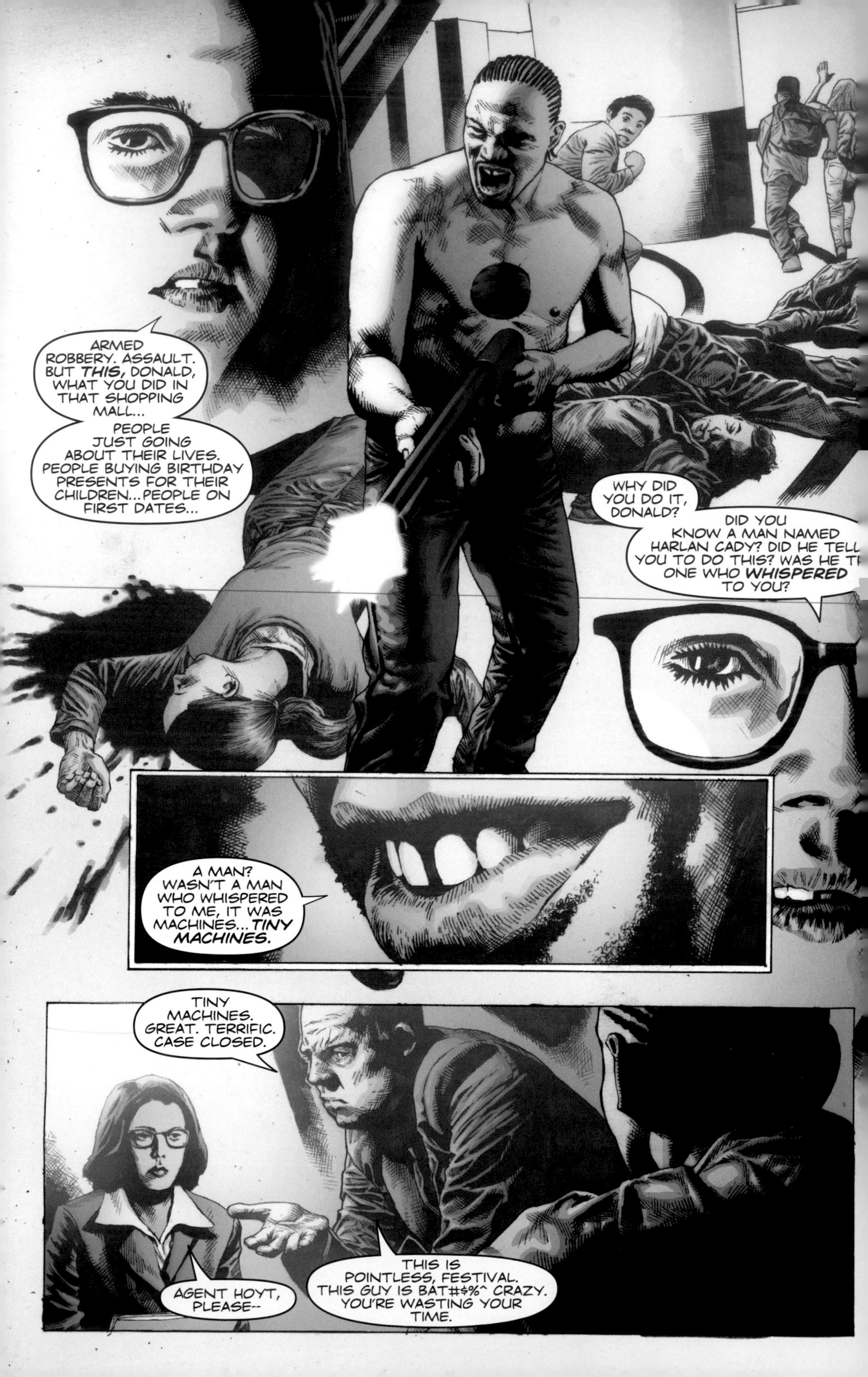
ARMED ROBBERY. ASSAULT. BUT THIS, DONALD, WHAT YOU DID IN THAT SHOPPING MALL...
PEOPLE JUST GOING ABOUT THEIR LIVES. PEOPLE BUYING BIRTHDAY PRESENTS FOR THEIR CHILDREN...PEOPLE ON FIRST DATES...
WHY DID YOU DO IT, DONALD?
DID YOU KNOW A MAN NAMED HARLAN CADY? DID HE TELL YOU TO DO THIS? WAS HE THE ONE WHO WHISPERED TO YOU?
A MAN? WASN'T A MAN WHO WHISPERED TO ME, IT WAS MACHINES...TINY MACHINES.
TINY MACHINES. GREAT. TERRIFIC. CASE CLOSED.
AGENT HOYT, PLEASE--
THIS IS POINTLESS, FESTIVAL. THIS GUY IS BAT#$%^ CRAZY. YOU'RE WASTING YOUR TIME.

YOU'RE NOT HELPING, HOYT.

OH, *EXCUSE ME,* CAPTAIN WUNDERKIND.

I'LL JUST STAY OUT HERE SO YOU AND THAT PSYCHO CAN DISCUSS THE IMPENDING ROBOT INVASION.

DONALD CHESTER IS UNHINGED. CLEARLY. BUT THERE IS SOMETHING ELSE GOING ON HERE, HOYT.

THE LAB RESULTS STILL AREN'T BACK, BUT THAT IS NOT MAKEUP ON HIS SKIN, OR CONTACTS IN THE EYES.

HE'S DONE SOMETHING TO HIMSELF...OR SOMEONE'S DONE SOMETHING TO HIM.

YOU THINK HARLAN CADY DID THAT TO HIM? SOME KIND OF MURDER CULT THING?

I DON'T KNOW WHAT TO THINK.

ALL I KNOW IS THAT WE HAVE TWO MASS SHOOTINGS WITHIN TWO DAYS OF EACH OTHER AND HARLAN CADY IS DEAD.

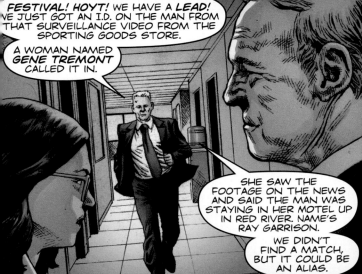

FESTIVAL! HOYT! WE HAVE A *LEAD!* WE JUST GOT AN I.D. ON THE MAN FROM THAT SURVEILLANCE VIDEO FROM THE SPORTING GOODS STORE.

A WOMAN NAMED *GENE TREMONT* CALLED IT IN.

SHE SAW THE FOOTAGE ON THE NEWS AND SAID THE MAN WAS STAYING IN HER MOTEL UP IN RED RIVER. NAME'S RAY GARRISON.

WE DIDN'T FIND A MATCH, BUT IT COULD BE AN ALIAS.

JESUS! YOU DON'T REALLY THINK THERE'S ANOTHER ONE OUT THERE, DO YOU?

IF THERE IS WE'RE GOING TO FIND HIM BEFORE HE CAN HURT ANYONE ELSE!

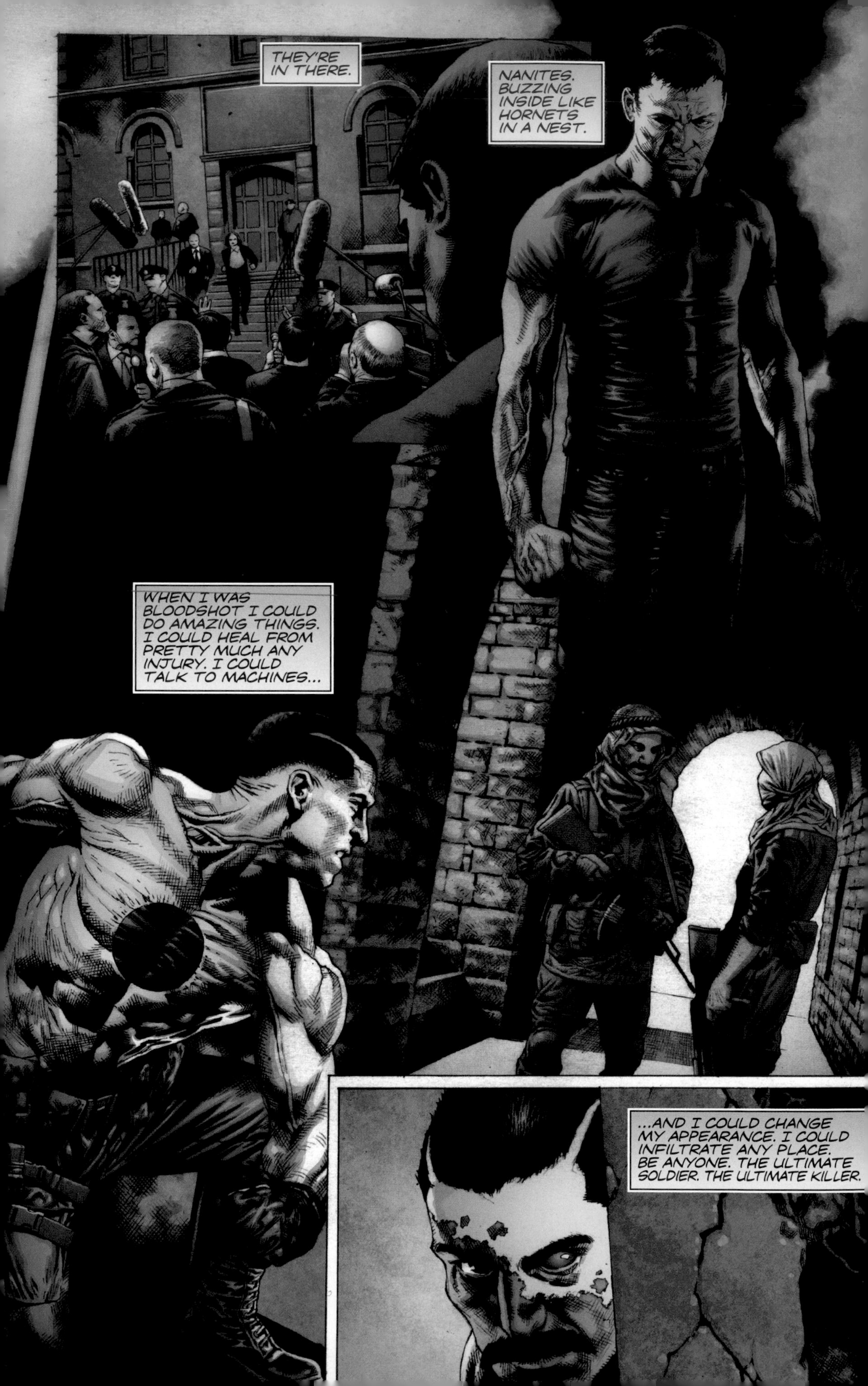
THEY'RE IN THERE.
NANITES. BUZZING INSIDE LIKE HORNETS IN A NEST.
WHEN I WAS BLOODSHOT I COULD DO AMAZING THINGS. I COULD HEAL FROM PRETTY MUCH ANY INJURY. I COULD TALK TO MACHINES...
...AND I COULD CHANGE MY APPEARANCE. I COULD INFILTRATE ANY PLACE. BE ANYONE. THE ULTIMATE SOLDIER. THE ULTIMATE KILLER.

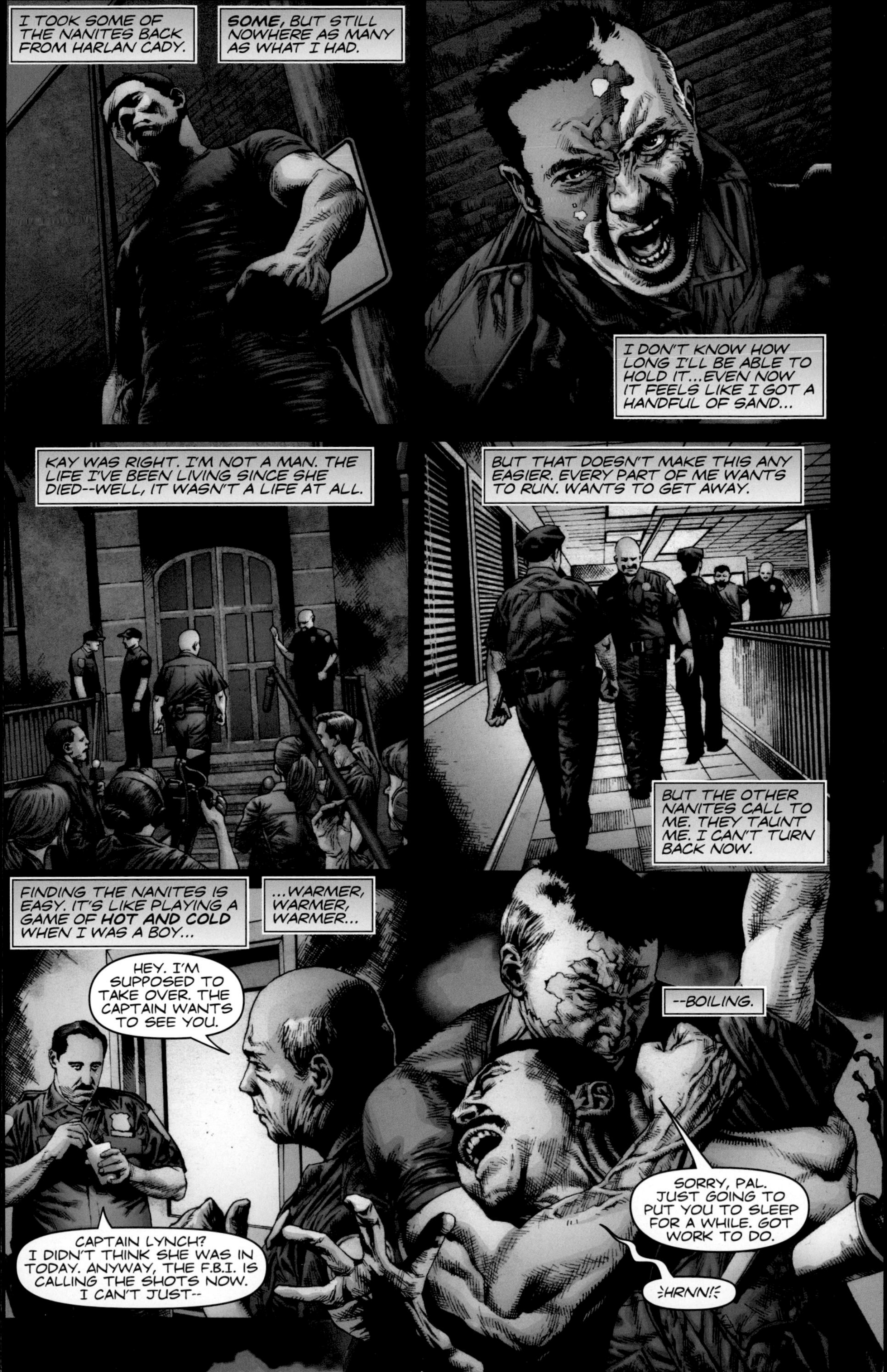

I TOOK SOME OF THE NANITES BACK FROM HARLAN CADY.
SOME, BUT STILL NOWHERE AS MANY AS WHAT I HAD.
I DON'T KNOW HOW LONG I'LL BE ABLE TO HOLD IT...EVEN NOW IT FEELS LIKE I GOT A HANDFUL OF SAND...
KAY WAS RIGHT. I'M NOT A MAN. THE LIFE I'VE BEEN LIVING SINCE SHE DIED--WELL, IT WASN'T A LIFE AT ALL.
BUT THAT DOESN'T MAKE THIS ANY EASIER. EVERY PART OF ME WANTS TO RUN. WANTS TO GET AWAY.
BUT THE OTHER NANITES CALL TO ME. THEY TAUNT ME. I CAN'T TURN BACK NOW.
FINDING THE NANITES IS EASY. IT'S LIKE PLAYING A GAME OF **HOT AND COLD** WHEN I WAS A BOY...
...WARMER, WARMER, WARMER...
HEY. I'M SUPPOSED TO TAKE OVER. THE CAPTAIN WANTS TO SEE YOU.
CAPTAIN LYNCH? I DIDN'T THINK SHE WAS IN TODAY. ANYWAY, THE F.B.I. IS CALLING THE SHOTS NOW. I CAN'T JUST--
--BOILING.
SORRY, PAL. JUST GOING TO PUT YOU TO SLEEP FOR A WHILE. GOT WORK TO DO.
HRNN!

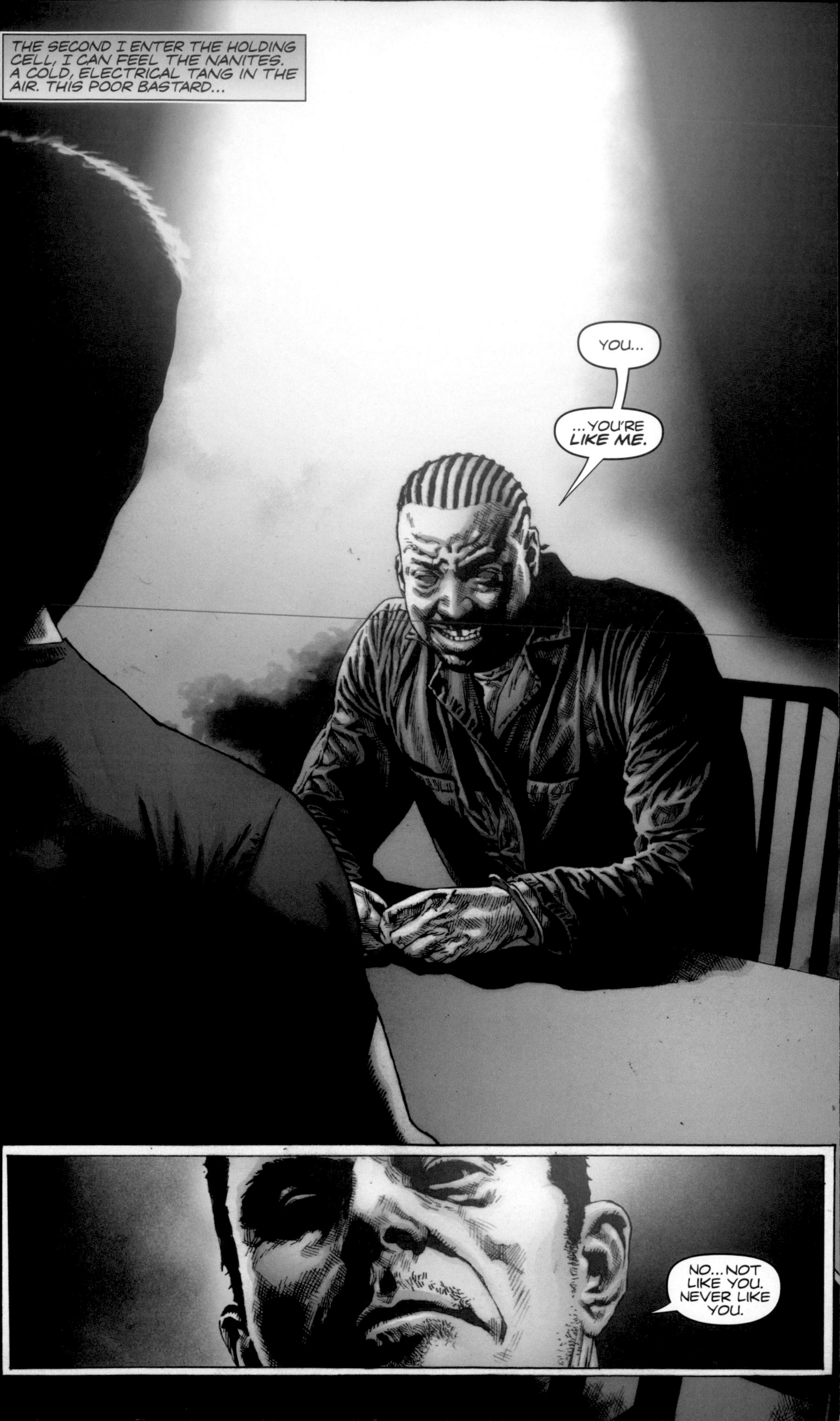
THE SECOND I ENTER THE HOLDING CELL, I CAN FEEL THE NANITES. A COLD, ELECTRICAL TANG IN THE AIR. THIS POOR BASTARD...
YOU...
...YOU'RE LIKE ME.
NO...NOT LIKE YOU. NEVER LIKE YOU.

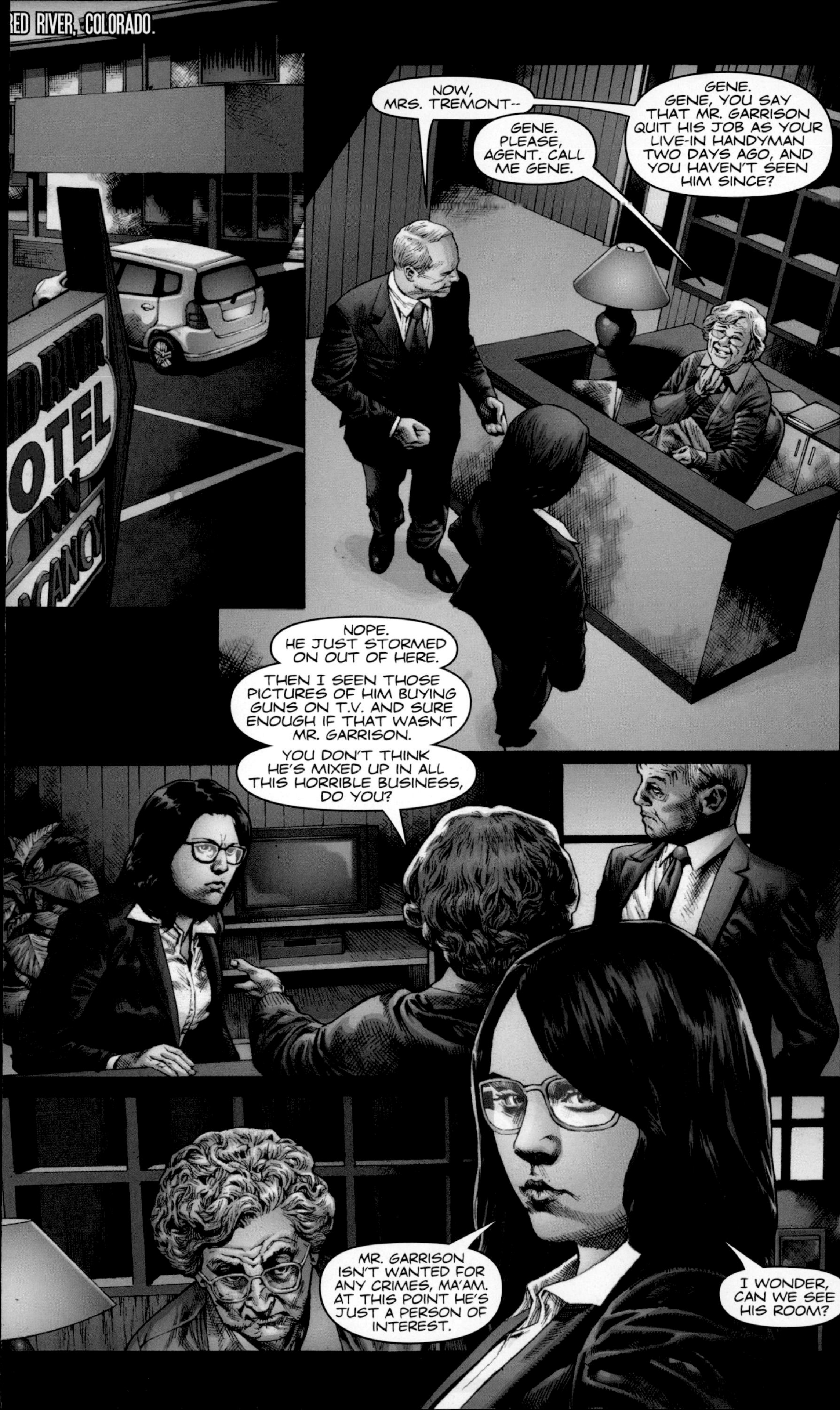
RED RIVER, COLORADO.
OTEL
INN
NOW, MRS. TREMONT--
GENE. PLEASE, AGENT. CALL ME GENE.
GENE. GENE, YOU SAY THAT MR. GARRISON QUIT HIS JOB AS YOUR LIVE-IN HANDYMAN TWO DAYS AGO, AND YOU HAVEN'T SEEN HIM SINCE?
NOPE. HE JUST STORMED ON OUT OF HERE.
THEN I SEEN THOSE PICTURES OF HIM BUYING GUNS ON T.V. AND SURE ENOUGH IF THAT WASN'T MR. GARRISON.
YOU DON'T THINK HE'S MIXED UP IN ALL THIS HORRIBLE BUSINESS, DO YOU?
MR. GARRISON ISN'T WANTED FOR ANY CRIMES, MA'AM. AT THIS POINT HE'S JUST A PERSON OF INTEREST.
I WONDER, CAN WE SEE HIS ROOM?

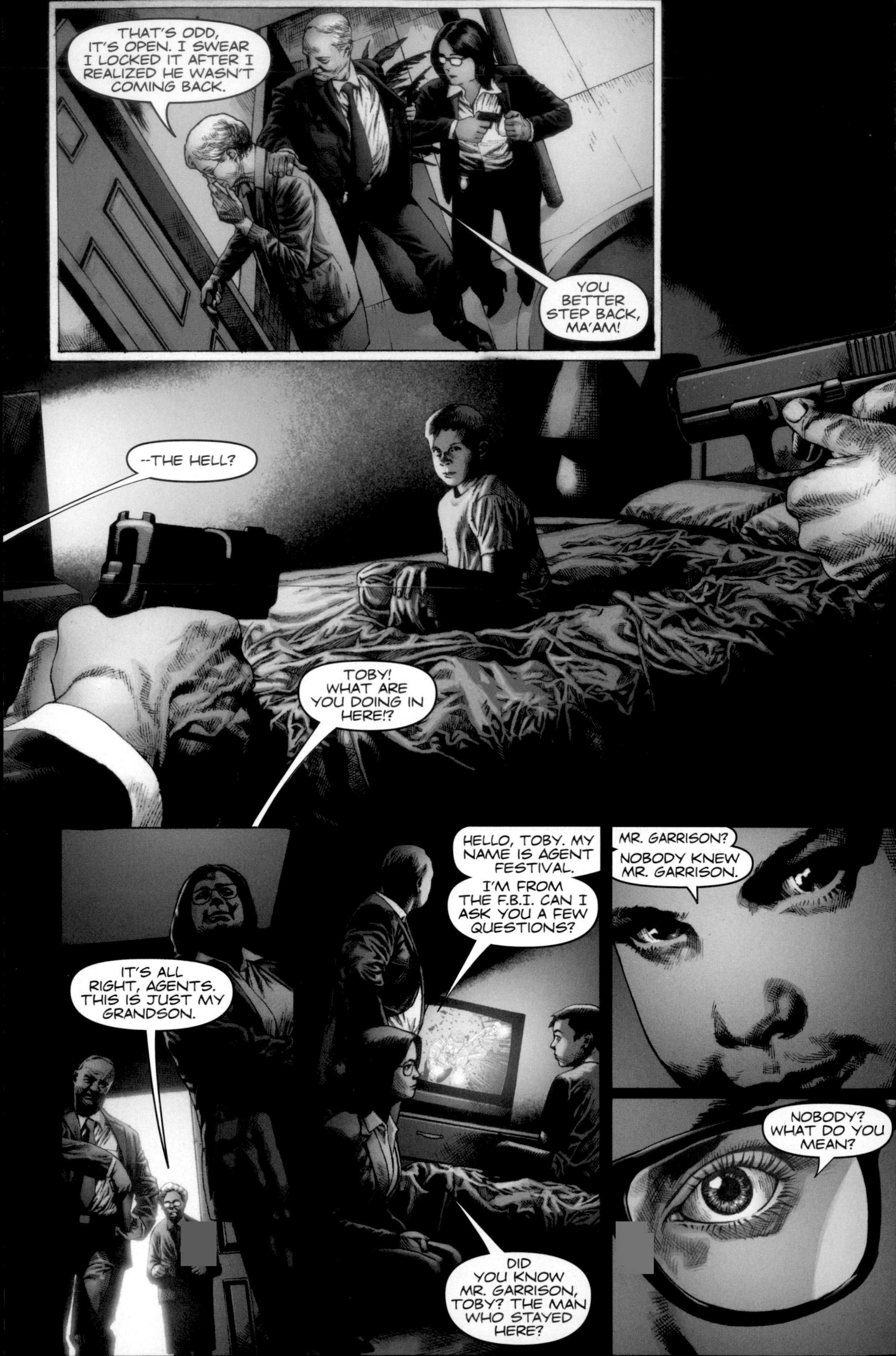
THAT'S ODD, IT'S OPEN. I SWEAR I LOCKED IT AFTER I REALIZED HE WASN'T COMING BACK.
YOU BETTER STEP BACK, MA'AM!
--THE HELL?
TOBY! WHAT ARE YOU DOING IN HERE!?
IT'S ALL RIGHT, AGENTS. THIS IS JUST MY GRANDSON.
HELLO, TOBY. MY NAME IS AGENT FESTIVAL.
I'M FROM THE F.B.I. CAN I ASK YOU A FEW QUESTIONS?
DID YOU KNOW MR. GARRISON, TOBY? THE MAN WHO STAYED HERE?
MR. GARRISON?
NOBODY KNEW MR. GARRISON.
NOBODY? WHAT DO YOU MEAN?

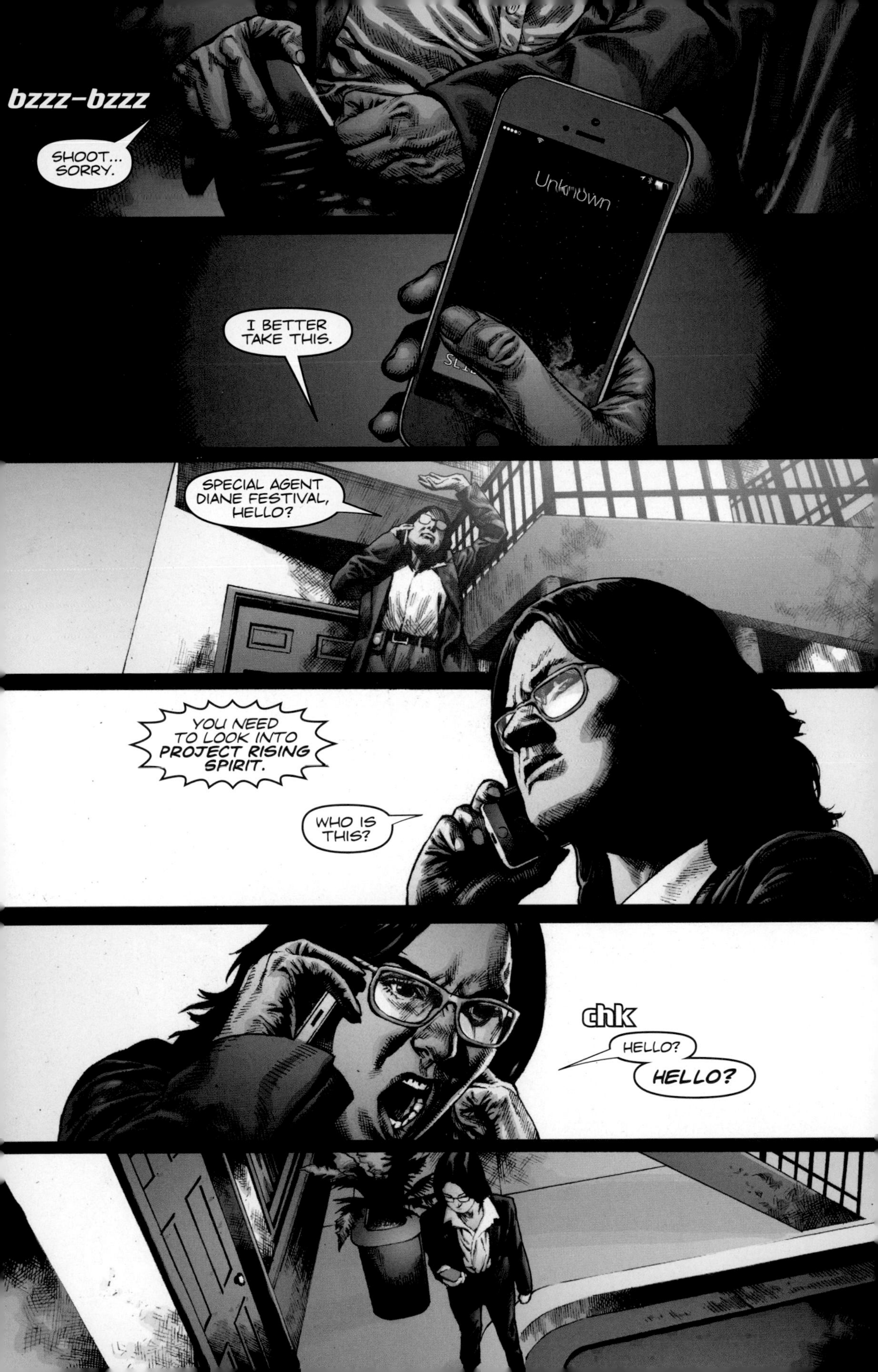
bzzz-bzzz
SHOOT... SORRY.
Unknown
I BETTER TAKE THIS.
SPECIAL AGENT DIANE FESTIVAL, HELLO?
YOU NEED TO LOOK INTO PROJECT RISING SPIRIT.
WHO IS THIS?
chk
HELLO?
HELLO?

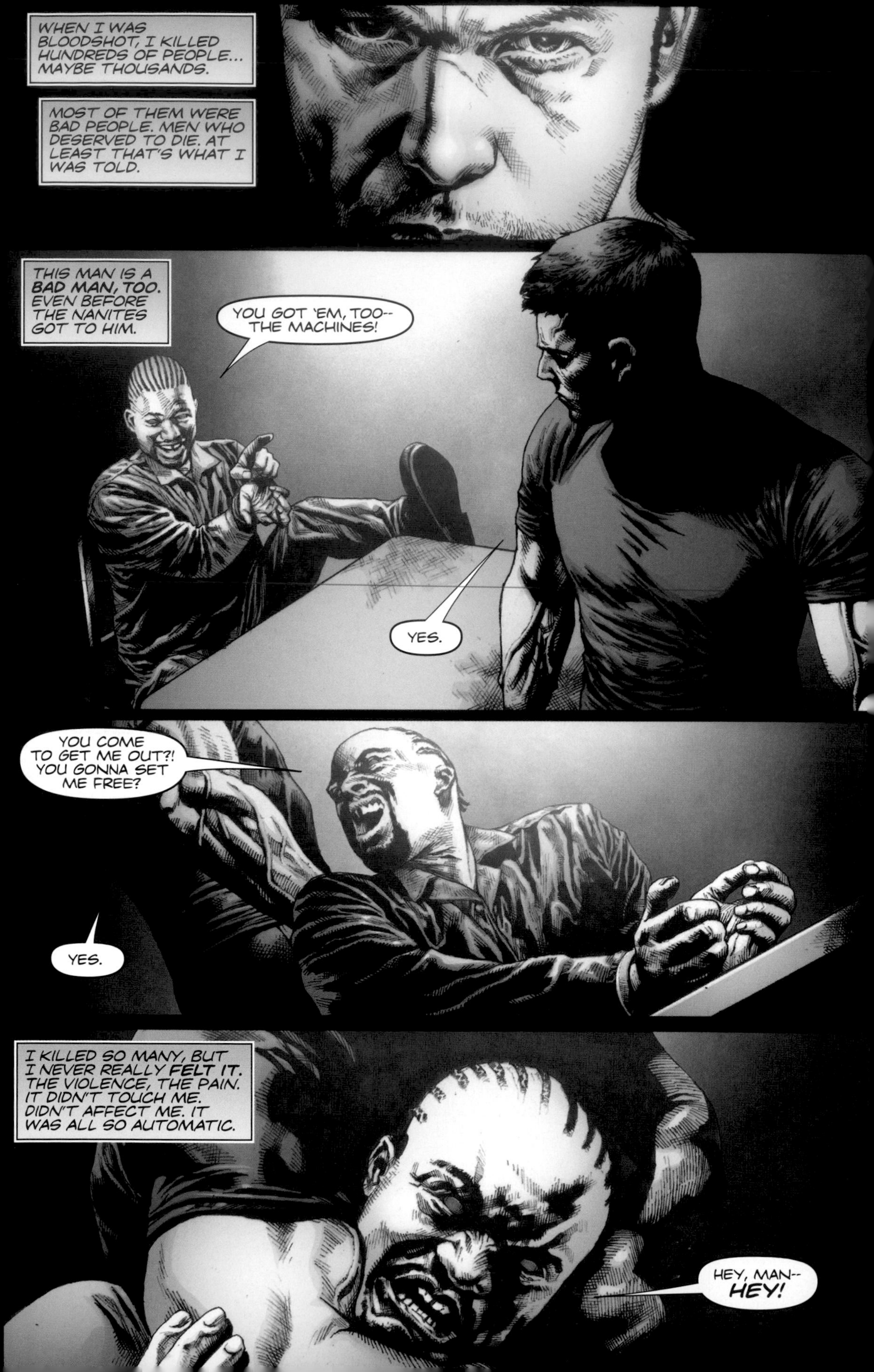

WHEN I WAS BLOODSHOT, I KILLED HUNDREDS OF PEOPLE... MAYBE THOUSANDS.
MOST OF THEM WERE BAD PEOPLE. MEN WHO DESERVED TO DIE. AT LEAST THAT'S WHAT I WAS TOLD.
THIS MAN IS A BAD MAN, TOO. EVEN BEFORE THE NANITES GOT TO HIM.
YOU GOT 'EM, TOO-- THE MACHINES!
YES.
YOU COME TO GET ME OUT?! YOU GONNA SET ME FREE?
YES.
I KILLED SO MANY, BUT I NEVER REALLY FELT IT. THE VIOLENCE, THE PAIN. IT DIDN'T TOUCH ME. DIDN'T AFFECT ME. IT WAS ALL SO AUTOMATIC.
HEY, MAN-- HEY!

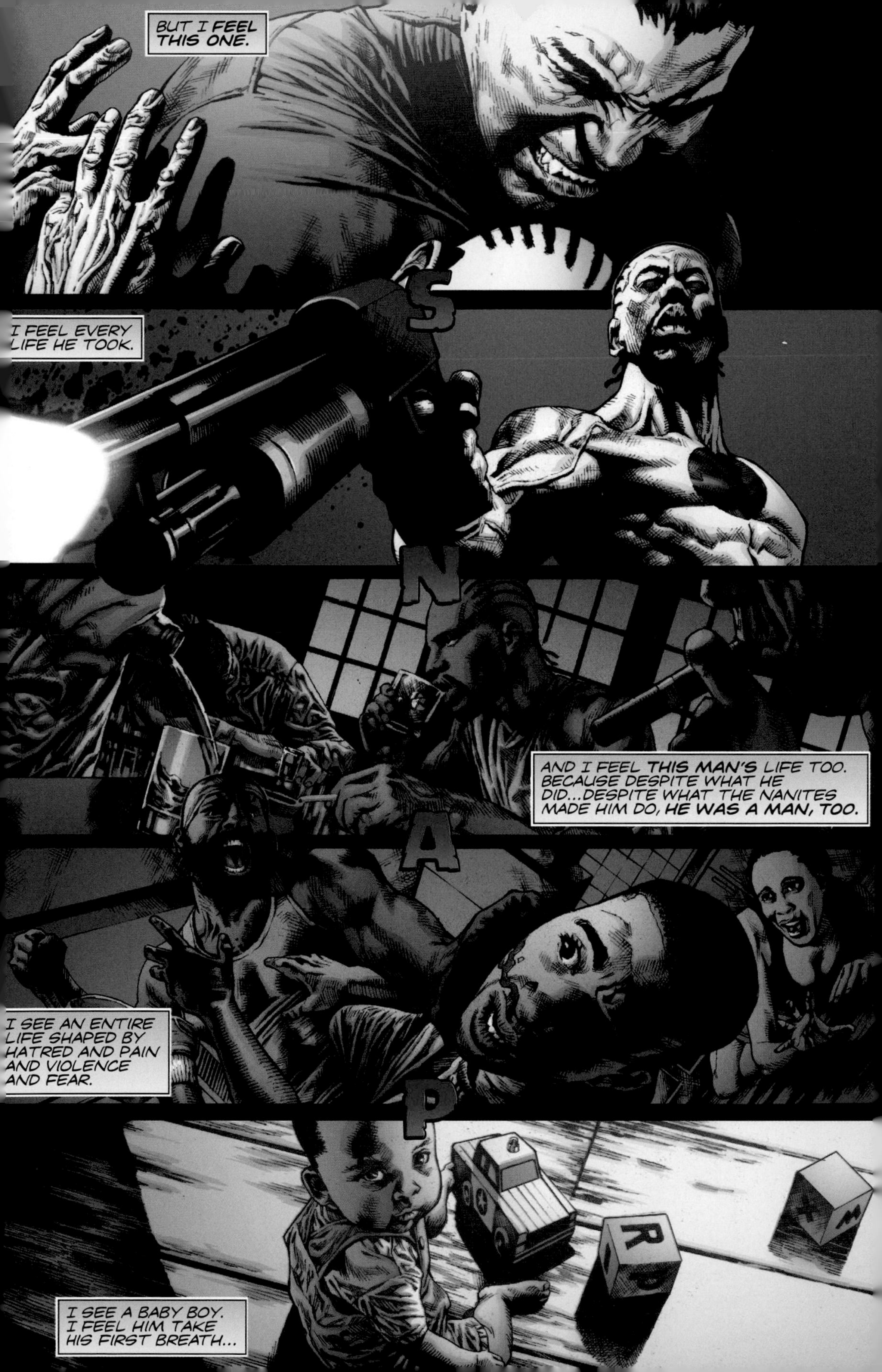
BUT I FEEL THIS ONE.
I FEEL EVERY LIFE HE TOOK.
S
N
AND I FEEL THIS MAN'S LIFE TOO. BECAUSE DESPITE WHAT HE DID...DESPITE WHAT THE NANITES MADE HIM DO, HE WAS A MAN, TOO.
A
I SEE AN ENTIRE LIFE SHAPED BY HATRED AND PAIN AND VIOLENCE AND FEAR.
P
I SEE A BABY BOY. I FEEL HIM TAKE HIS FIRST BREATH...

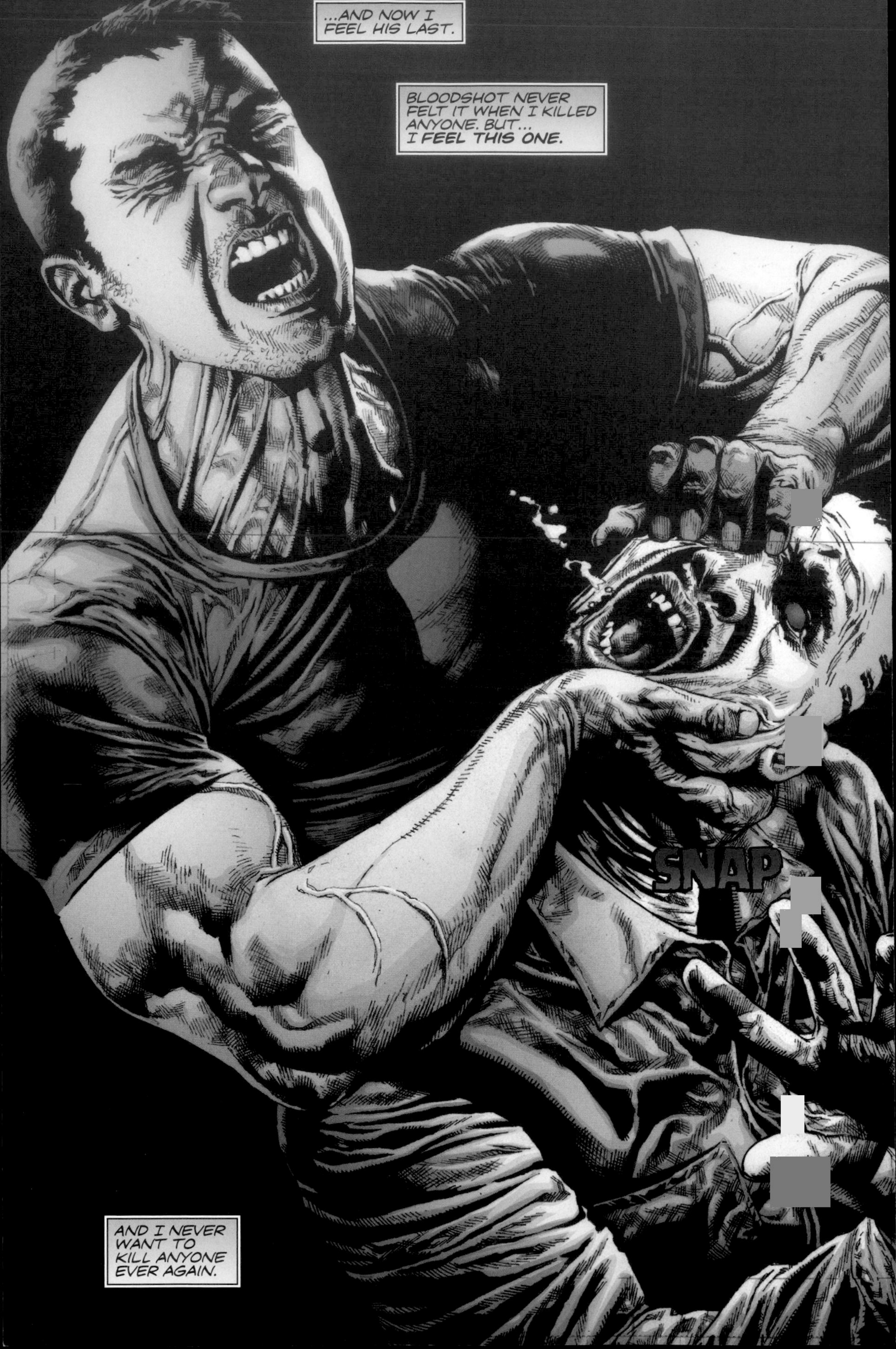
...AND NOW I FEEL HIS LAST.
BLOODSHOT NEVER FELT IT WHEN I KILLED ANYONE. BUT... I FEEL THIS ONE.
SNAP
AND I NEVER WANT TO KILL ANYONE EVER AGAIN.

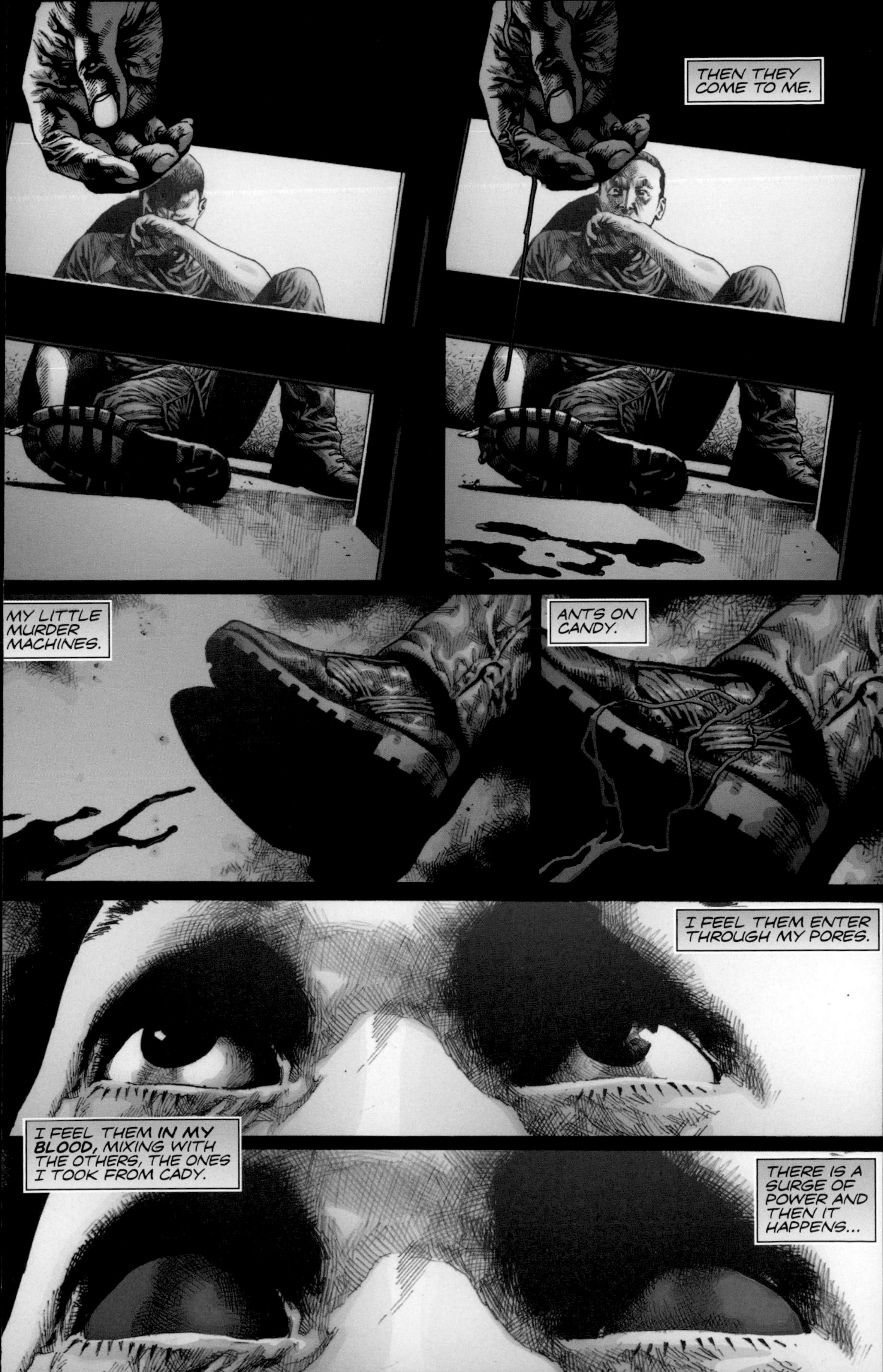
THEN THEY COME TO ME.
MY LITTLE MURDER MACHINES.
ANTS ON CANDY.
I FEEL THEM ENTER THROUGH MY PORES.
I FEEL THEM **IN MY BLOOD**, MIXING WITH THE OTHERS, THE ONES I TOOK FROM CADY.
THERE IS A SURGE OF POWER AND THEN IT HAPPENS...

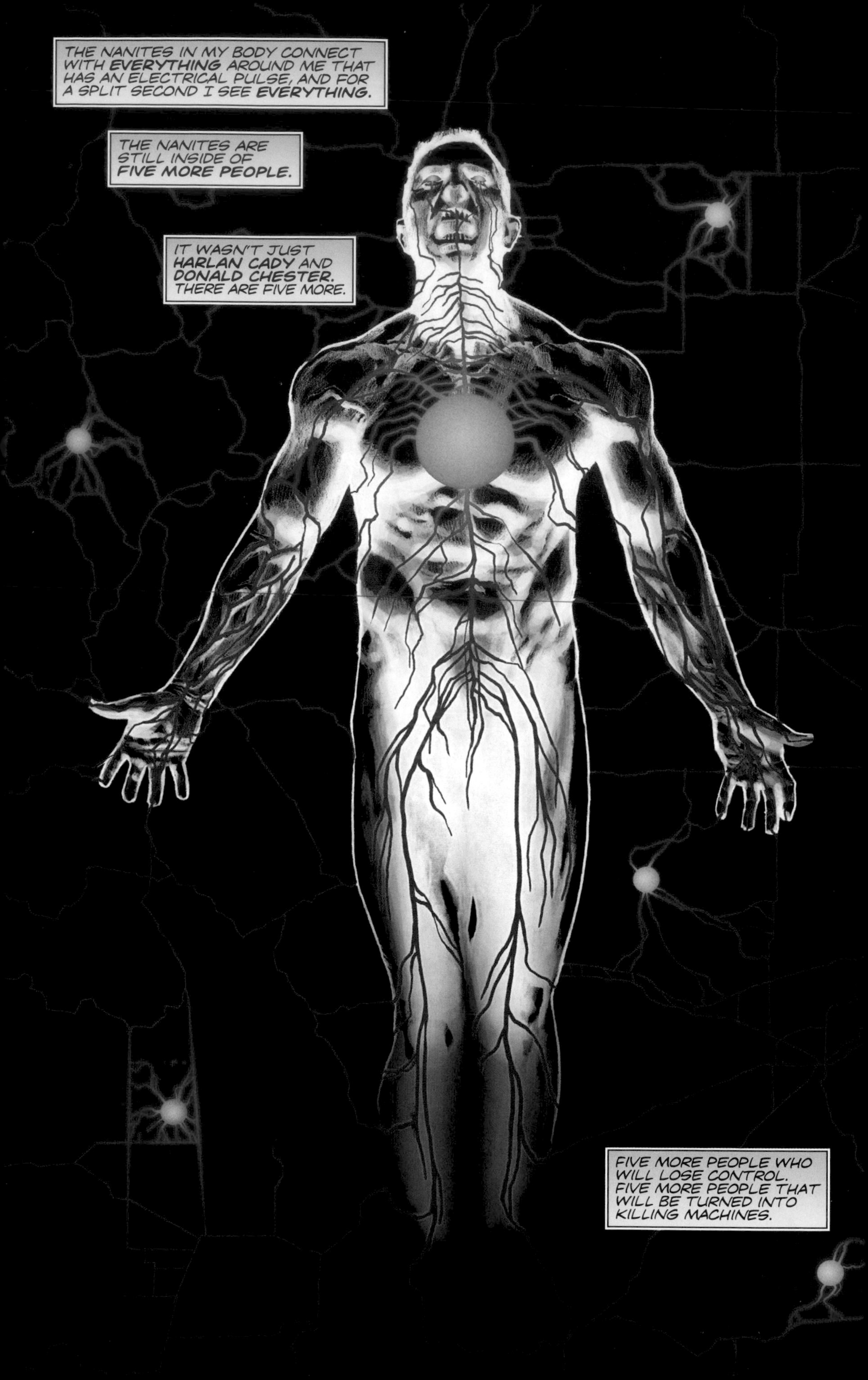
THE NANITES IN MY BODY CONNECT WITH EVERYTHING AROUND ME THAT HAS AN ELECTRICAL PULSE, AND FOR A SPLIT SECOND I SEE EVERYTHING.
THE NANITES ARE STILL INSIDE OF FIVE MORE PEOPLE.
IT WASN'T JUST HARLAN CADY AND DONALD CHESTER. THERE ARE FIVE MORE.
FIVE MORE PEOPLE WHO WILL LOSE CONTROL. FIVE MORE PEOPLE THAT WILL BE TURNED INTO KILLING MACHINES.

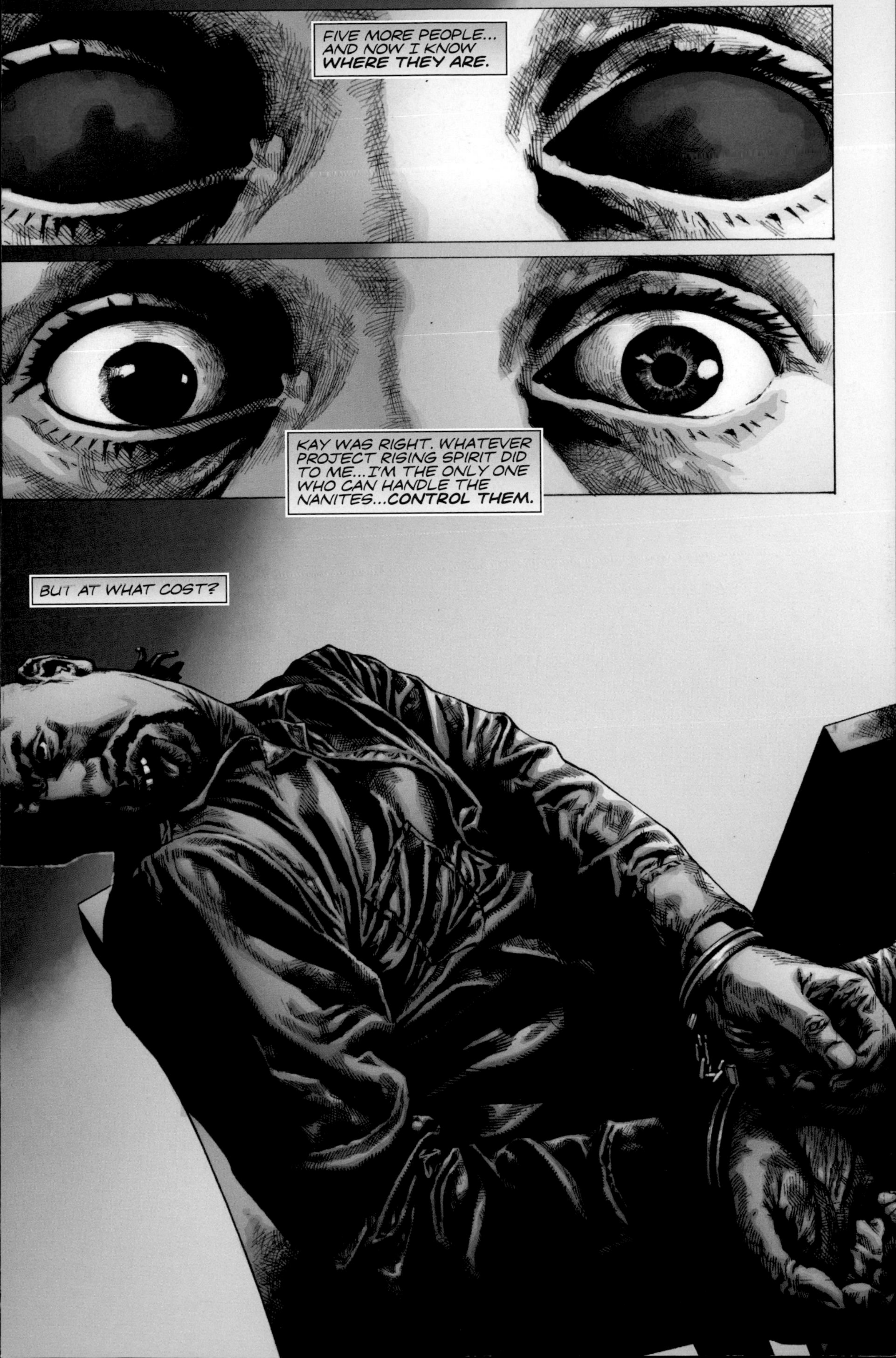
FIVE MORE PEOPLE... AND NOW I KNOW WHERE THEY ARE.
KAY WAS RIGHT. WHATEVER PROJECT RISING SPIRIT DID TO ME...I'M THE ONLY ONE WHO CAN HANDLE THE NANITES...CONTROL THEM.
BUT AT WHAT COST?

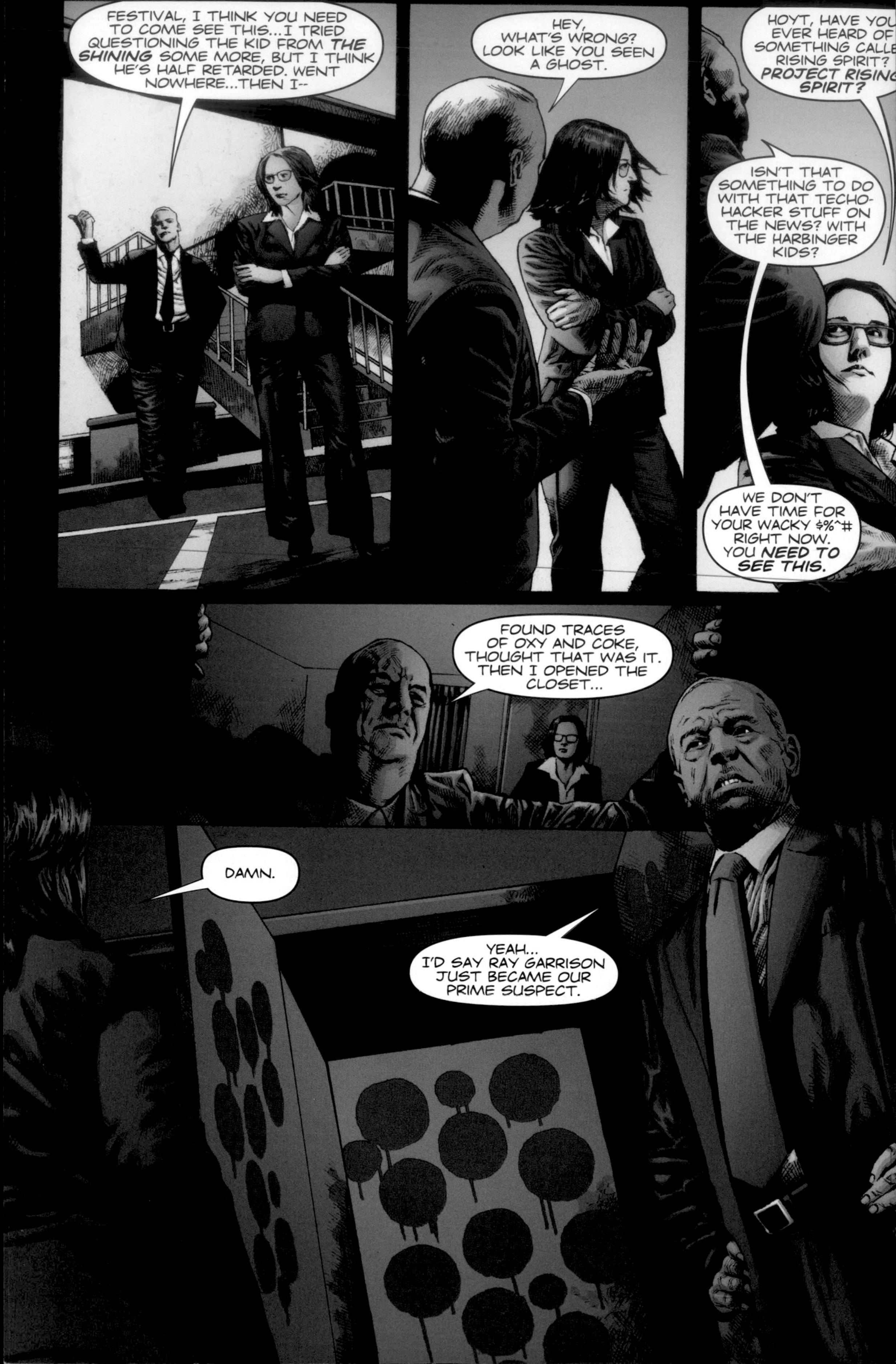
FESTIVAL, I THINK YOU NEED TO COME SEE THIS...I TRIED QUESTIONING THE KID FROM **THE SHINING** SOME MORE, BUT I THINK HE'S HALF RETARDED. WENT NOWHERE...THEN I--
HEY, WHAT'S WRONG? LOOK LIKE YOU SEEN A GHOST.
HOYT, HAVE YOU EVER HEARD OF SOMETHING CALLE RISING SPIRIT? **PROJECT RISING SPIRIT?**
ISN'T THAT SOMETHING TO DO WITH THAT TECHO-HACKER STUFF ON THE NEWS? WITH THE HARBINGER KIDS?
WE DON'T HAVE TIME FOR YOUR WACKY $%^# RIGHT NOW. YOU **NEED TO SEE THIS.**
FOUND TRACES OF OXY AND COKE, THOUGHT THAT WAS IT. THEN I OPENED THE CLOSET...
DAMN.
YEAH... I'D SAY RAY GARRISON JUST BECAME OUR PRIME SUSPECT.

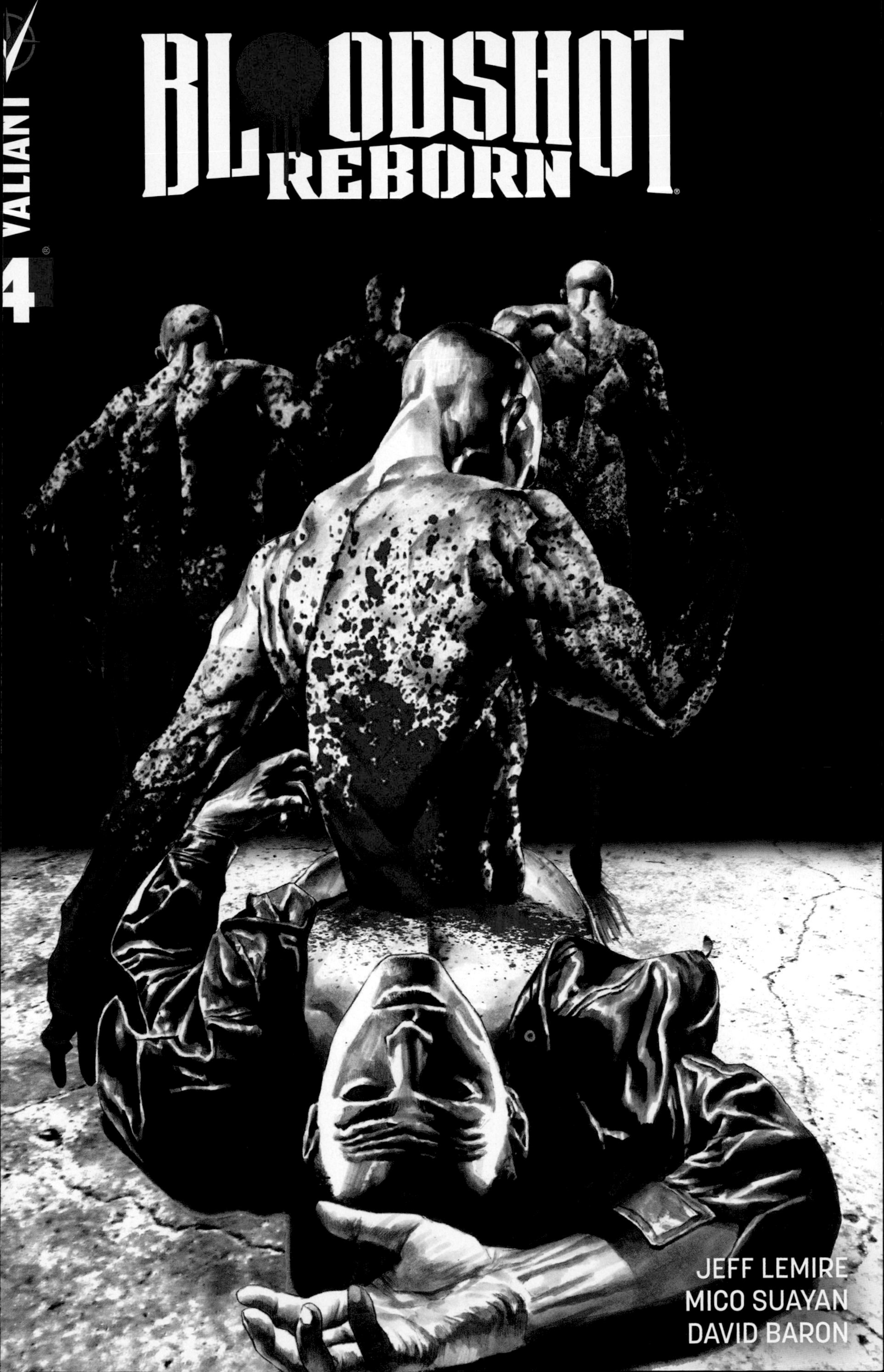
VALIANT
4
BLOODSHOT REBORN
JEFF LEMIRE
MICO SUAYAN
DAVID BARON

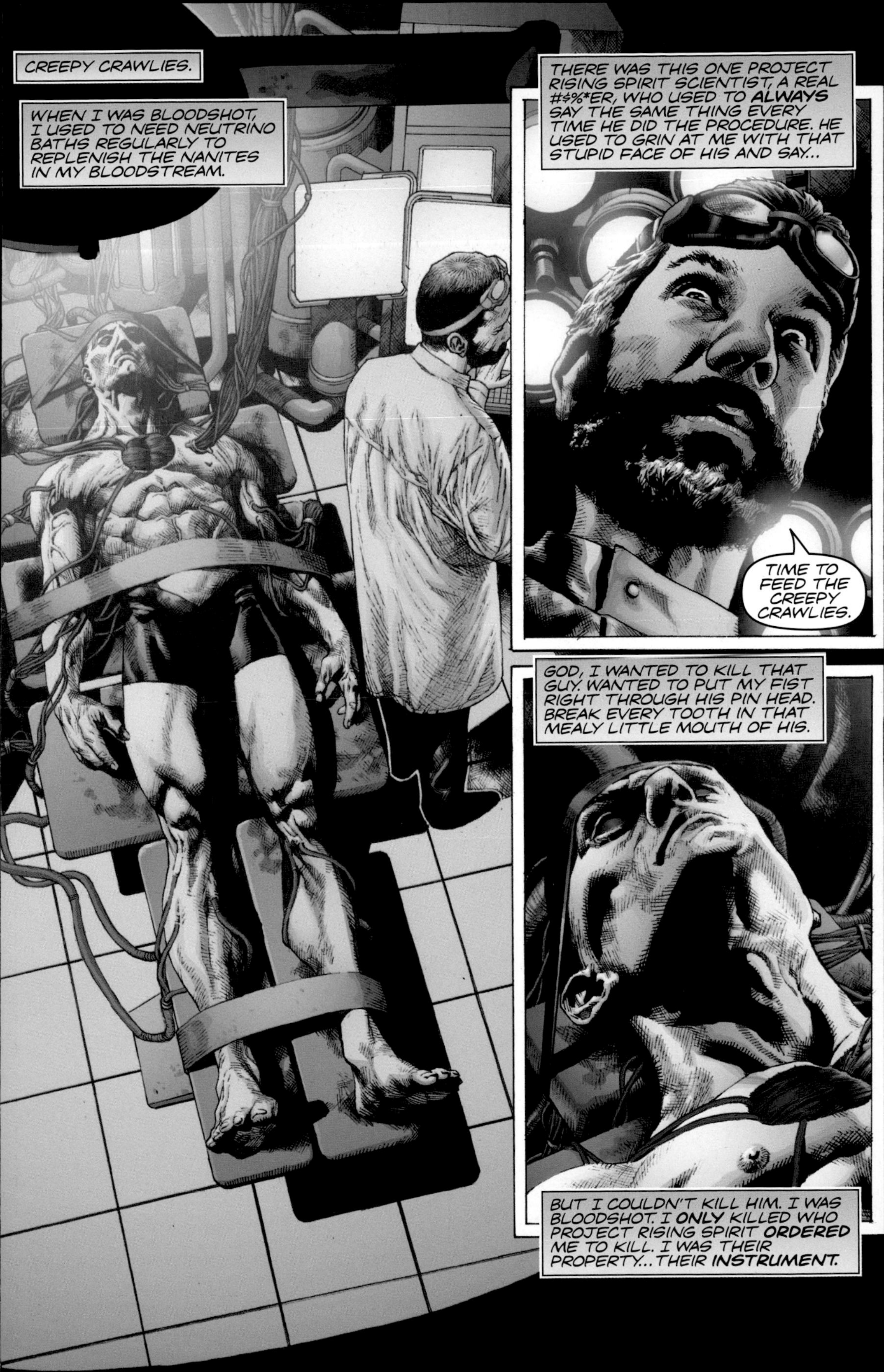
CREEPY CRAWLIES.
WHEN I WAS BLOODSHOT, I USED TO NEED NEUTRINO BATHS REGULARLY TO REPLENISH THE NANITES IN MY BLOODSTREAM.
THERE WAS THIS ONE PROJECT RISING SPIRIT SCIENTIST, A REAL #$%*ER, WHO USED TO ALWAYS SAY THE SAME THING EVERY TIME HE DID THE PROCEDURE. HE USED TO GRIN AT ME WITH THAT STUPID FACE OF HIS AND SAY...
TIME TO FEED THE CREEPY CRAWLIES.
GOD, I WANTED TO KILL THAT GUY. WANTED TO PUT MY FIST RIGHT THROUGH HIS PIN HEAD. BREAK EVERY TOOTH IN THAT MEALY LITTLE MOUTH OF HIS.
BUT I COULDN'T KILL HIM. I WAS BLOODSHOT. I ONLY KILLED WHO PROJECT RISING SPIRIT ORDERED ME TO KILL. I WAS THEIR PROPERTY... THEIR INSTRUMENT.

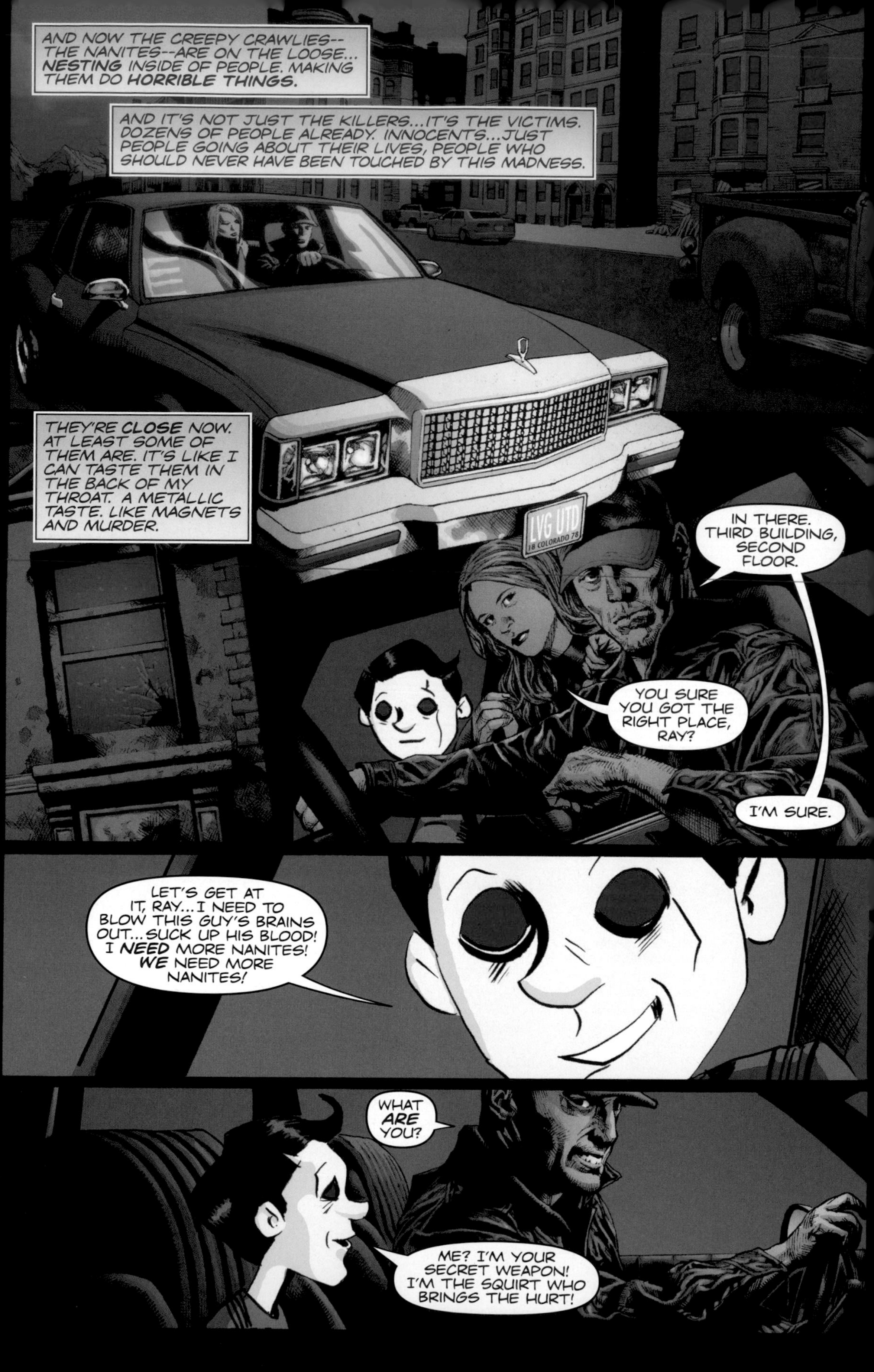
AND NOW THE CREEPY CRAWLIES--THE NANITES--ARE ON THE LOOSE... NESTING INSIDE OF PEOPLE. MAKING THEM DO HORRIBLE THINGS.
AND IT'S NOT JUST THE KILLERS...IT'S THE VICTIMS. DOZENS OF PEOPLE ALREADY. INNOCENTS...JUST PEOPLE GOING ABOUT THEIR LIVES, PEOPLE WHO SHOULD NEVER HAVE BEEN TOUCHED BY THIS MADNESS.
THEY'RE CLOSE NOW. AT LEAST SOME OF THEM ARE. IT'S LIKE I CAN TASTE THEM IN THE BACK OF MY THROAT. A METALLIC TASTE. LIKE MAGNETS AND MURDER.
LVG UTD
18 COLORADO 78
IN THERE. THIRD BUILDING, SECOND FLOOR.
YOU SURE YOU GOT THE RIGHT PLACE, RAY?
I'M SURE.
LET'S GET AT IT, RAY...I NEED TO BLOW THIS GUY'S BRAINS OUT...SUCK UP HIS BLOOD! I NEED MORE NANITES! WE NEED MORE NANITES!
WHAT ARE YOU?
ME? I'M YOUR SECRET WEAPON! I'M THE SQUIRT WHO BRINGS THE HURT!

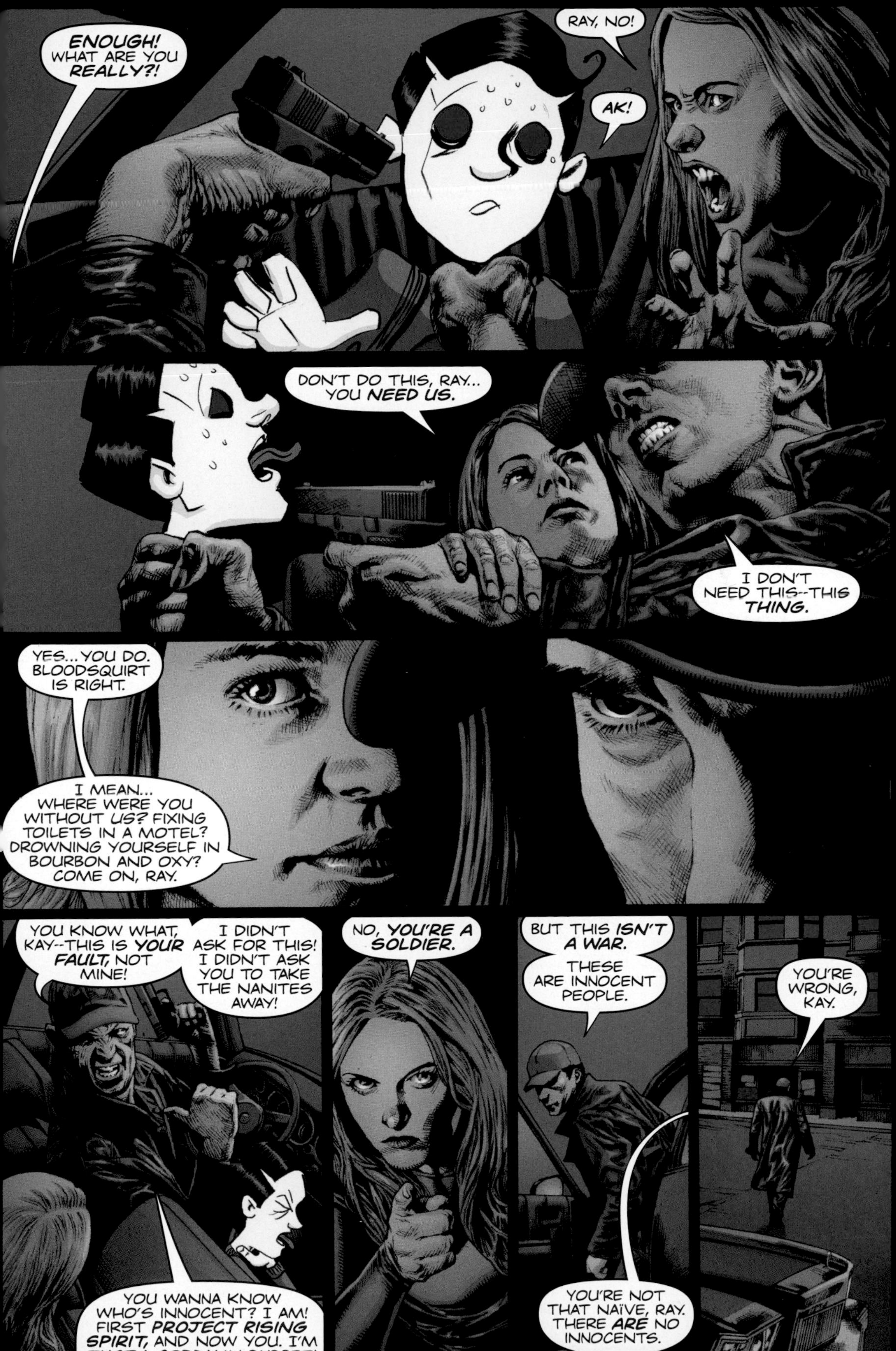

ENOUGH! WHAT ARE YOU REALLY?!
RAY, NO!
AK!
DON'T DO THIS, RAY... YOU NEED US.
I DON'T NEED THIS--THIS THING.
YES... YOU DO. BLOODSQUIRT IS RIGHT.
I MEAN... WHERE WERE YOU WITHOUT US? FIXING TOILETS IN A MOTEL? DROWNING YOURSELF IN BOURBON AND OXY? COME ON, RAY.
YOU KNOW WHAT, KAY--THIS IS YOUR FAULT, NOT MINE!
I DIDN'T ASK FOR THIS! I DIDN'T ASK YOU TO TAKE THE NANITES AWAY!
YOU WANNA KNOW WHO'S INNOCENT? I AM! FIRST PROJECT RISING SPIRIT, AND NOW YOU. I'M JUST A GODDAMN PUPPET!
NO, YOU'RE A SOLDIER.
BUT THIS ISN'T A WAR.
THESE ARE INNOCENT PEOPLE.
YOU'RE NOT THAT NAÏVE, RAY. THERE ARE NO INNOCENTS.
YOU'RE WRONG, KAY.

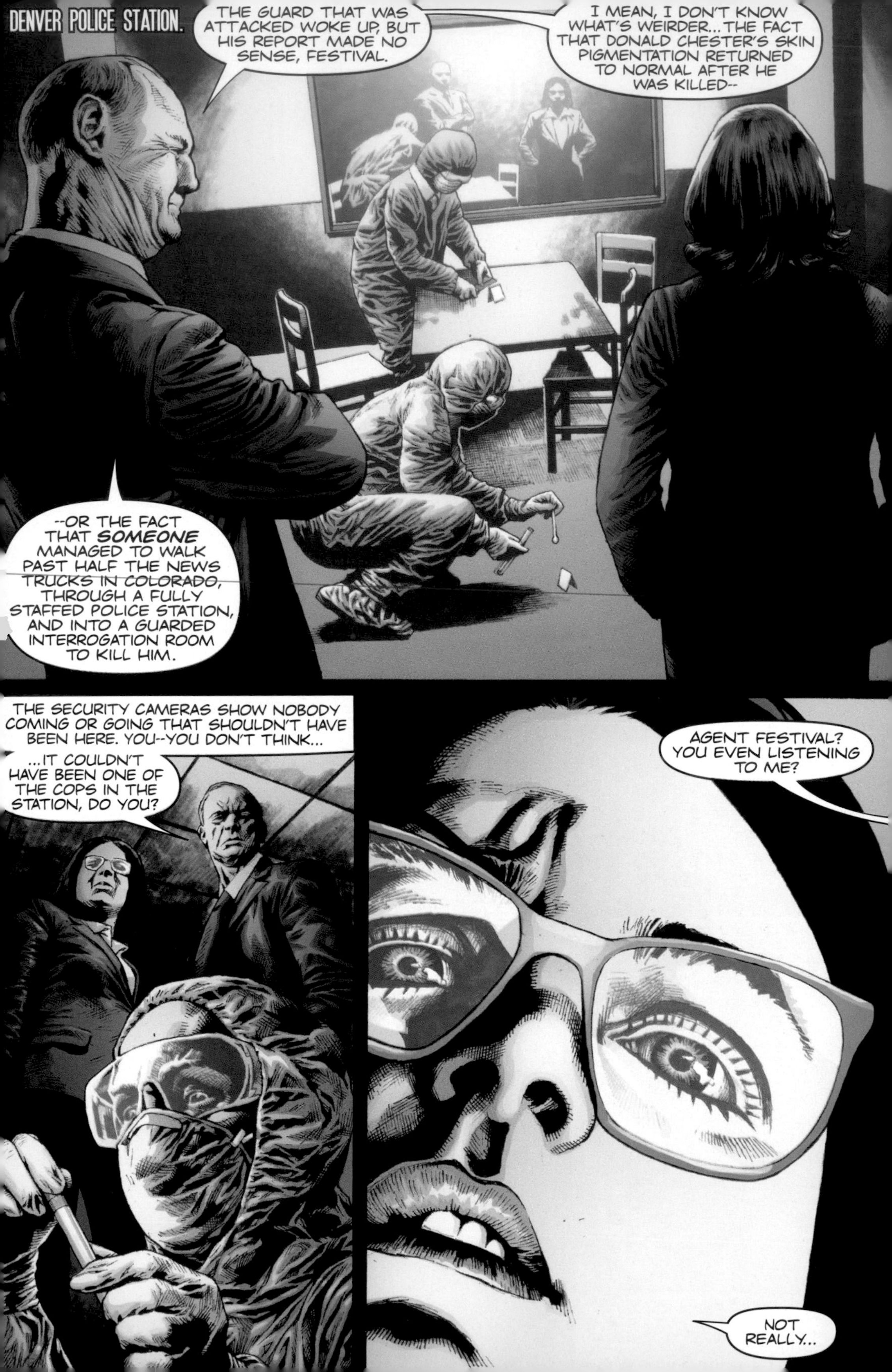
DENVER POLICE STATION.
THE GUARD THAT WAS ATTACKED WOKE UP, BUT HIS REPORT MADE NO SENSE, FESTIVAL.
I MEAN, I DON'T KNOW WHAT'S WEIRDER... THE FACT THAT DONALD CHESTER'S SKIN PIGMENTATION RETURNED TO NORMAL AFTER HE WAS KILLED--
--OR THE FACT THAT SOMEONE MANAGED TO WALK PAST HALF THE NEWS TRUCKS IN COLORADO, THROUGH A FULLY STAFFED POLICE STATION, AND INTO A GUARDED INTERROGATION ROOM TO KILL HIM.
THE SECURITY CAMERAS SHOW NOBODY COMING OR GOING THAT SHOULDN'T HAVE BEEN HERE. YOU--YOU DON'T THINK...
...IT COULDN'T HAVE BEEN ONE OF THE COPS IN THE STATION, DO YOU?
AGENT FESTIVAL? YOU EVEN LISTENING TO ME?
NOT REALLY...

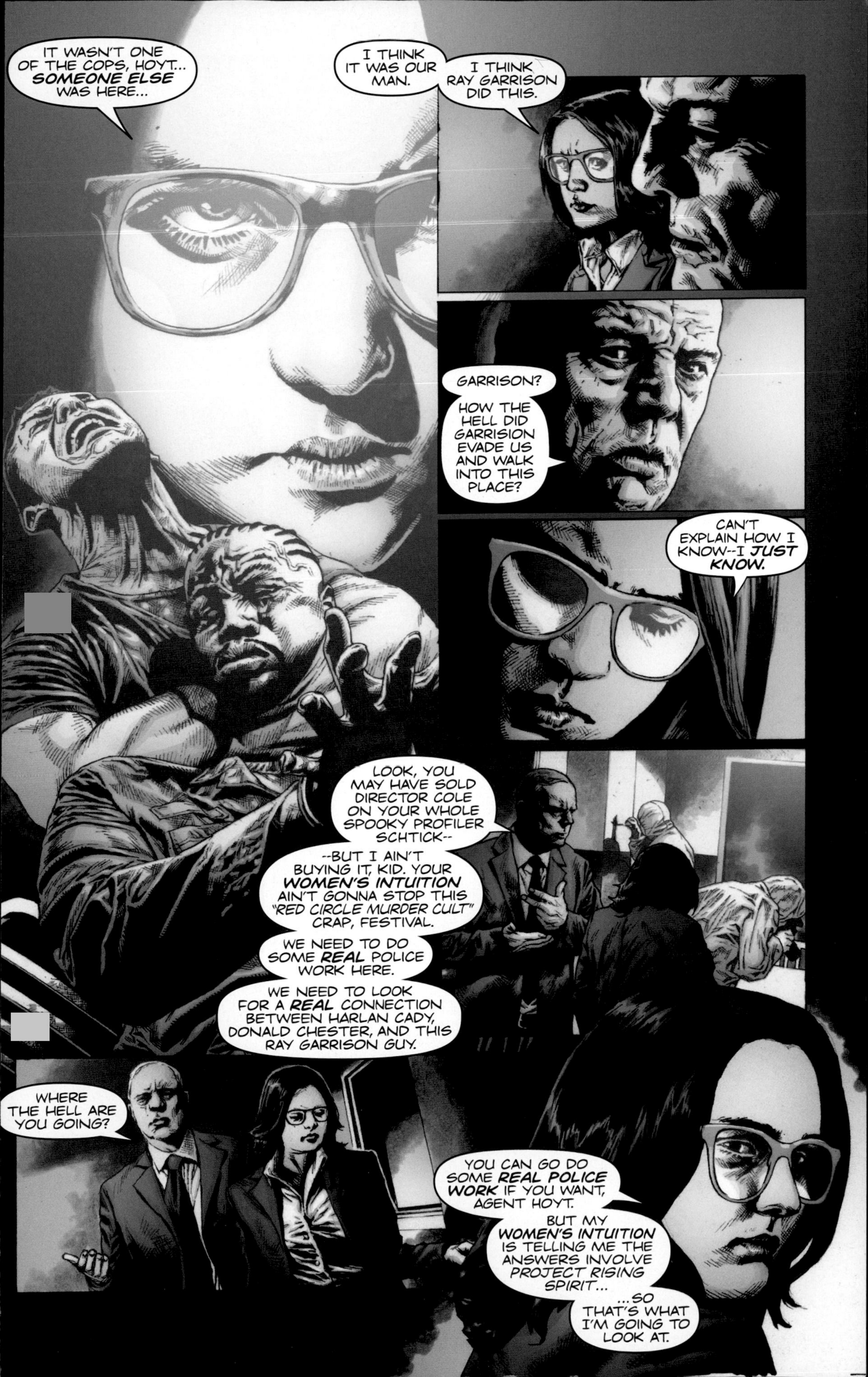

IT WASN'T ONE OF THE COPS, HOYT... SOMEONE ELSE WAS HERE...
I THINK IT WAS OUR MAN.
I THINK RAY GARRISON DID THIS.
GARRISON?
HOW THE HELL DID GARRISION EVADE US AND WALK INTO THIS PLACE?
CAN'T EXPLAIN HOW I KNOW--I JUST KNOW.
LOOK, YOU MAY HAVE SOLD DIRECTOR COLE ON YOUR WHOLE SPOOKY PROFILER SCHTICK--
--BUT I AIN'T BUYING IT, KID. YOUR WOMEN'S INTUITION AIN'T GONNA STOP THIS "RED CIRCLE MURDER CULT" CRAP, FESTIVAL.
WE NEED TO DO SOME REAL POLICE WORK HERE.
WE NEED TO LOOK FOR A REAL CONNECTION BETWEEN HARLAN CADY, DONALD CHESTER, AND THIS RAY GARRISON GUY.
WHERE THE HELL ARE YOU GOING?
YOU CAN GO DO SOME REAL POLICE WORK IF YOU WANT, AGENT HOYT.
BUT MY WOMEN'S INTUITION IS TELLING ME THE ANSWERS INVOLVE PROJECT RISING SPIRIT...
...SO THAT'S WHAT I'M GOING TO LOOK AT.

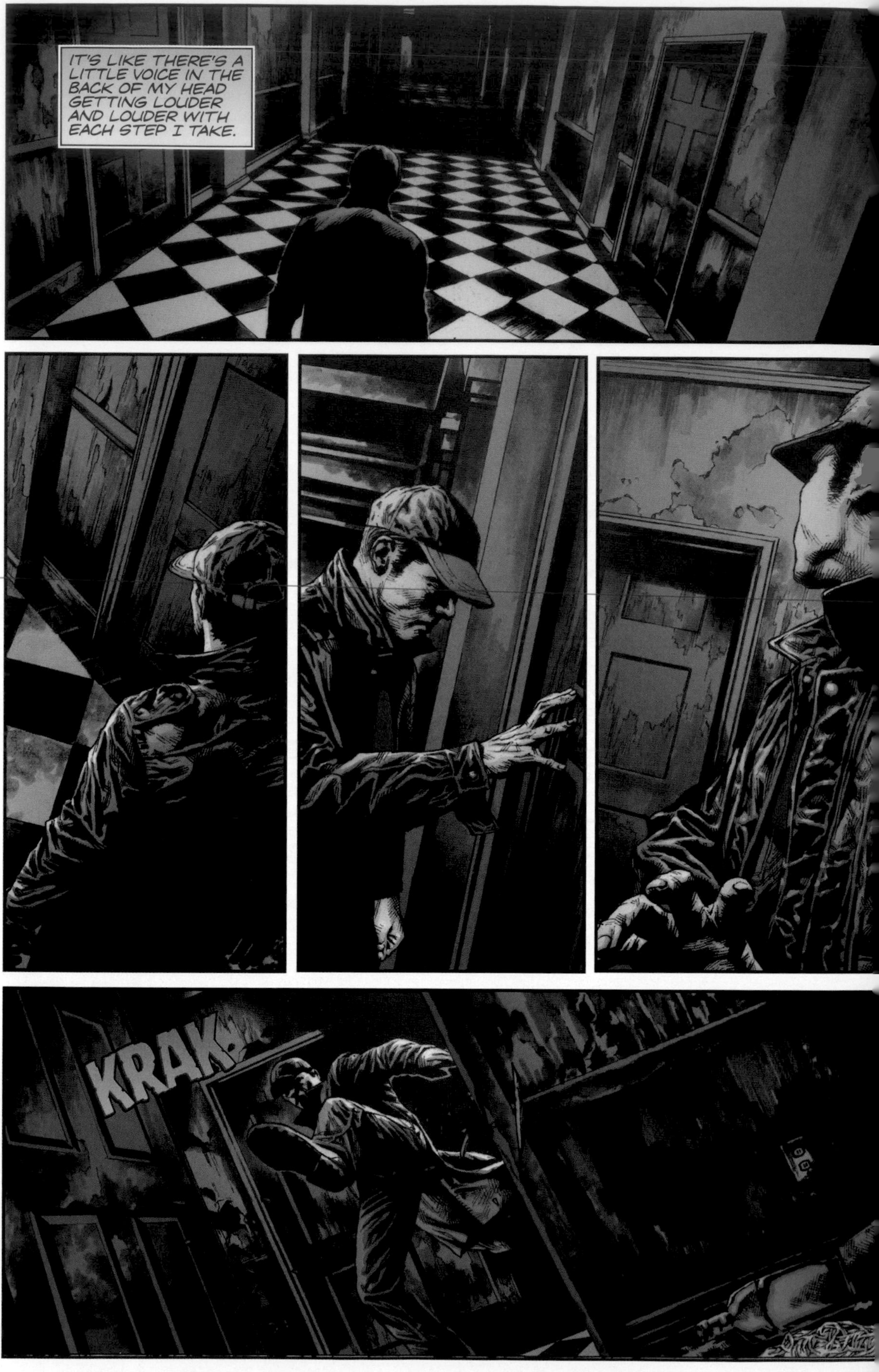
IT'S LIKE THERE'S A LITTLE VOICE IN THE BACK OF MY HEAD GETTING LOUDER AND LOUDER WITH EACH STEP I TAKE.
KRAK!

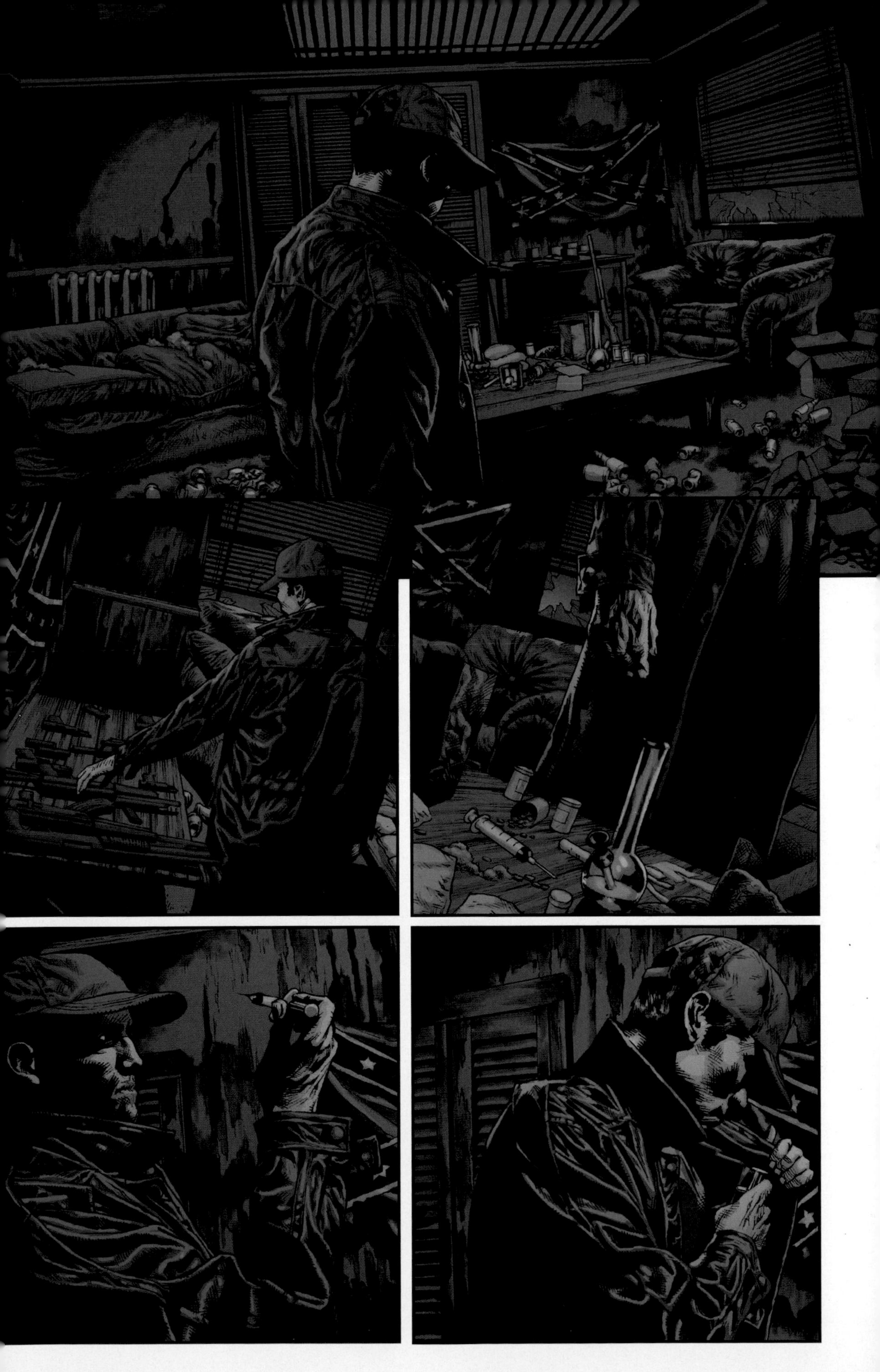

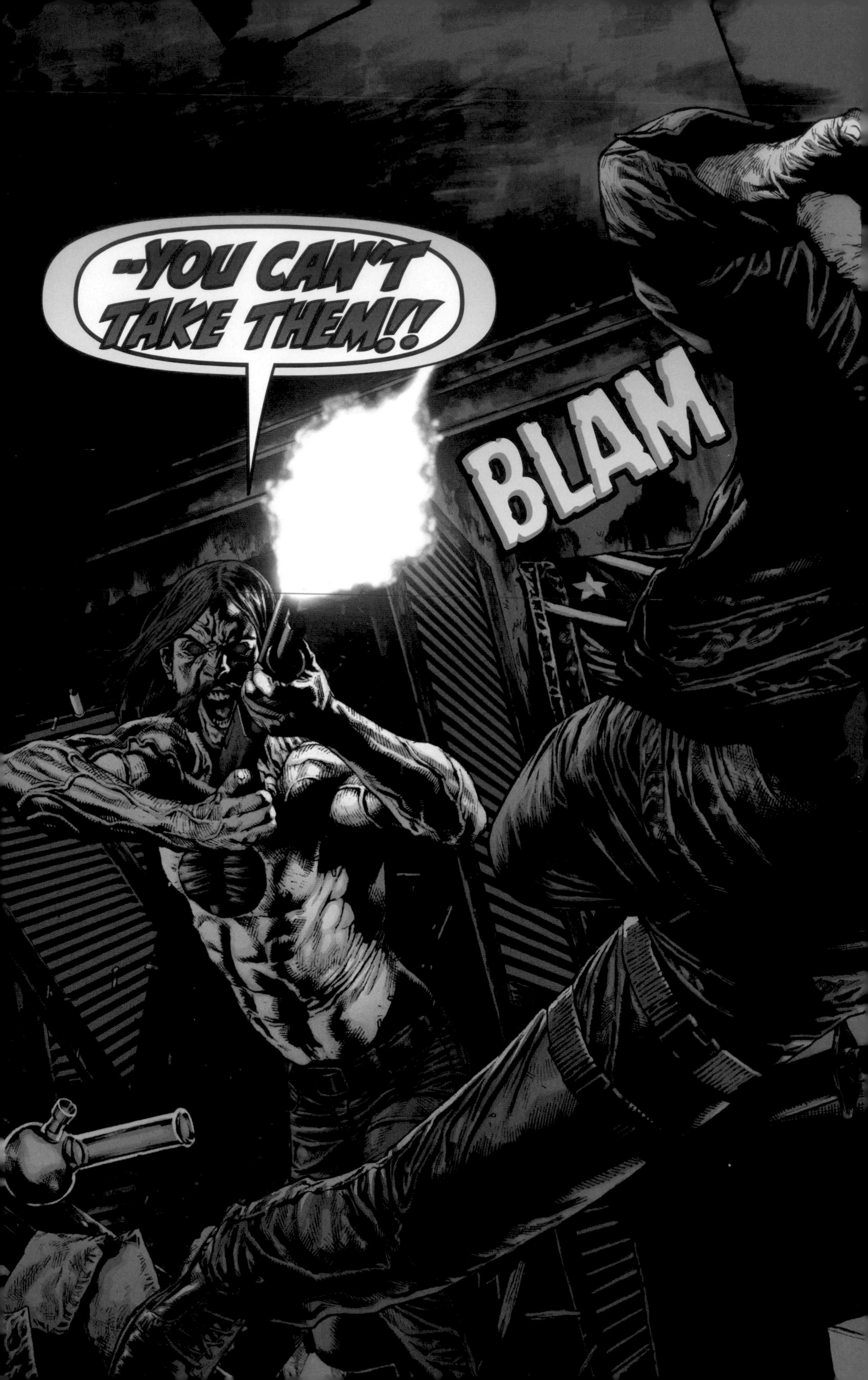
-YOU CAN'T TAKE THEM!!
BLAM

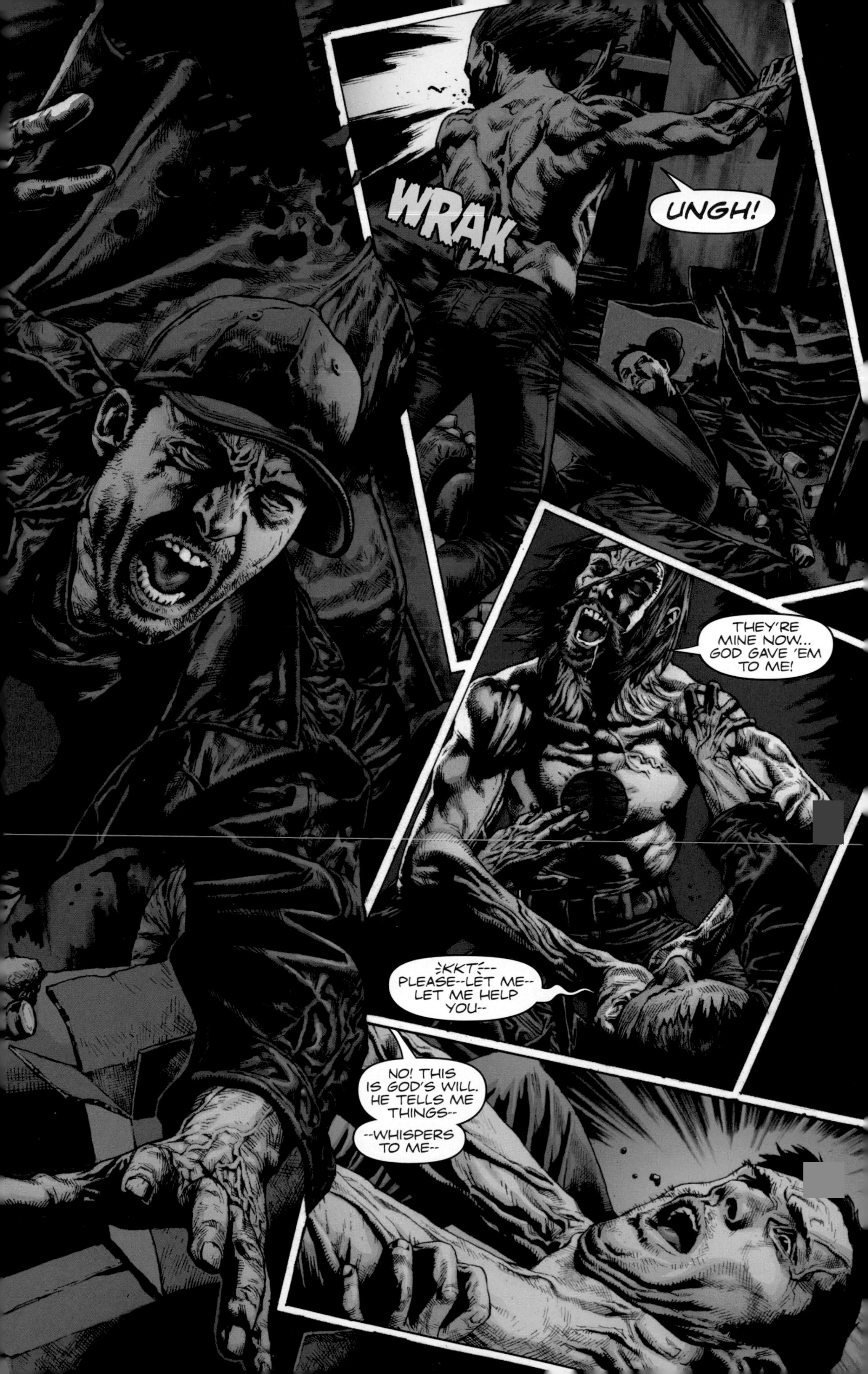
WRAK
UNGH!
THEY'RE MINE NOW... GOD GAVE 'EM TO ME!
KKT-- PLEASE--LET ME-- LET ME HELP YOU--
NO! THIS IS GOD'S WILL. HE TELLS ME THINGS--
--WHISPERS TO ME--

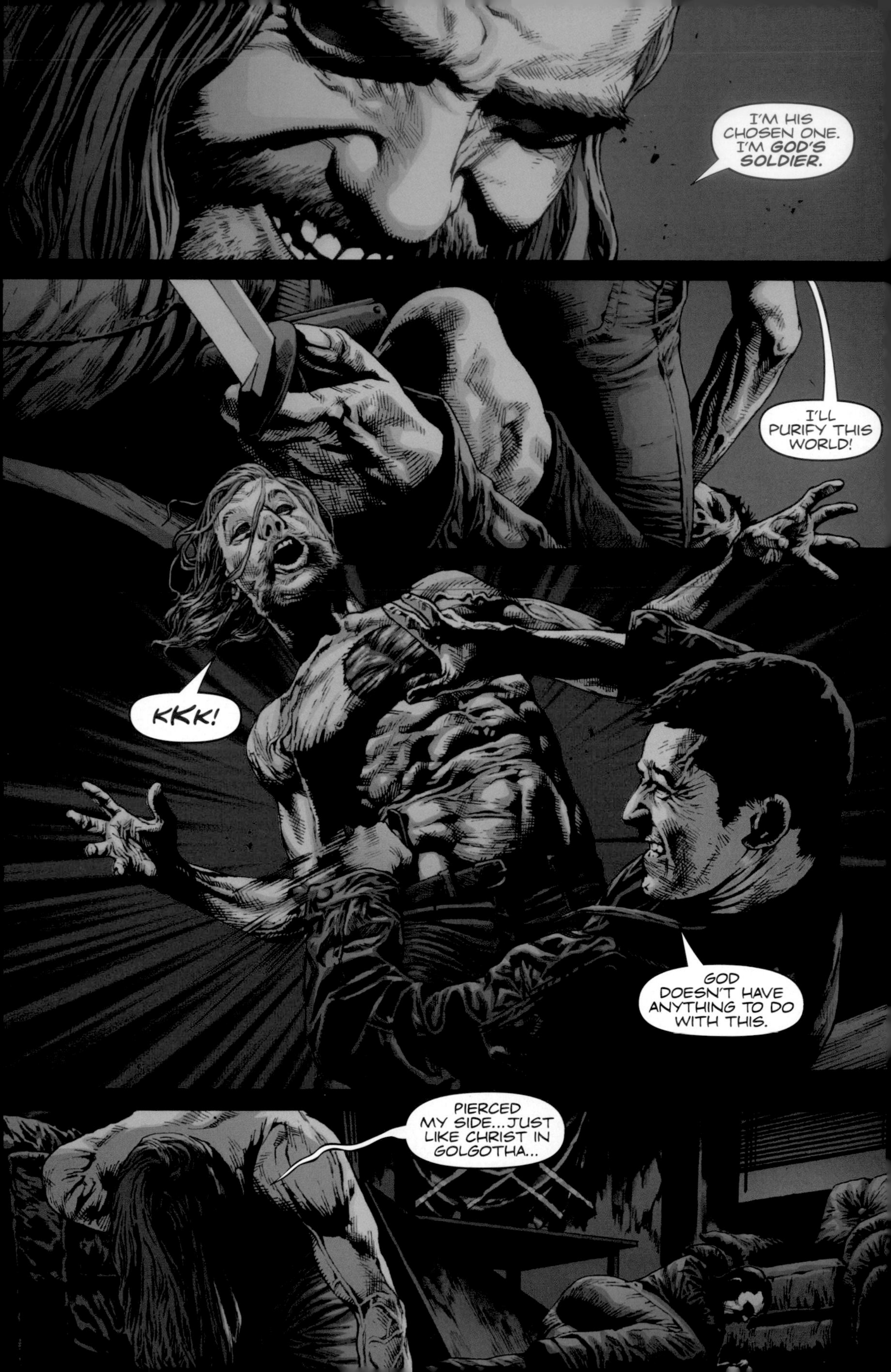
I'M HIS CHOSEN ONE. I'M GOD'S SOLDIER.
I'LL PURIFY THIS WORLD!
KKK!
GOD DOESN'T HAVE ANYTHING TO DO WITH THIS.
PIERCED MY SIDE...JUST LIKE CHRIST IN GOLGOTHA...

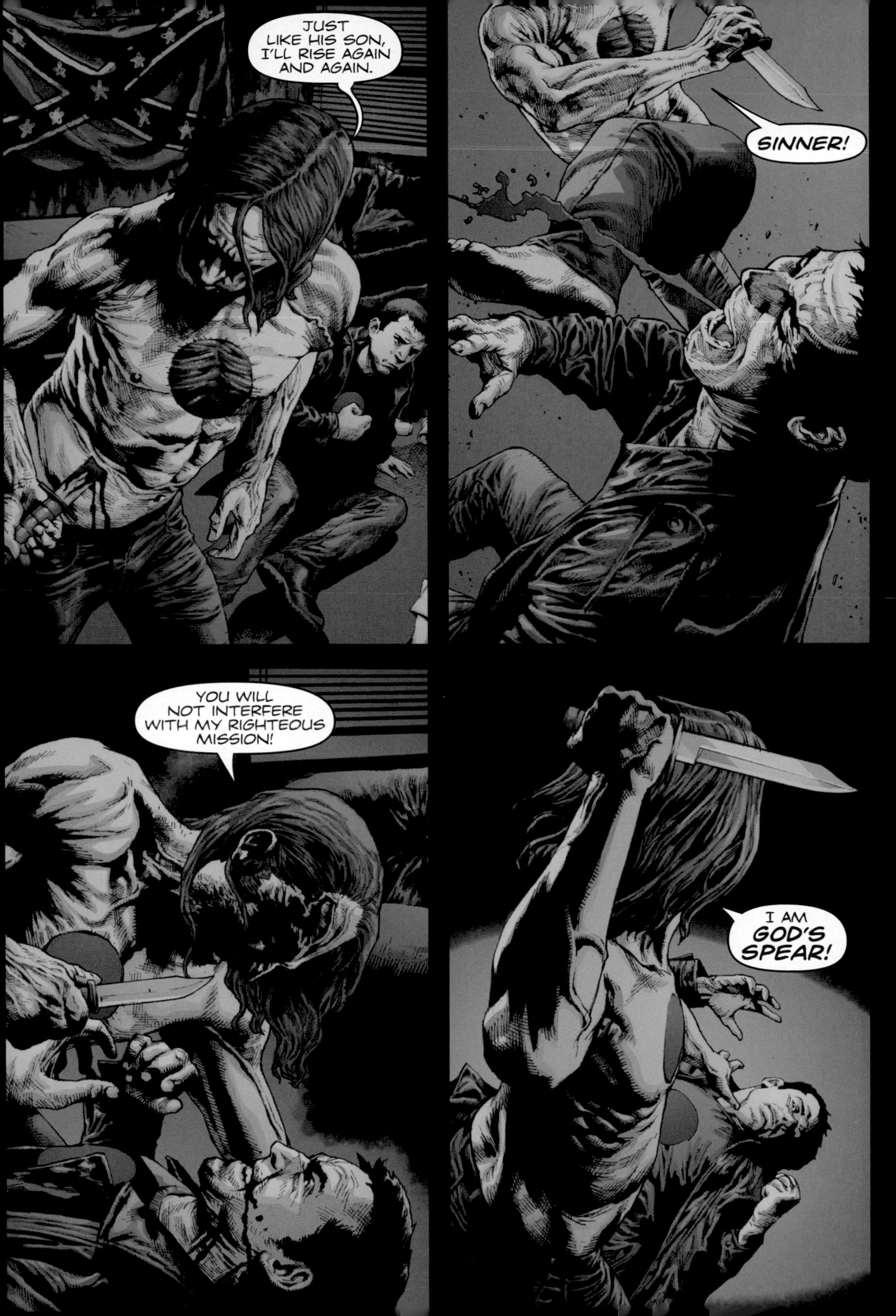
JUST LIKE HIS SON, I'LL RISE AGAIN AND AGAIN.
SINNER!
YOU WILL NOT INTERFERE WITH MY RIGHTEOUS MISSION!
I AM GOD'S SPEAR!

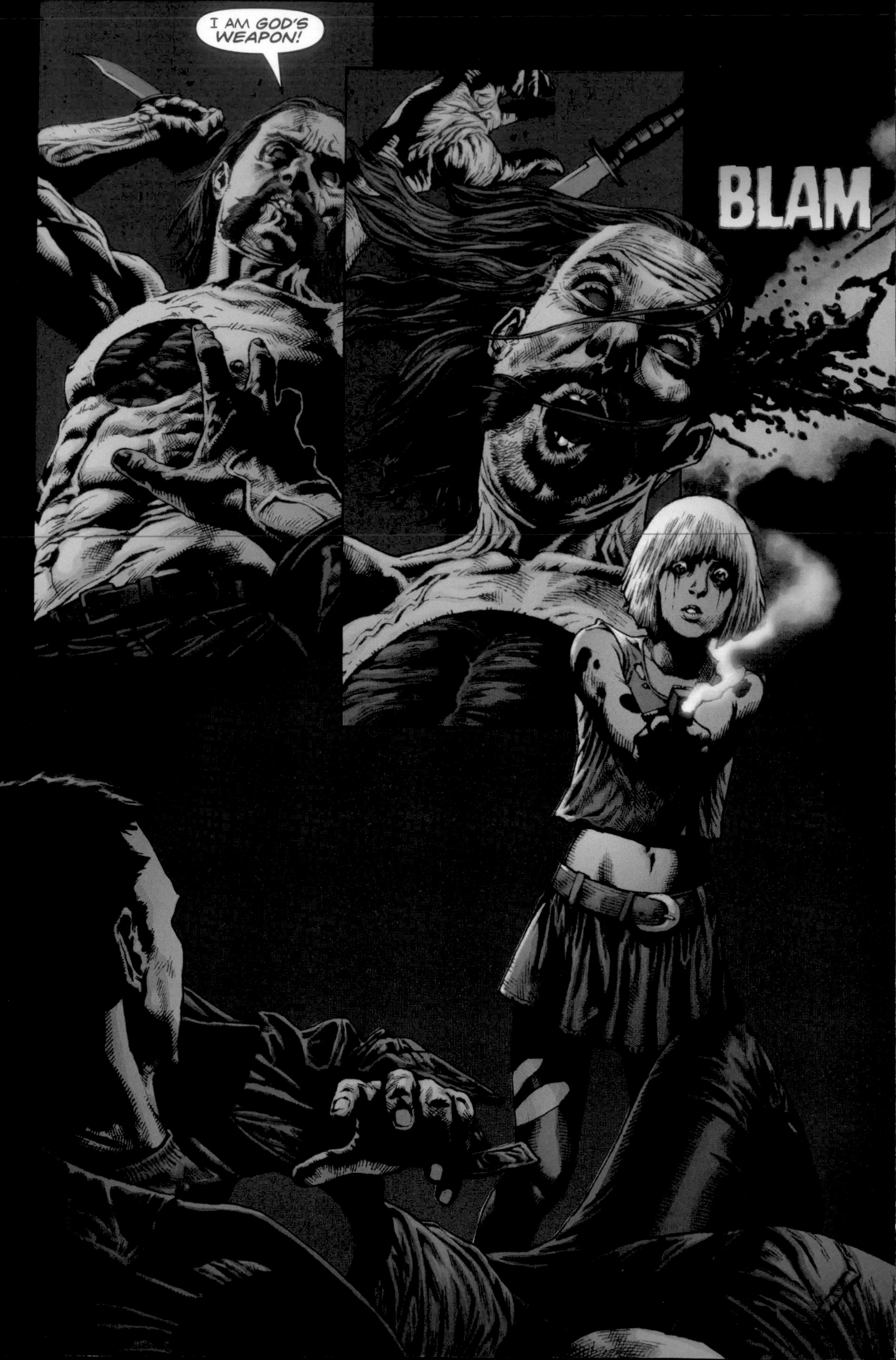
I AM GOD'S WEAPON!
BLAM

tak tak

DEPARTMENT OF JUSTICE
FEDERAL BUREAU OF INVESTIGATION

FEDERAL AGENT RESTRICTED PERSONEL

DIANE FESTIVAL___

SEARCH

BUREAU OF INVES

ERAL AGENT RESTRICTED PERSO

DIANE FESTIVAL___

SEARCH

D.O.B.: JUNE 12, 1989
BIRTHPLACE: LIVONIA, MI
HAIR: BROWN
EYES: BROWN
HEIGHT: 5'4"
WEIGHT: 125 lbs.

KNOWN RELATIVES:
DELORES JEAN FESTIVAL
(MOTHER, DECEASED)
EVERETT JACK FESTIVAL
(FATHER, DECEASED)

WITNESSED THE
VIOLENT MURDER OF
BOTH PARENTS AT
THE AGE OF THIRTEEN.

HER **FATHER KILLED HER MOTHER,**
HIS WIFE, AND **SHOT THE THIRTEEN-
YEAR-OLD** DIANE FESTIVAL IN THE
CLAVICLE AND STOMACH BEFORE
TURNING THE GUN ON HIMSELF.

ENTERED QUANTICO'S
ADVANCED PROGRAM AT
THE EARLY AGE OF
SEVENTEEN AFTER
DEMONSTRATING **UNIQUE
DEDUCTIVE AND PROFILING
CAPACITY.** GRADUATED
WITH HONORS, MAY 2010.

HOYT!

WHA-?!

I'VE BEEN
LOOKING ALL OVER
FOR YOU!!
REPORTS OF SHOTS
FIRED AT AN APARTMENT
COMPLEX! THE CALLER
DESCRIBED A MAN THAT
MATCHES RAY GARRISON
ENTERING THE
BUILDING.

LET'S
MOVE!

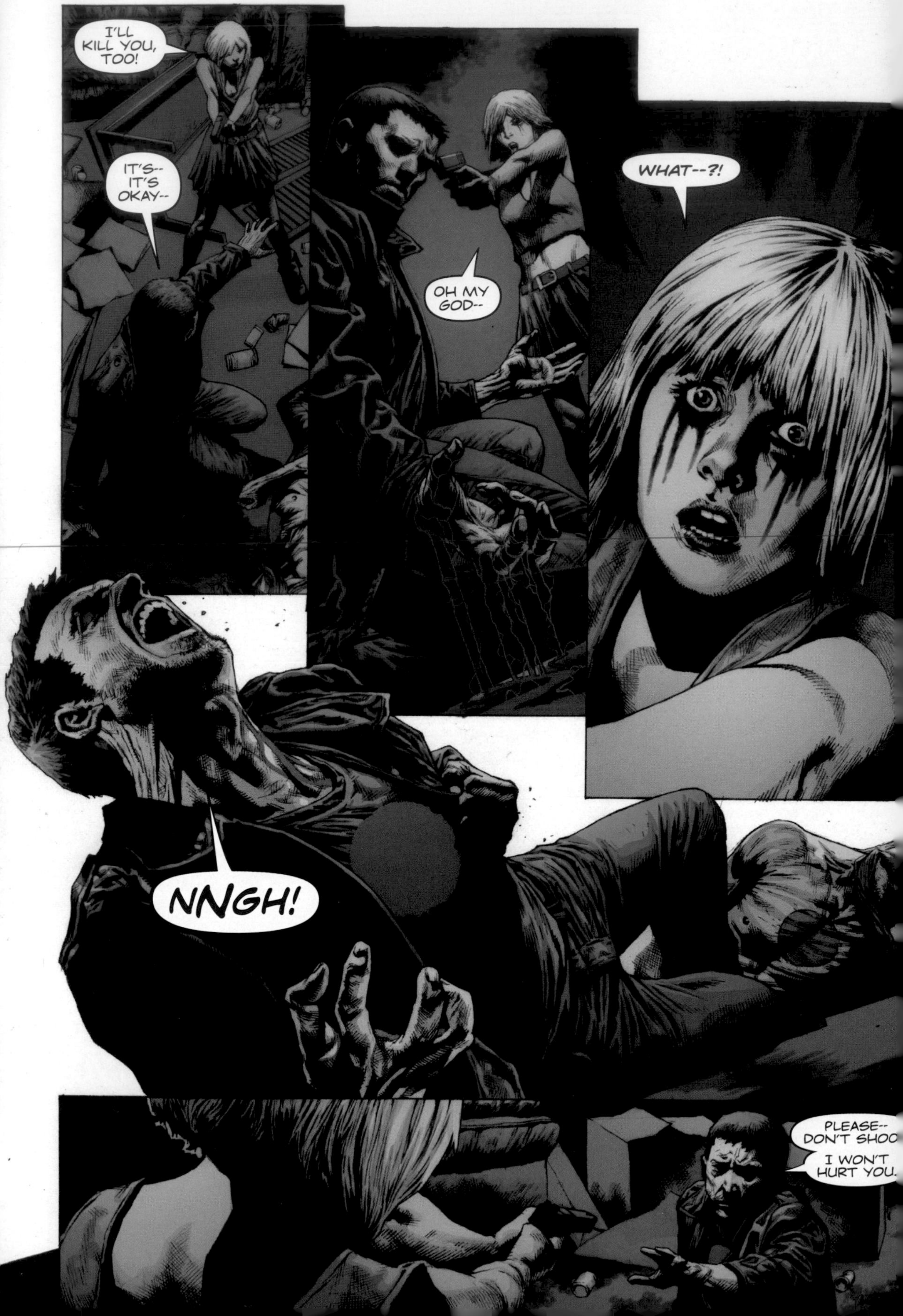

I'LL KILL YOU, TOO!
IT'S-- IT'S OKAY--
OH MY GOD--
WHAT--?!
NNGH!
PLEASE-- DON'T SHOO
I WON'T HURT YOU.

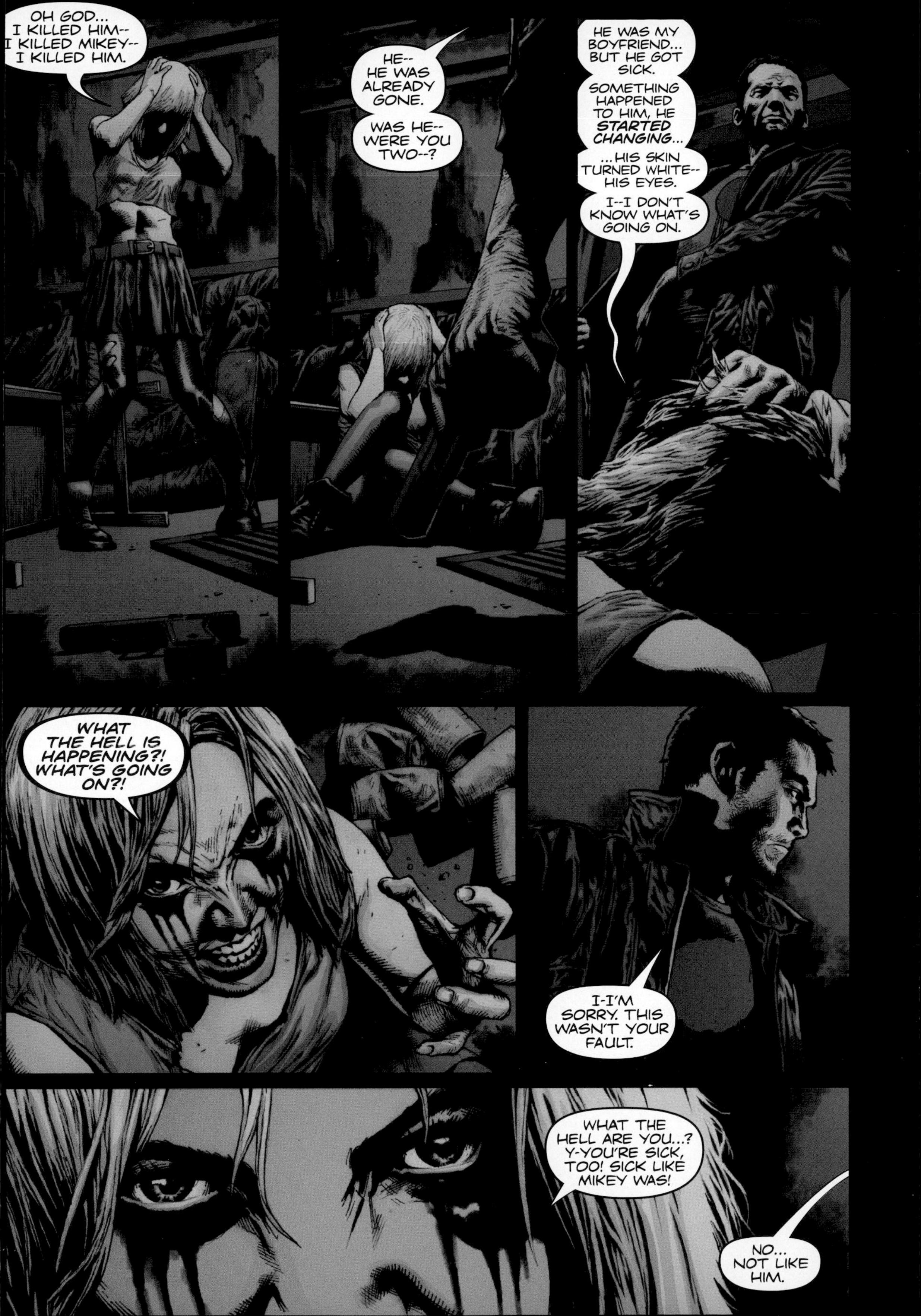
OH GOD... I KILLED HIM-- I KILLED MIKEY-- I KILLED HIM.
HE-- HE WAS ALREADY GONE.
WAS HE-- WERE YOU TWO--?
HE WAS MY BOYFRIEND... BUT HE GOT SICK.
SOMETHING HAPPENED TO HIM, HE STARTED CHANGING...
...HIS SKIN TURNED WHITE-- HIS EYES.
I--I DON'T KNOW WHAT'S GOING ON.
WHAT THE HELL IS HAPPENING?! WHAT'S GOING ON?!
I-I'M SORRY. THIS WASN'T YOUR FAULT.
WHAT THE HELL ARE YOU...? Y-YOU'RE SICK, TOO! SICK LIKE MIKEY WAS!
NO... NOT LIKE HIM.

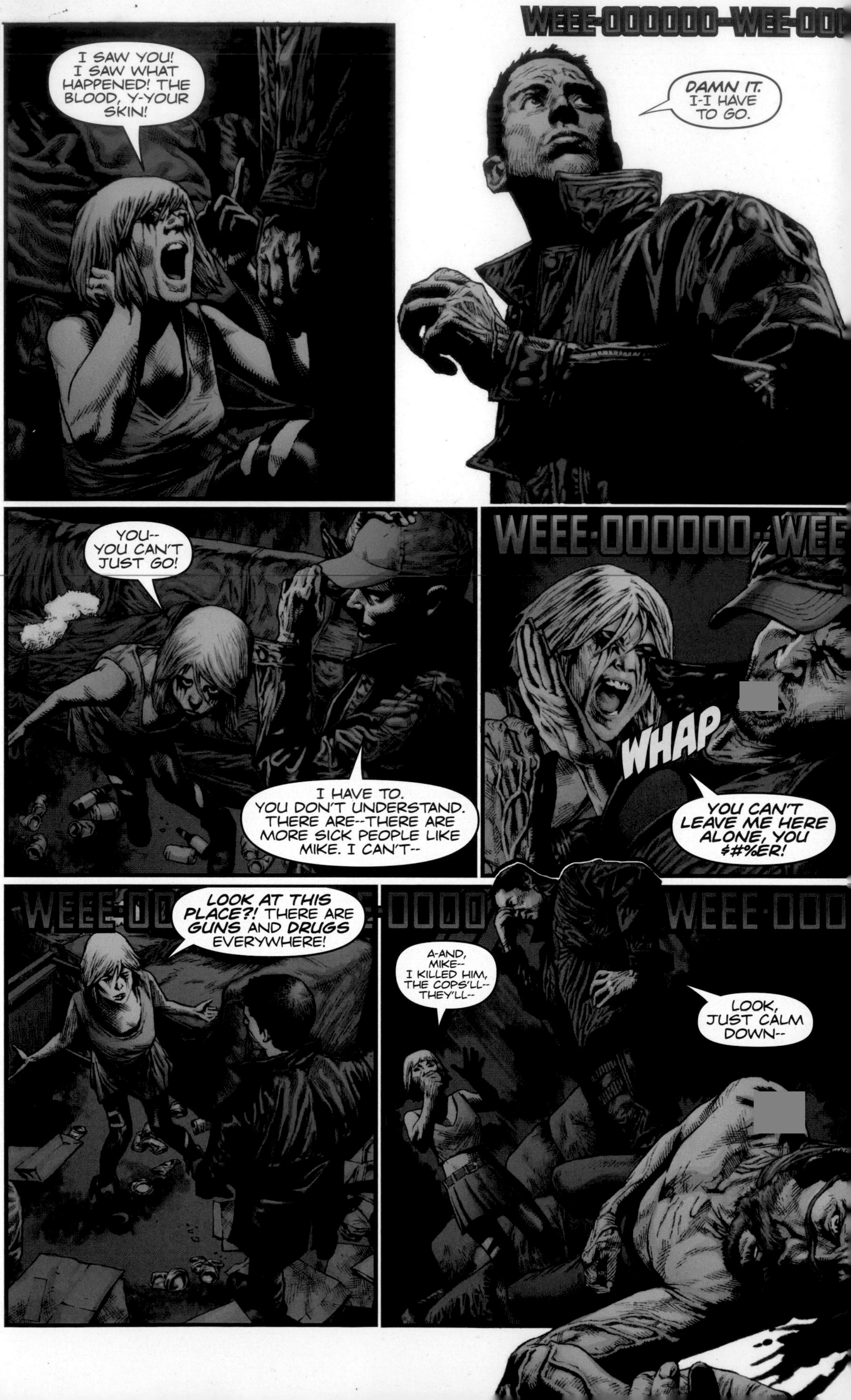
I SAW YOU! I SAW WHAT HAPPENED! THE BLOOD, Y-YOUR SKIN!
WEEE-OOOOOO--WEE-OO
DAMN IT. I-I HAVE TO GO.
YOU-- YOU CAN'T JUST GO!
I HAVE TO. YOU DON'T UNDERSTAND. THERE ARE--THERE ARE MORE SICK PEOPLE LIKE MIKE. I CAN'T--
WEEE-OOOOOO--WEE
WHAP
YOU CAN'T LEAVE ME HERE ALONE, YOU $#%ER!
LOOK AT THIS PLACE?! THERE ARE GUNS AND DRUGS EVERYWHERE!
A-AND, MIKE-- I KILLED HIM, THE COPS'LL-- THEY'LL--
LOOK, JUST CALM DOWN--

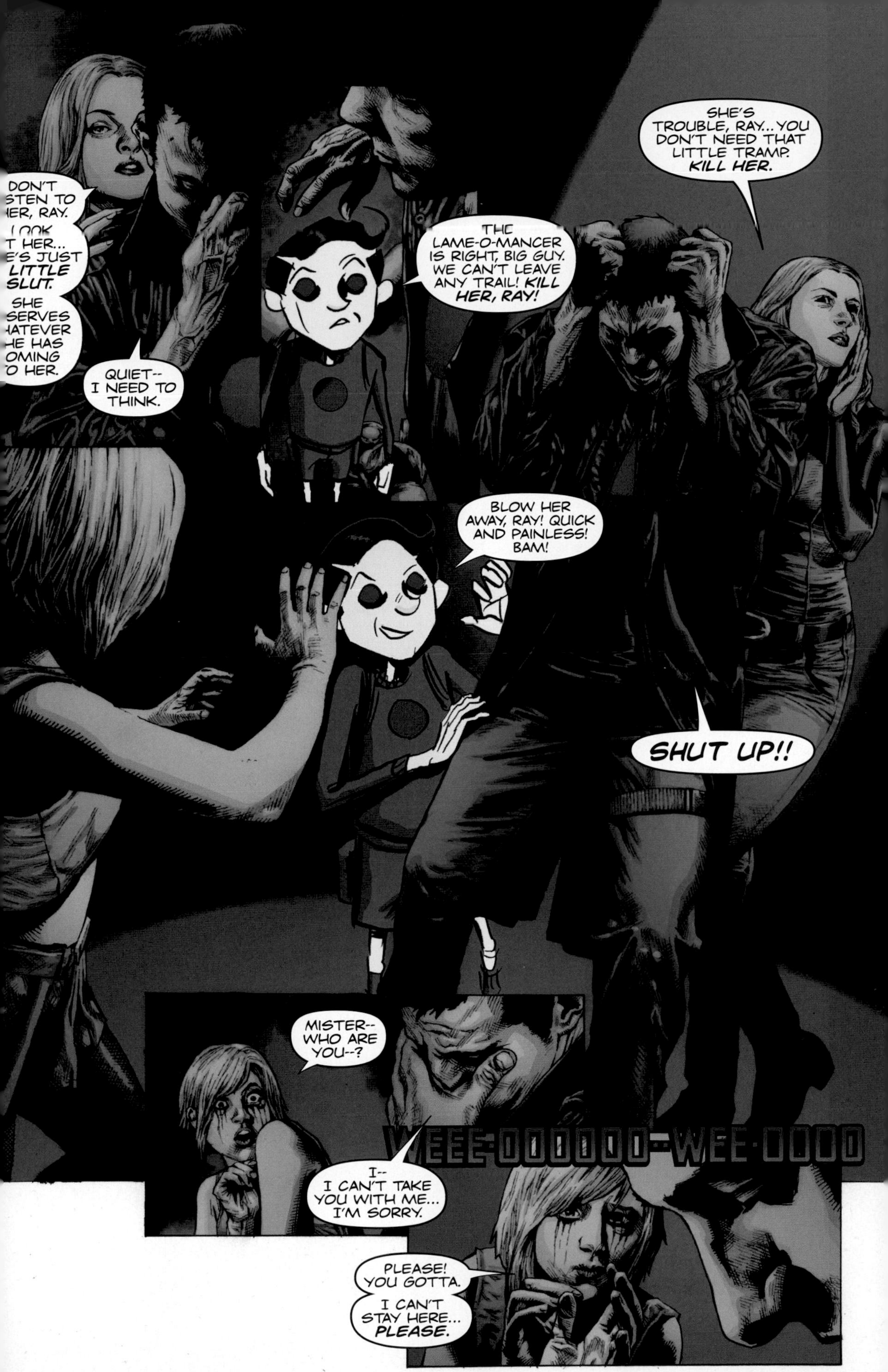
DON'T STEN TO HER, RAY.
LOOK T HER... E'S JUST LITTLE SLUT.
SHE SERVES HATEVER HE HAS OMING O HER.
QUIET-- I NEED TO THINK.
THE LAME-O-MANCER IS RIGHT, BIG GUY. WE CAN'T LEAVE ANY TRAIL! KILL HER, RAY!
SHE'S TROUBLE, RAY... YOU DON'T NEED THAT LITTLE TRAMP. KILL HER.
BLOW HER AWAY, RAY! QUICK AND PAINLESS! BAM!
SHUT UP!!
MISTER-- WHO ARE YOU--?
WEEE-OOOOOO-WEE-OOOO
I-- I CAN'T TAKE YOU WITH ME... I'M SORRY.
PLEASE! YOU GOTTA.
I CAN'T STAY HERE... PLEASE.

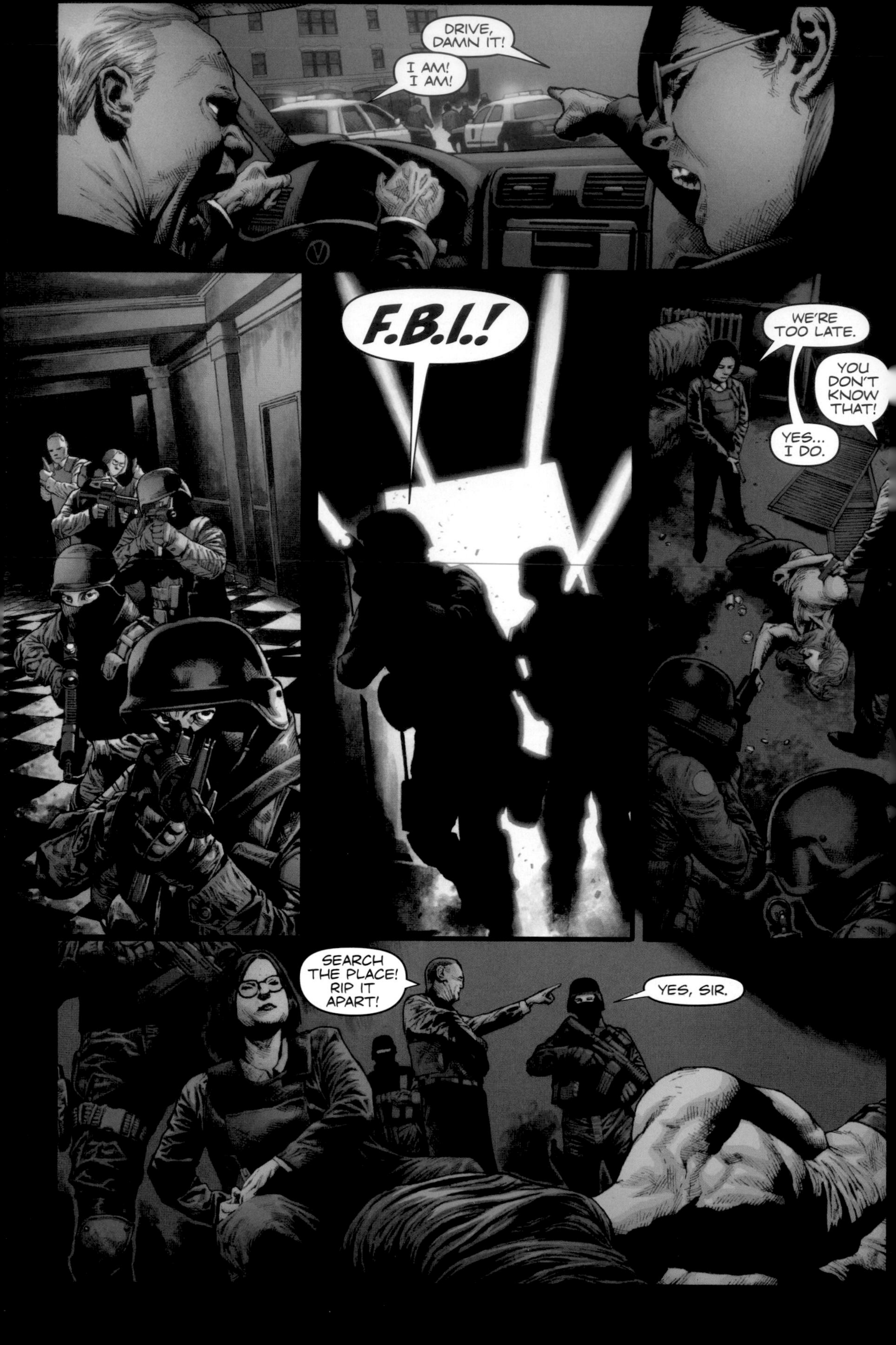
DRIVE, DAMN IT!
I AM! I AM!
F.B.I.!
WE'RE TOO LATE.
YOU DON'T KNOW THAT!
YES... I DO.
SEARCH THE PLACE! RIP IT APART!
YES, SIR.

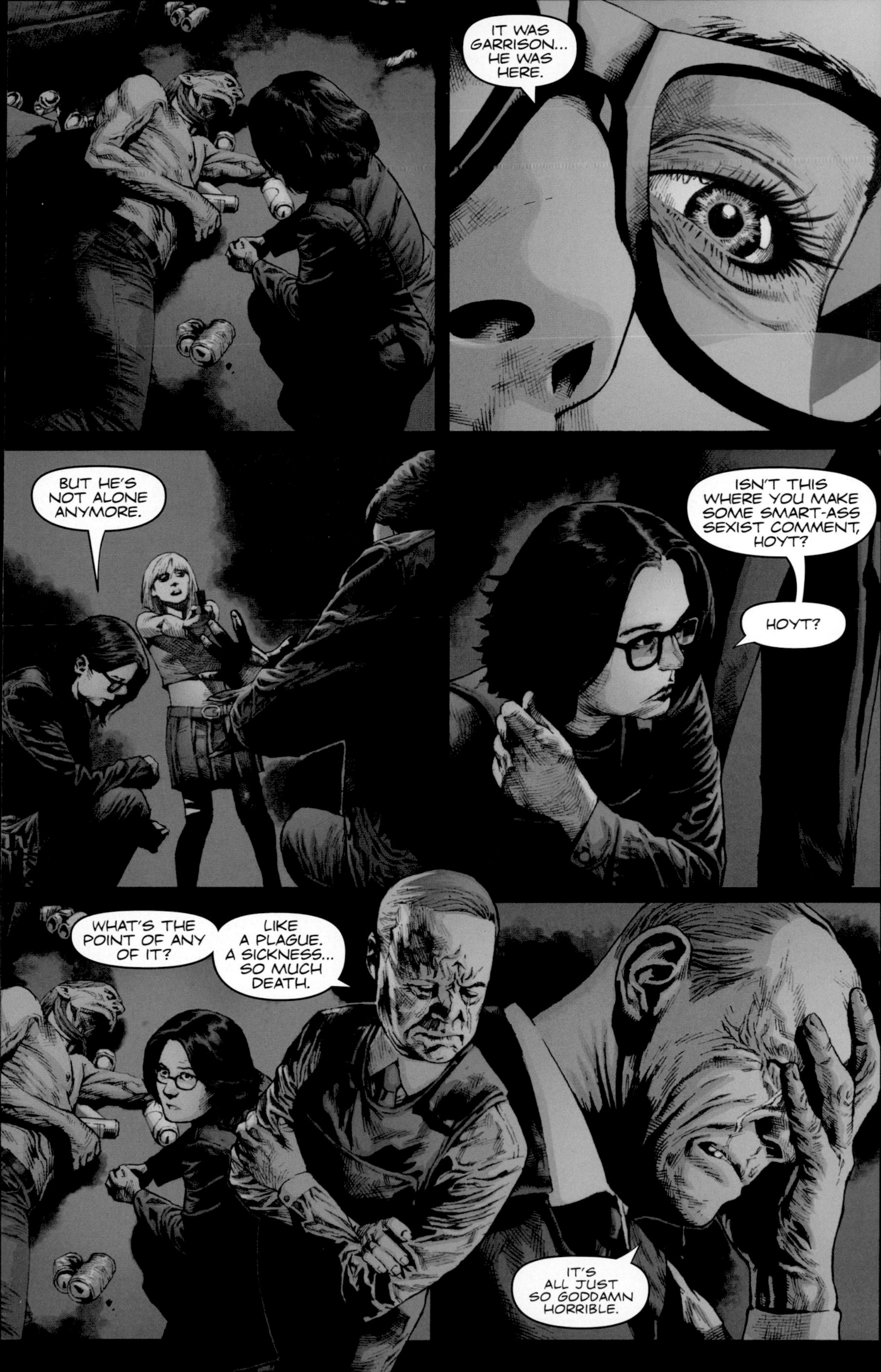
IT WAS GARRISON... HE WAS HERE.
BUT HE'S NOT ALONE ANYMORE.
ISN'T THIS WHERE YOU MAKE SOME SMART-ASS SEXIST COMMENT, HOYT?
HOYT?
WHAT'S THE POINT OF ANY OF IT?
LIKE A PLAGUE. A SICKNESS... SO MUCH DEATH.
IT'S ALL JUST SO GODDAMN HORRIBLE.

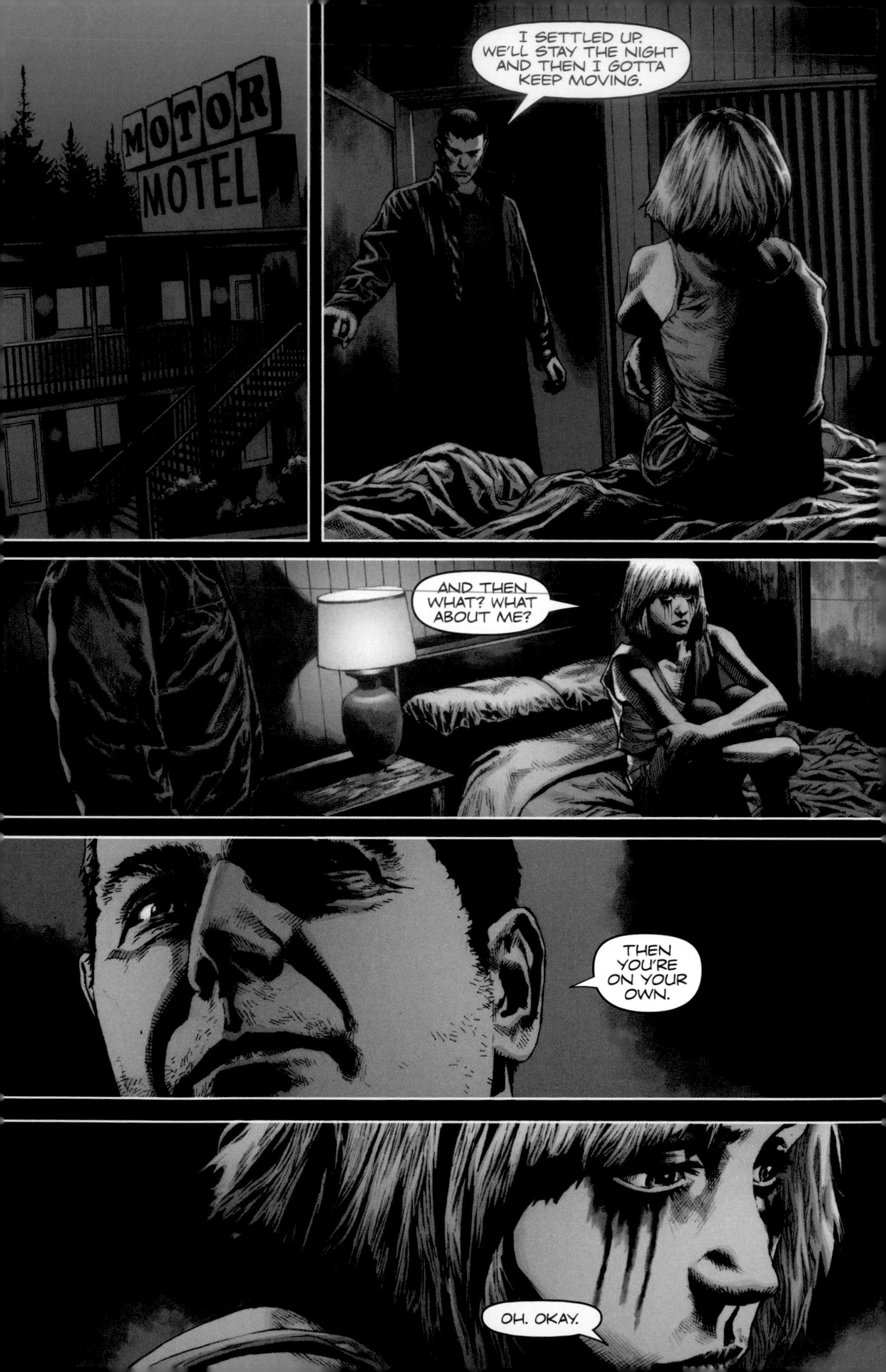
MOTOR
MOTEL
I SETTLED UP. WE'LL STAY THE NIGHT AND THEN I GOTTA KEEP MOVING.
AND THEN WHAT? WHAT ABOUT ME?
THEN YOU'RE ON YOUR OWN.
OH. OKAY.

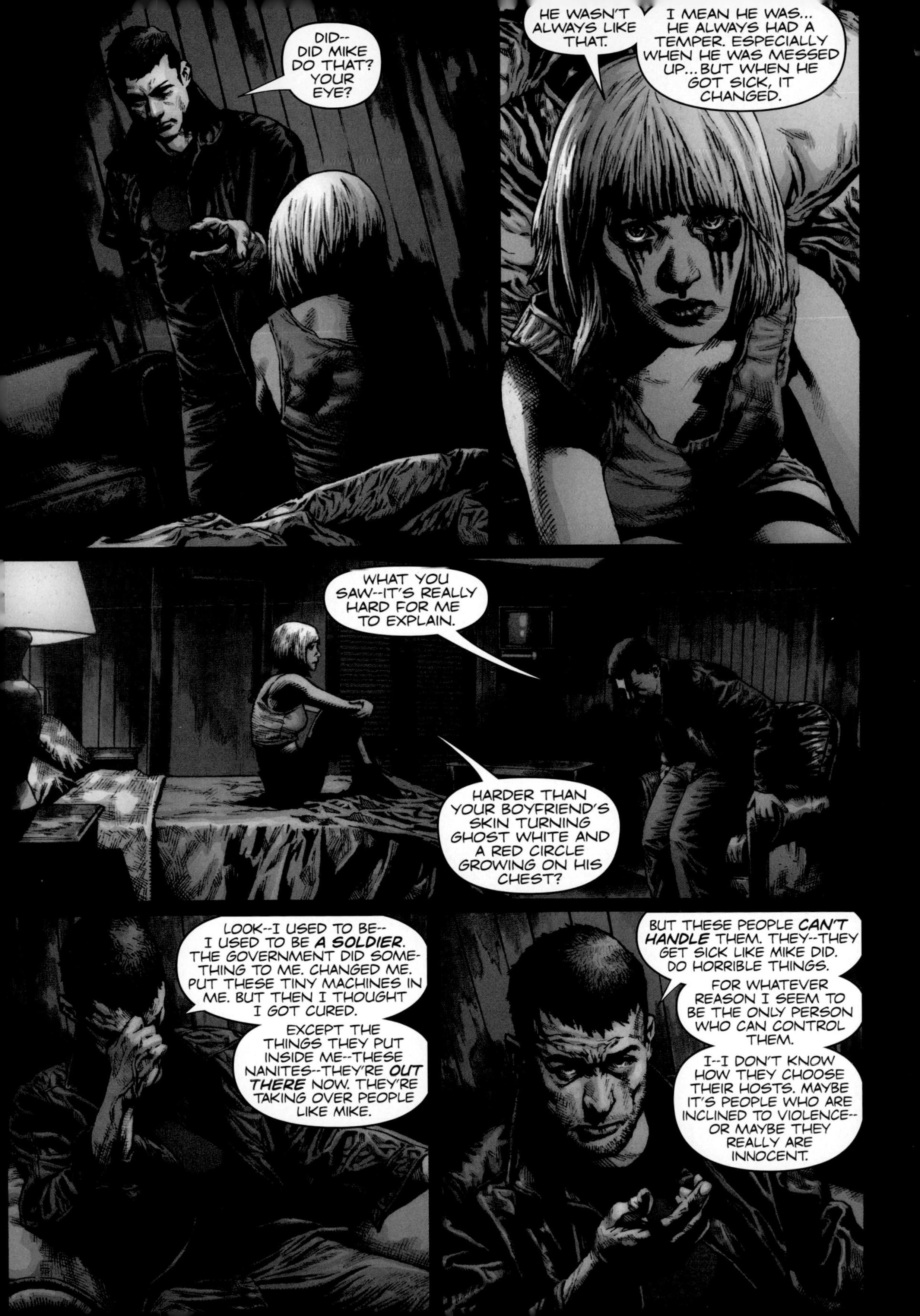
DID-- DID MIKE DO THAT? YOUR EYE?
HE WASN'T ALWAYS LIKE THAT.
I MEAN HE WAS... HE ALWAYS HAD A TEMPER. ESPECIALLY WHEN HE WAS MESSED UP...BUT WHEN HE GOT SICK, IT CHANGED.
WHAT YOU SAW--IT'S REALLY HARD FOR ME TO EXPLAIN.
HARDER THAN YOUR BOYFRIEND'S SKIN TURNING GHOST WHITE AND A RED CIRCLE GROWING ON HIS CHEST?
LOOK--I USED TO BE-- I USED TO BE A SOLDIER. THE GOVERNMENT DID SOMETHING TO ME. CHANGED ME. PUT THESE TINY MACHINES IN ME. BUT THEN I THOUGHT I GOT CURED.
EXCEPT THE THINGS THEY PUT INSIDE ME--THESE NANITES--THEY'RE OUT THERE NOW. THEY'RE TAKING OVER PEOPLE LIKE MIKE.
BUT THESE PEOPLE CAN'T HANDLE THEM. THEY--THEY GET SICK LIKE MIKE DID. DO HORRIBLE THINGS.
FOR WHATEVER REASON I SEEM TO BE THE ONLY PERSON WHO CAN CONTROL THEM.
I--I DON'T KNOW HOW THEY CHOOSE THEIR HOSTS. MAYBE IT'S PEOPLE WHO ARE INCLINED TO VIOLENCE-- OR MAYBE THEY REALLY ARE INNOCENT.

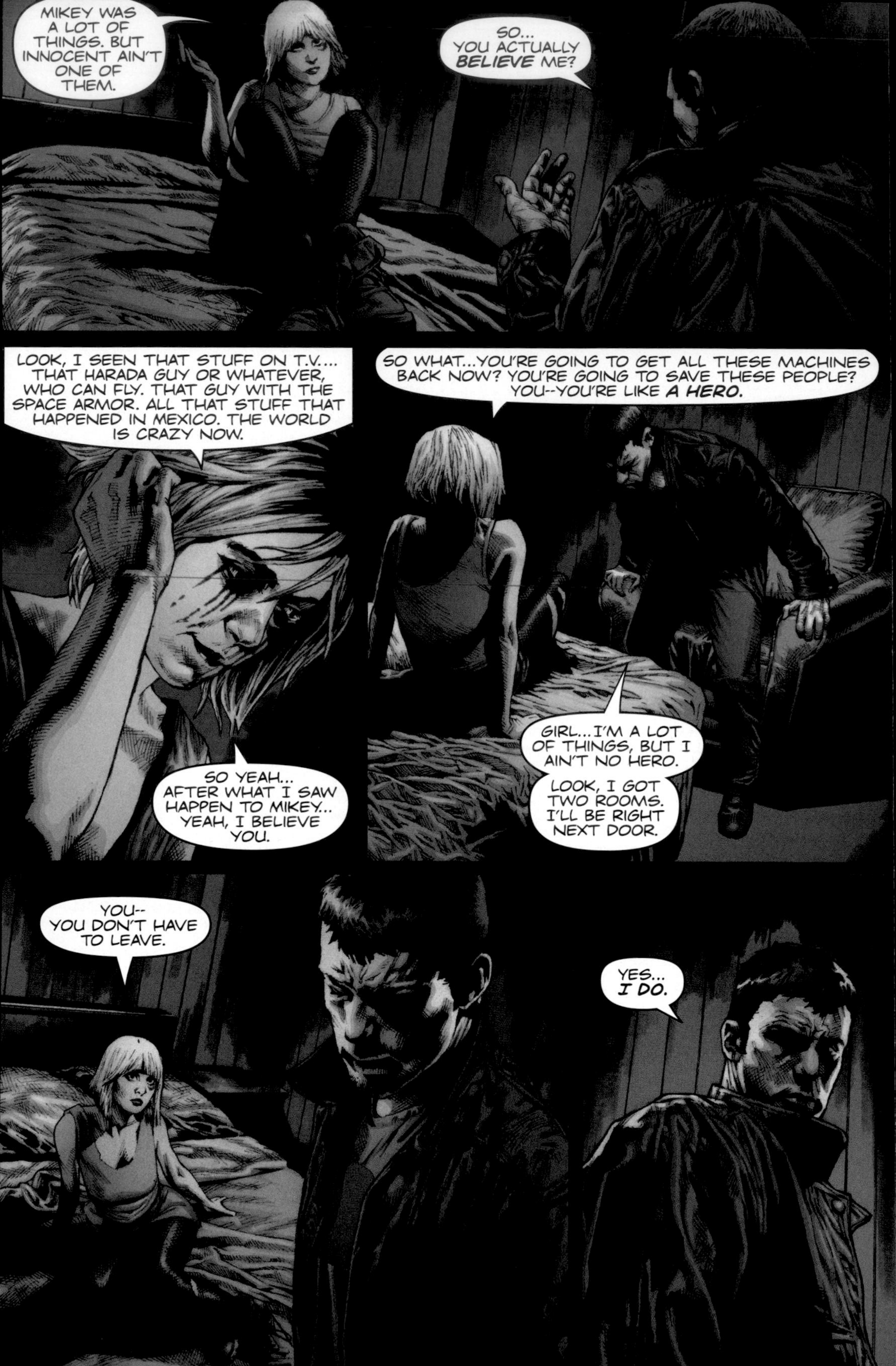
MIKEY WAS A LOT OF THINGS. BUT INNOCENT AIN'T ONE OF THEM.
SO... YOU ACTUALLY BELIEVE ME?
LOOK, I SEEN THAT STUFF ON T.V.... THAT HARADA GUY OR WHATEVER, WHO CAN FLY. THAT GUY WITH THE SPACE ARMOR. ALL THAT STUFF THAT HAPPENED IN MEXICO. THE WORLD IS CRAZY NOW.
SO YEAH... AFTER WHAT I SAW HAPPEN TO MIKEY... YEAH, I BELIEVE YOU.
SO WHAT...YOU'RE GOING TO GET ALL THESE MACHINES BACK NOW? YOU'RE GOING TO SAVE THESE PEOPLE? YOU--YOU'RE LIKE A HERO.
GIRL...I'M A LOT OF THINGS, BUT I AIN'T NO HERO.
LOOK, I GOT TWO ROOMS. I'LL BE RIGHT NEXT DOOR.
YOU-- YOU DON'T HAVE TO LEAVE.
YES... I DO.

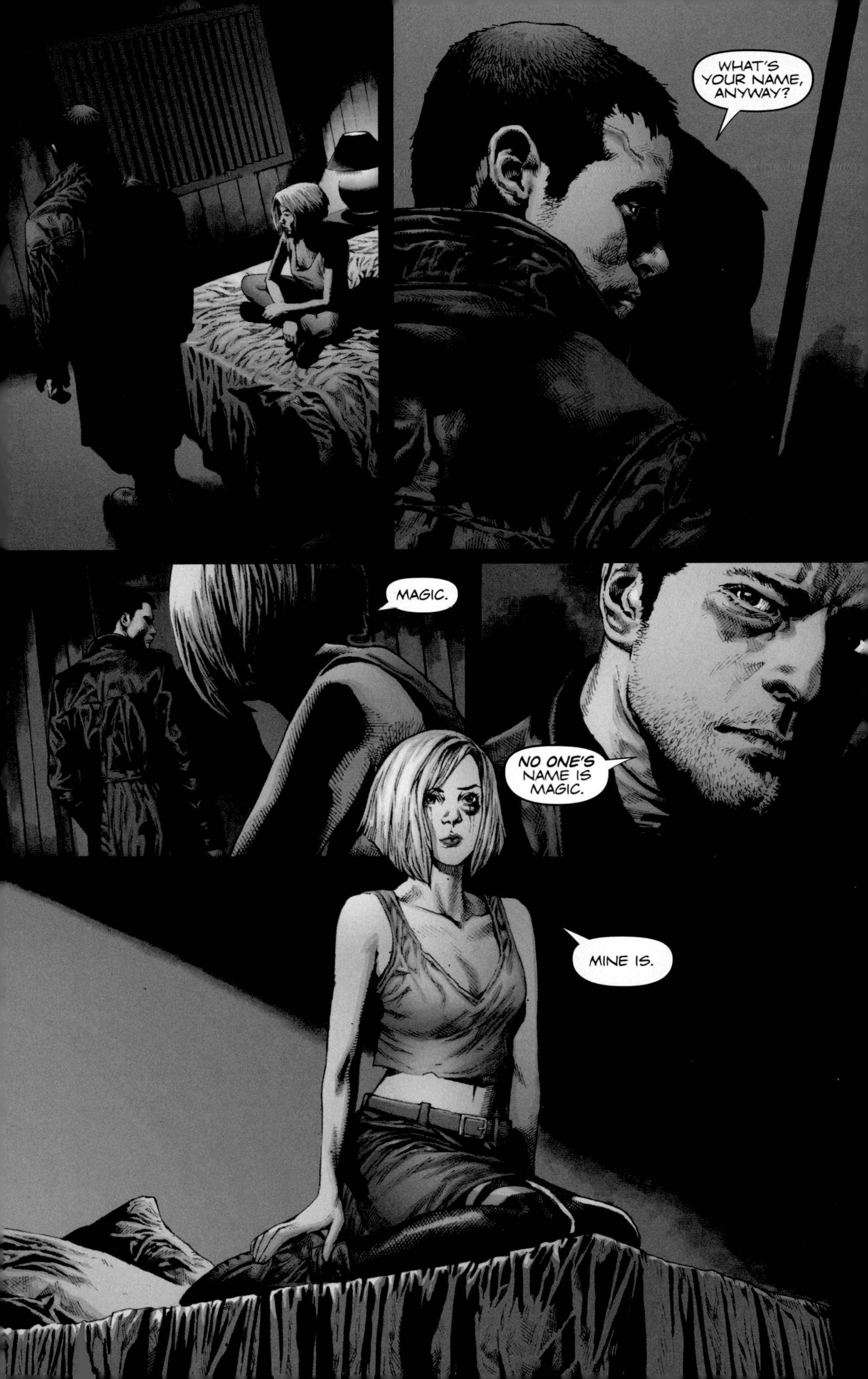
WHAT'S YOUR NAME, ANYWAY?
MAGIC.
NO ONE'S NAME IS MAGIC.
MINE IS.

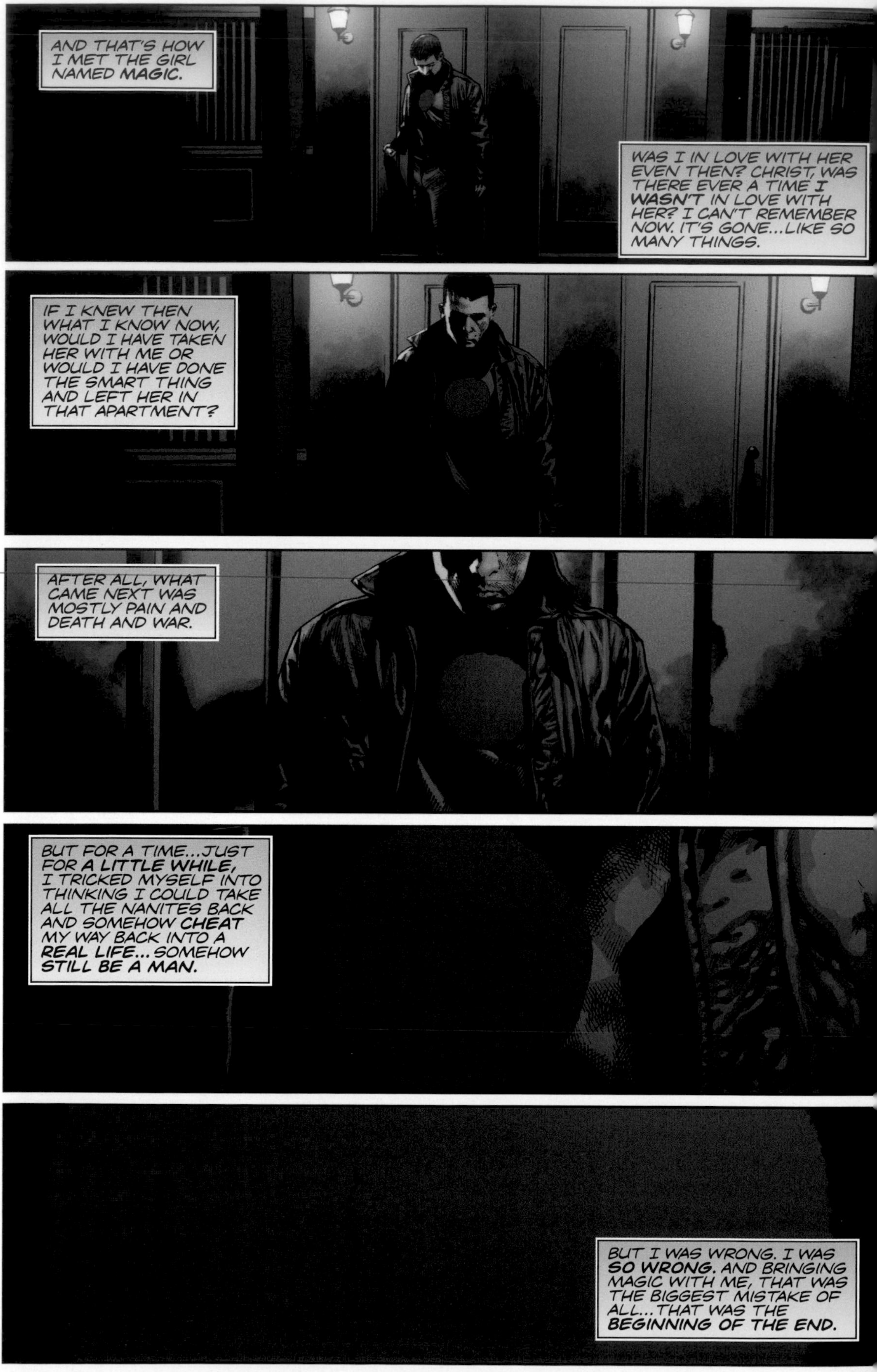
AND THAT'S HOW I MET THE GIRL NAMED MAGIC.
WAS I IN LOVE WITH HER EVEN THEN? CHRIST, WAS THERE EVER A TIME I WASN'T IN LOVE WITH HER? I CAN'T REMEMBER NOW. IT'S GONE...LIKE SO MANY THINGS.
IF I KNEW THEN WHAT I KNOW NOW, WOULD I HAVE TAKEN HER WITH ME OR WOULD I HAVE DONE THE SMART THING AND LEFT HER IN THAT APARTMENT?
AFTER ALL, WHAT CAME NEXT WAS MOSTLY PAIN AND DEATH AND WAR.
BUT FOR A TIME...JUST FOR A LITTLE WHILE, I TRICKED MYSELF INTO THINKING I COULD TAKE ALL THE NANITES BACK AND SOMEHOW CHEAT MY WAY BACK INTO A REAL LIFE...SOMEHOW STILL BE A MAN.
BUT I WAS WRONG. I WAS SO WRONG. AND BRINGING MAGIC WITH ME, THAT WAS THE BIGGEST MISTAKE OF ALL...THAT WAS THE BEGINNING OF THE END.

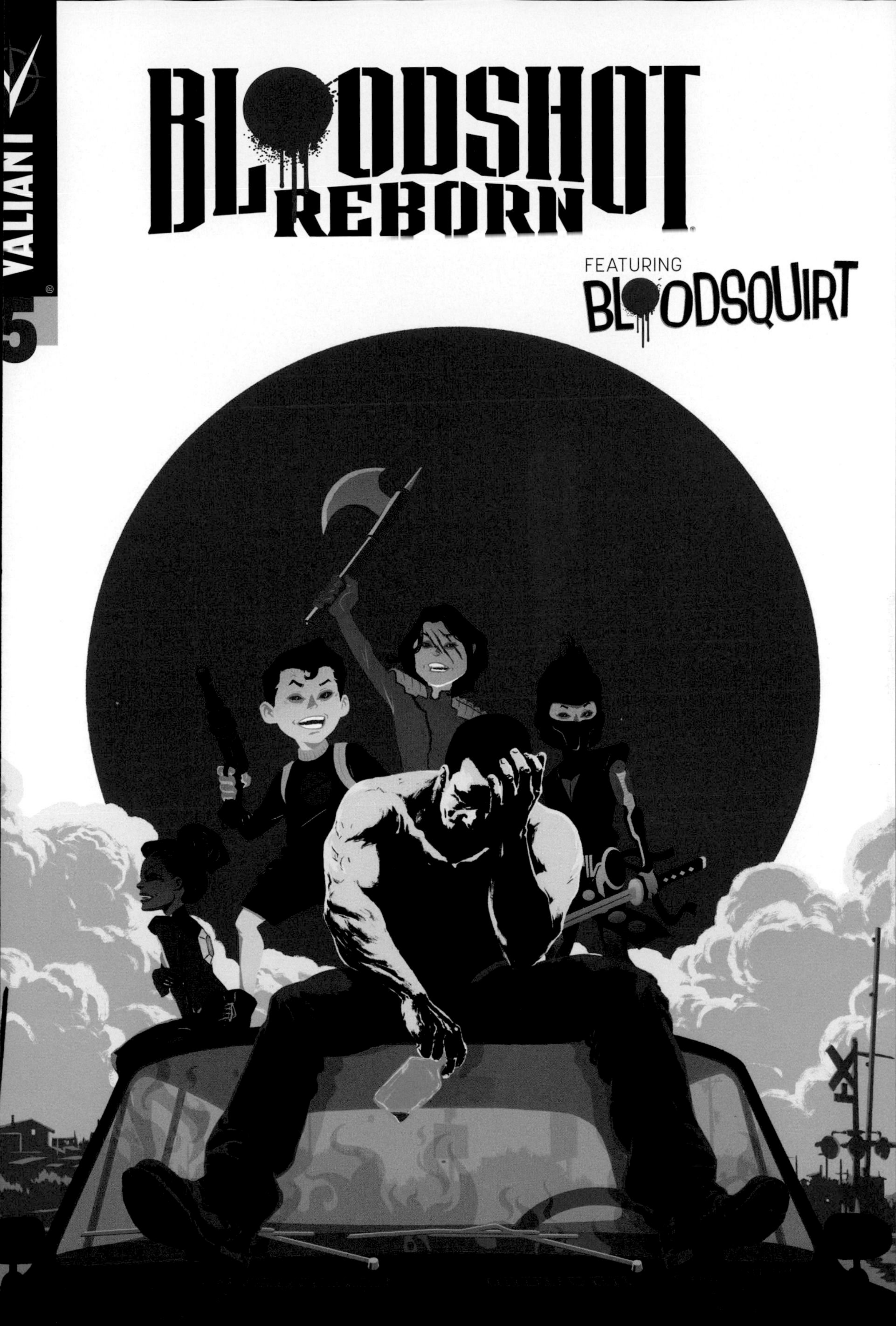
VALIANT
5
BLOODSHOT
REBORN
FEATURING
BLOODSQUIRT

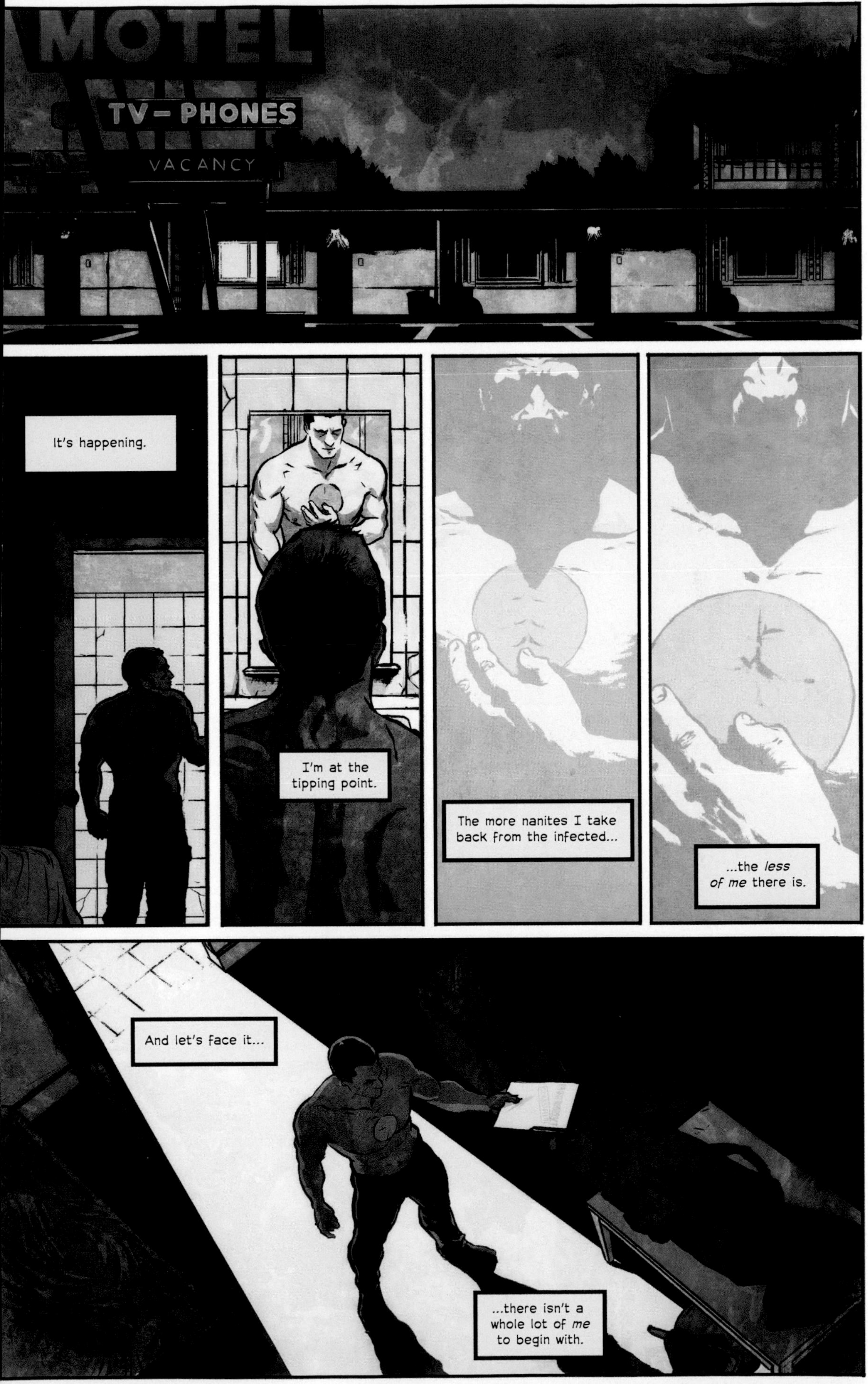
MOTEL
TV–PHONES
VACANCY
It's happening.
I'm at the tipping point.
The more nanites I take back from the infected...
...the *less of me* there is.
And let's face it...
...there isn't a whole lot of *me* to begin with.

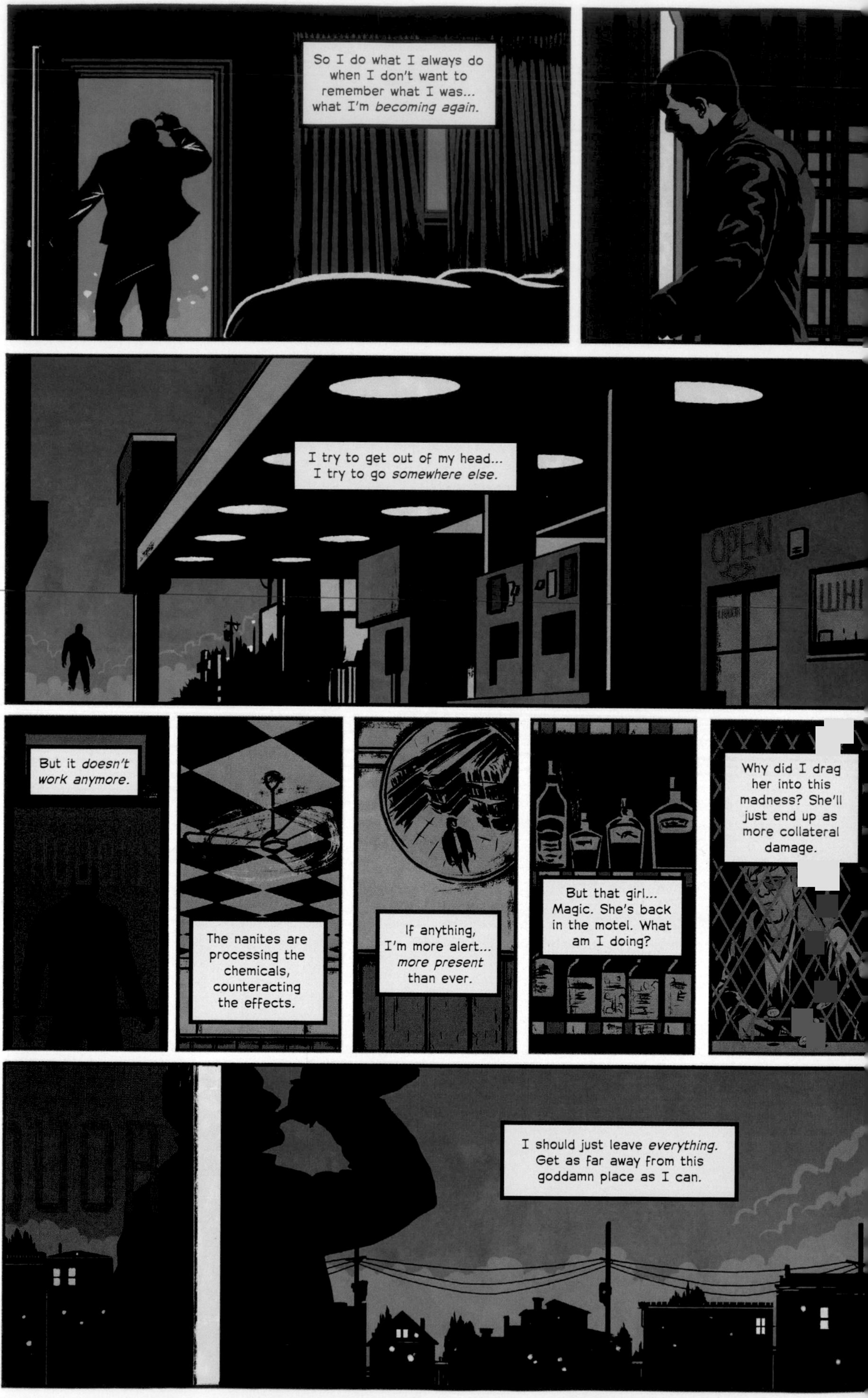
So I do what I always do when I don't want to remember what I was... what I'm *becoming again.*
I try to get out of my head... I try to go *somewhere else.*
OPEN
But it *doesn't work anymore.*
The nanites are processing the chemicals, counteracting the effects.
If anything, I'm more alert... *more present* than ever.
But that girl... Magic. She's back in the motel. What am I doing?
Why did I drag her into this madness? She'll just end up as more collateral damage.
I should just leave *everything.* Get as far away from this goddamn place as I can.

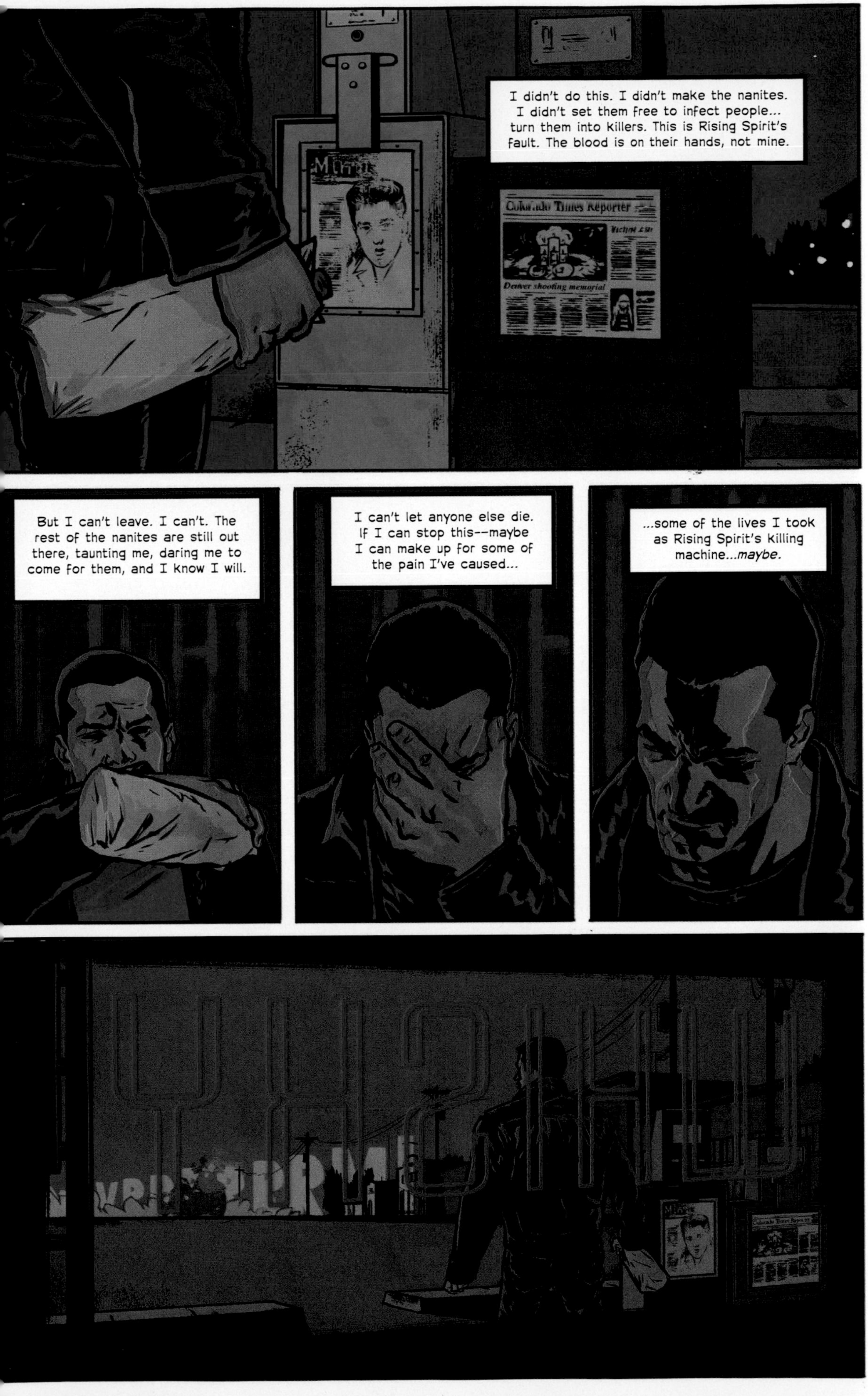

I didn't do this. I didn't make the nanites. I didn't set them free to infect people... turn them into killers. This is Rising Spirit's fault. The blood is on their hands, not mine.
Colorado Times Reporter
Denver shooting memorial
But I can't leave. I can't. The rest of the nanites are still out there, taunting me, daring me to come for them, and I know I will.
I can't let anyone else die. If I can stop this--maybe I can make up for some of the pain I've caused...
...some of the lives I took as Rising Spirit's killing machine...*maybe.*

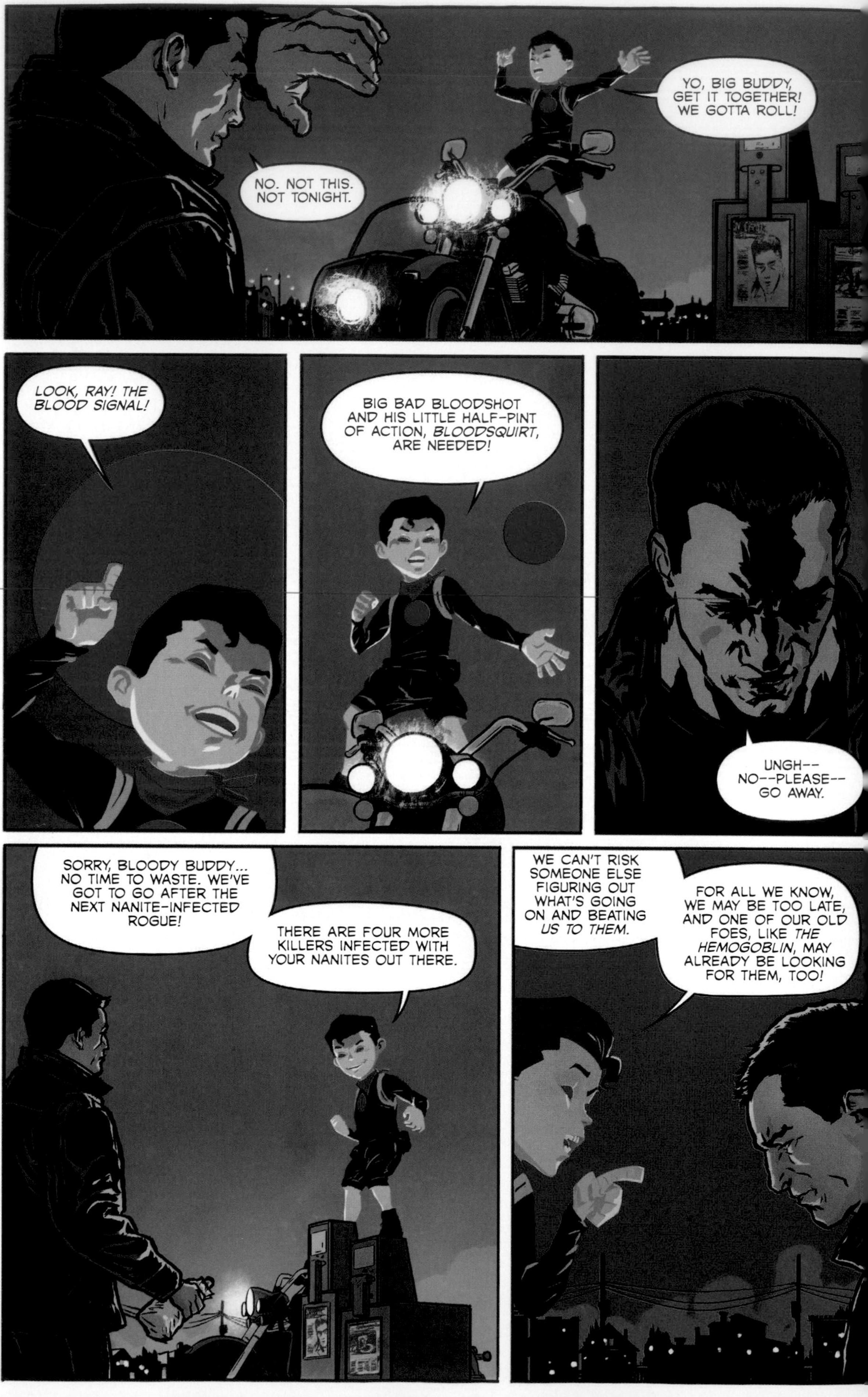
YO, BIG BUDDY, GET IT TOGETHER! WE GOTTA ROLL!
NO. NOT THIS. NOT TONIGHT.
LOOK, RAY! THE BLOOD SIGNAL!
BIG BAD BLOODSHOT AND HIS LITTLE HALF-PINT OF ACTION, BLOODSQUIRT, ARE NEEDED!
UNGH-- NO--PLEASE-- GO AWAY.
SORRY, BLOODY BUDDY... NO TIME TO WASTE. WE'VE GOT TO GO AFTER THE NEXT NANITE-INFECTED ROGUE!
THERE ARE FOUR MORE KILLERS INFECTED WITH YOUR NANITES OUT THERE.
WE CAN'T RISK SOMEONE ELSE FIGURING OUT WHAT'S GOING ON AND BEATING US TO THEM.
FOR ALL WE KNOW, WE MAY BE TOO LATE, AND ONE OF OUR OLD FOES, LIKE THE HEMOGOBLIN, MAY ALREADY BE LOOKING FOR THEM, TOO!

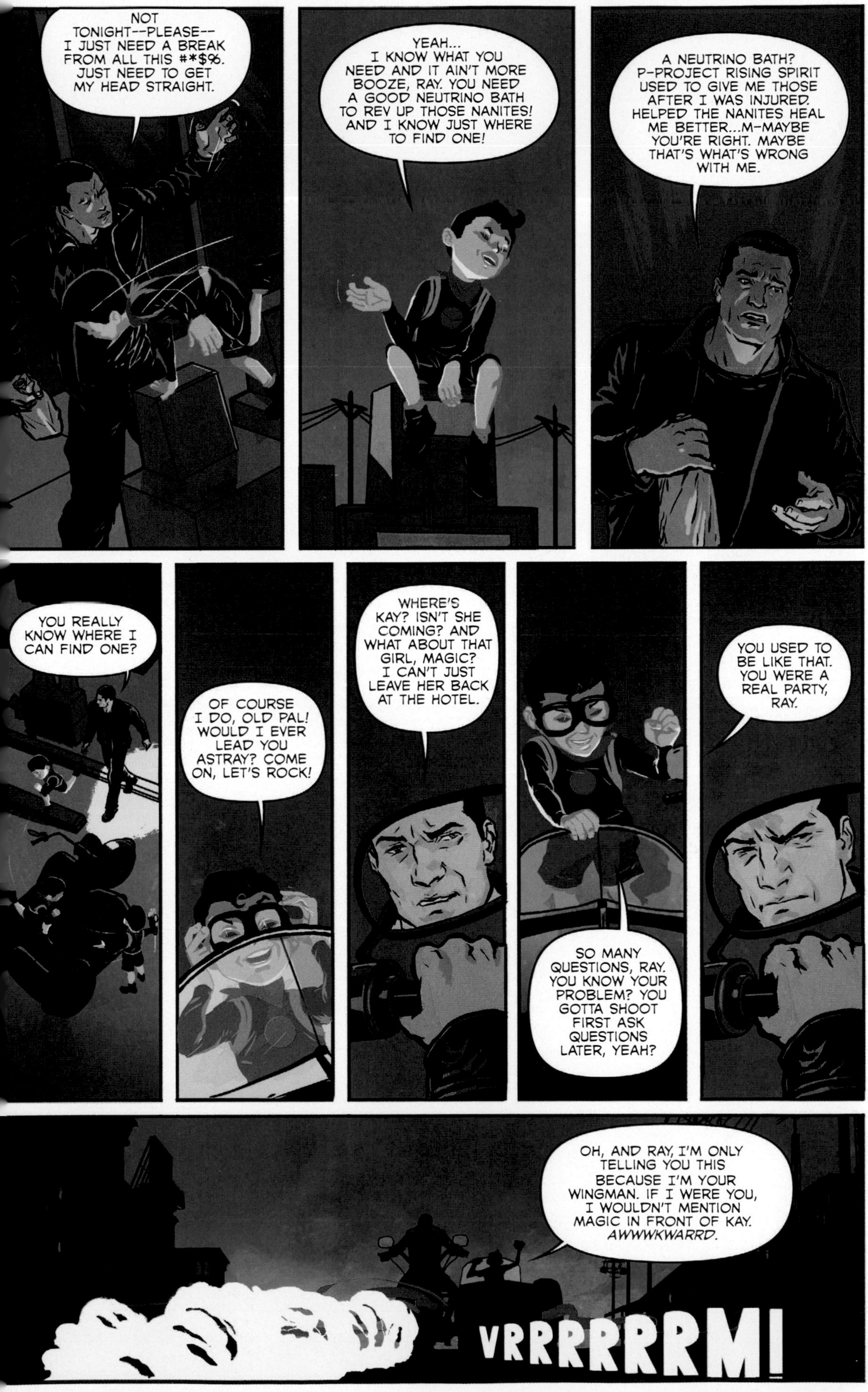
NOT TONIGHT--PLEASE-- I JUST NEED A BREAK FROM ALL THIS #*$%. JUST NEED TO GET MY HEAD STRAIGHT.
YEAH... I KNOW WHAT YOU NEED AND IT AIN'T MORE BOOZE, RAY. YOU NEED A GOOD NEUTRINO BATH TO REV UP THOSE NANITES! AND I KNOW JUST WHERE TO FIND ONE!
A NEUTRINO BATH? P-PROJECT RISING SPIRIT USED TO GIVE ME THOSE AFTER I WAS INJURED. HELPED THE NANITES HEAL ME BETTER...M-MAYBE YOU'RE RIGHT. MAYBE THAT'S WHAT'S WRONG WITH ME.
YOU REALLY KNOW WHERE I CAN FIND ONE?
OF COURSE I DO, OLD PAL! WOULD I EVER LEAD YOU ASTRAY? COME ON, LET'S ROCK!
WHERE'S KAY? ISN'T SHE COMING? AND WHAT ABOUT THAT GIRL, MAGIC? I CAN'T JUST LEAVE HER BACK AT THE HOTEL.
SO MANY QUESTIONS, RAY. YOU KNOW YOUR PROBLEM? YOU GOTTA SHOOT FIRST ASK QUESTIONS LATER, YEAH?
YOU USED TO BE LIKE THAT. YOU WERE A REAL PARTY, RAY.
OH, AND RAY, I'M ONLY TELLING YOU THIS BECAUSE I'M YOUR WINGMAN. IF I WERE YOU, I WOULDN'T MENTION MAGIC IN FRONT OF KAY. *AWWWKWARRD.*
VRRRRRRM!

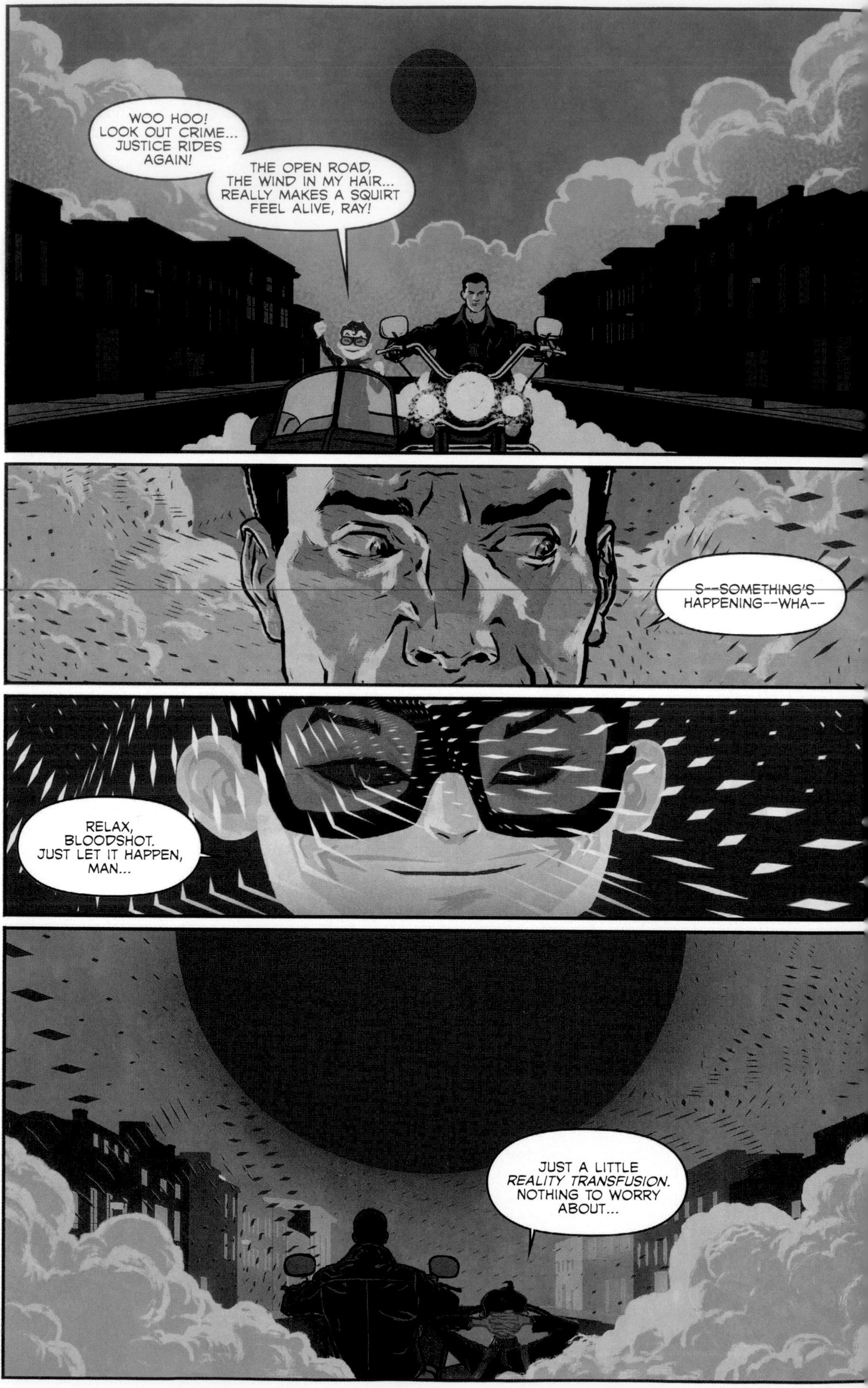
WOO HOO! LOOK OUT CRIME... JUSTICE RIDES AGAIN!
THE OPEN ROAD, THE WIND IN MY HAIR... REALLY MAKES A SQUIRT FEEL ALIVE, RAY!
S--SOMETHING'S HAPPENING--WHA--
RELAX, BLOODSHOT. JUST LET IT HAPPEN, MAN...
JUST A LITTLE *REALITY TRANSFUSION.* NOTHING TO WORRY ABOUT...

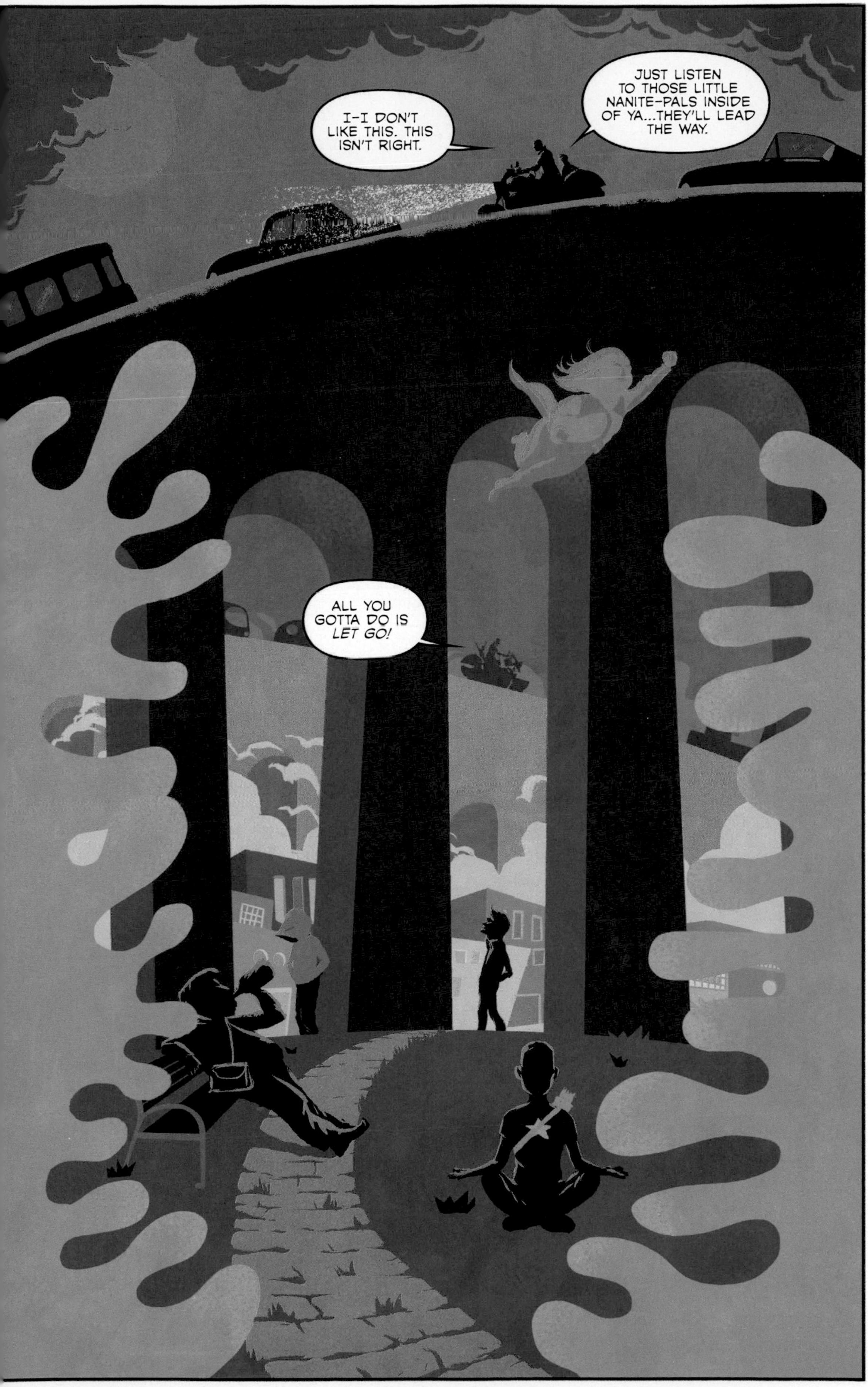
JUST LISTEN TO THOSE LITTLE NANITE-PALS INSIDE OF YA...THEY'LL LEAD THE WAY.
I-I DON'T LIKE THIS. THIS ISN'T RIGHT.
ALL YOU GOTTA DO IS *LET GO!*

THERE, RAY! THAT WAY!

SECTOR B

WHAT IS THIS? WHERE ARE WE HEADING?

WHERE DO YOU THINK, BLOODSHOT, OL' CHUM?

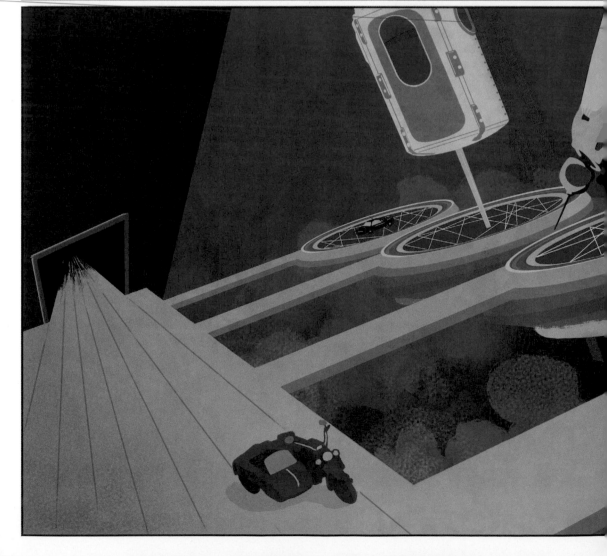

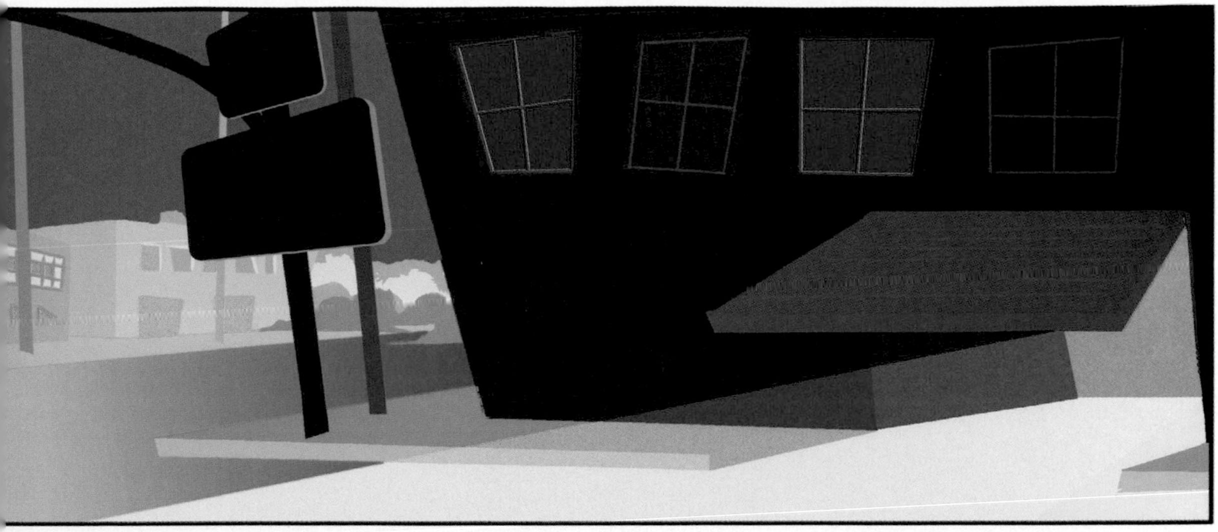

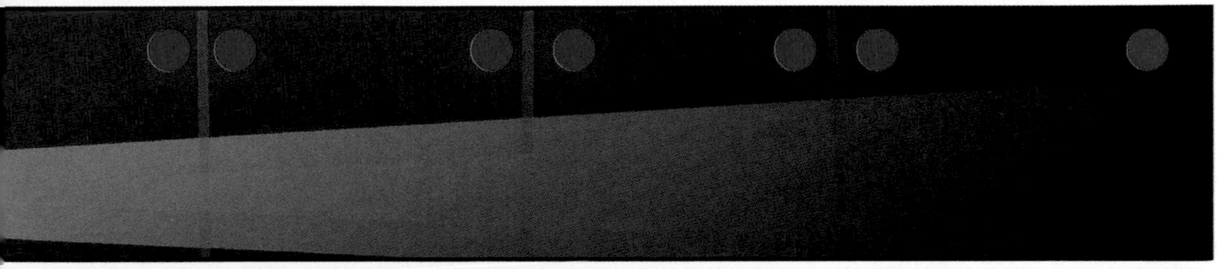

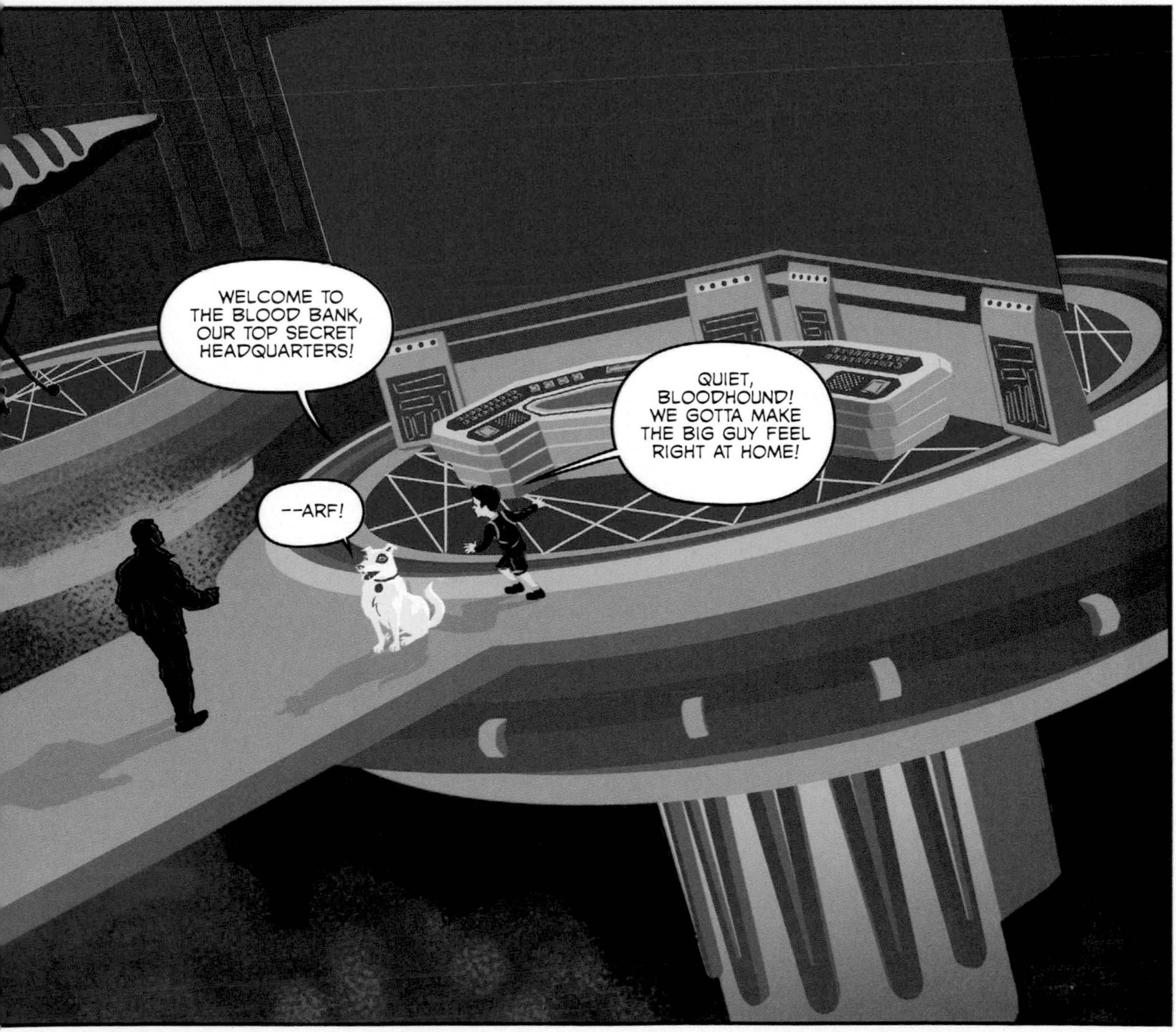
WELCOME TO THE BLOOD BANK, OUR TOP SECRET HEADQUARTERS!
QUIET, BLOODHOUND! WE GOTTA MAKE THE BIG GUY FEEL RIGHT AT HOME!
--ARF!

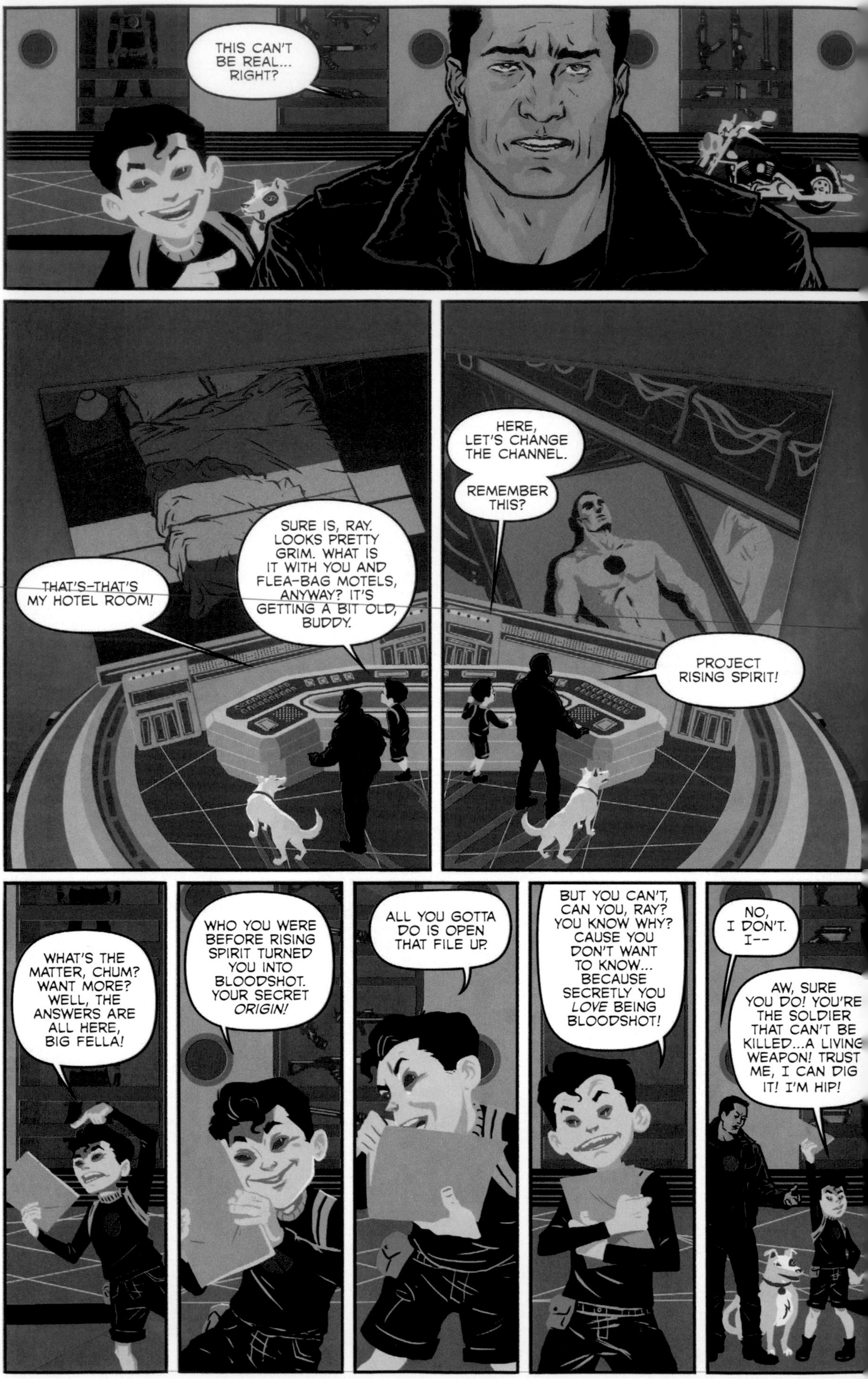
THIS CAN'T BE REAL... RIGHT?
THAT'S--THAT'S MY HOTEL ROOM!
SURE IS, RAY. LOOKS PRETTY GRIM. WHAT IS IT WITH YOU AND FLEA-BAG MOTELS, ANYWAY? IT'S GETTING A BIT OLD, BUDDY.
HERE, LET'S CHANGE THE CHANNEL.
REMEMBER THIS?
PROJECT RISING SPIRIT!
WHAT'S THE MATTER, CHUM? WANT MORE? WELL, THE ANSWERS ARE ALL HERE, BIG FELLA!
WHO YOU WERE BEFORE RISING SPIRIT TURNED YOU INTO BLOODSHOT. YOUR SECRET *ORIGIN!*
ALL YOU GOTTA DO IS OPEN THAT FILE UP.
BUT YOU CAN'T, CAN YOU, RAY? YOU KNOW WHY? CAUSE YOU DON'T WANT TO KNOW... BECAUSE SECRETLY YOU *LOVE* BEING BLOODSHOT!
NO, I DON'T. I--
AW, SURE YOU DO! YOU'RE THE SOLDIER THAT CAN'T BE KILLED...A LIVING WEAPON! TRUST ME, I CAN DIG IT! I'M HIP!

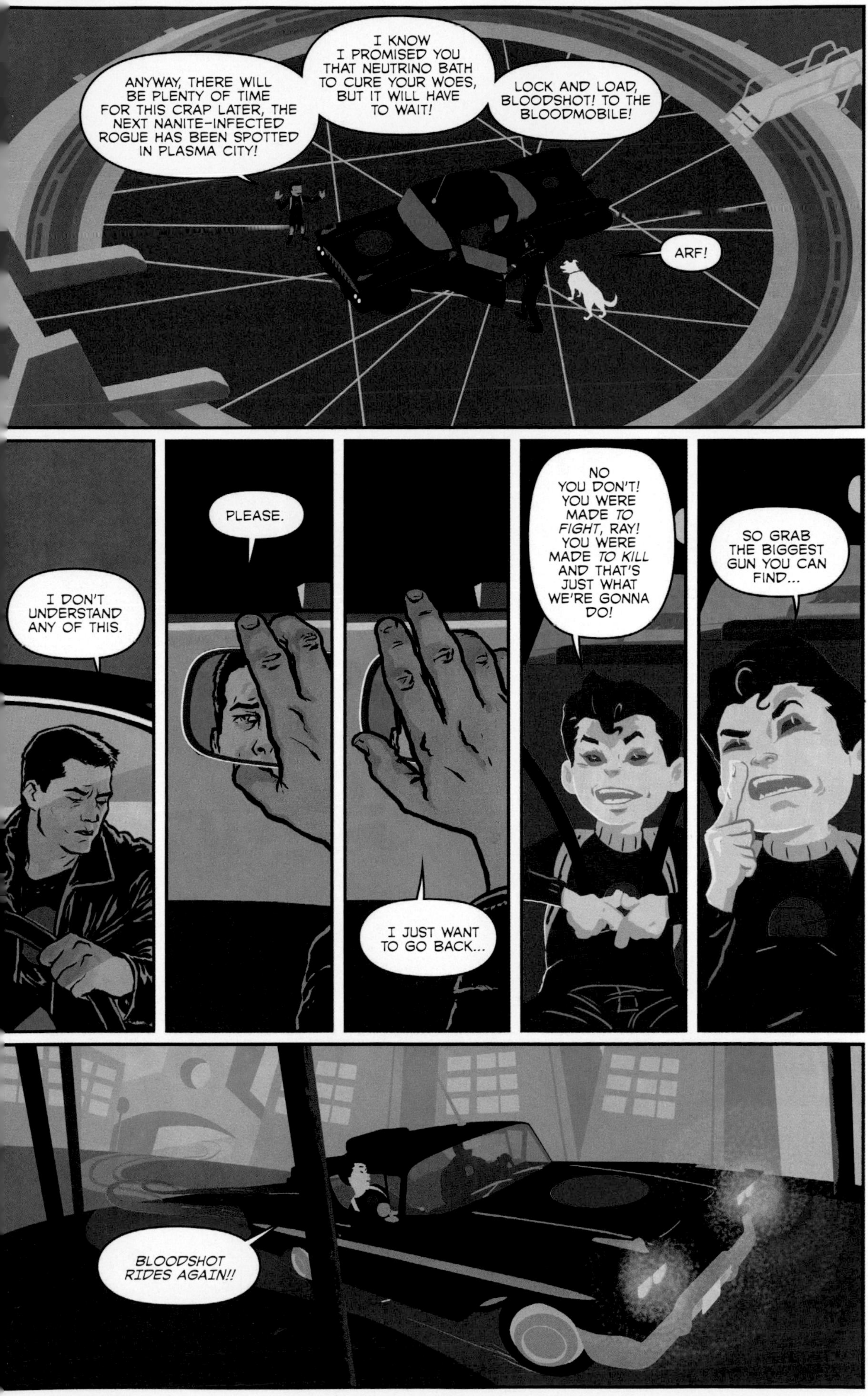
ANYWAY, THERE WILL BE PLENTY OF TIME FOR THIS CRAP LATER, THE NEXT NANITE-INFECTED ROGUE HAS BEEN SPOTTED IN PLASMA CITY!
I KNOW I PROMISED YOU THAT NEUTRINO BATH TO CURE YOUR WOES, BUT IT WILL HAVE TO WAIT!
LOCK AND LOAD, BLOODSHOT! TO THE BLOODMOBILE!
ARF!
I DON'T UNDERSTAND ANY OF THIS.
PLEASE.
I JUST WANT TO GO BACK...
NO YOU DON'T! YOU WERE MADE *TO FIGHT*, RAY! YOU WERE MADE *TO KILL* AND THAT'S JUST WHAT WE'RE GONNA DO!
SO GRAB THE BIGGEST GUN YOU CAN FIND...
BLOODSHOT RIDES AGAIN!!

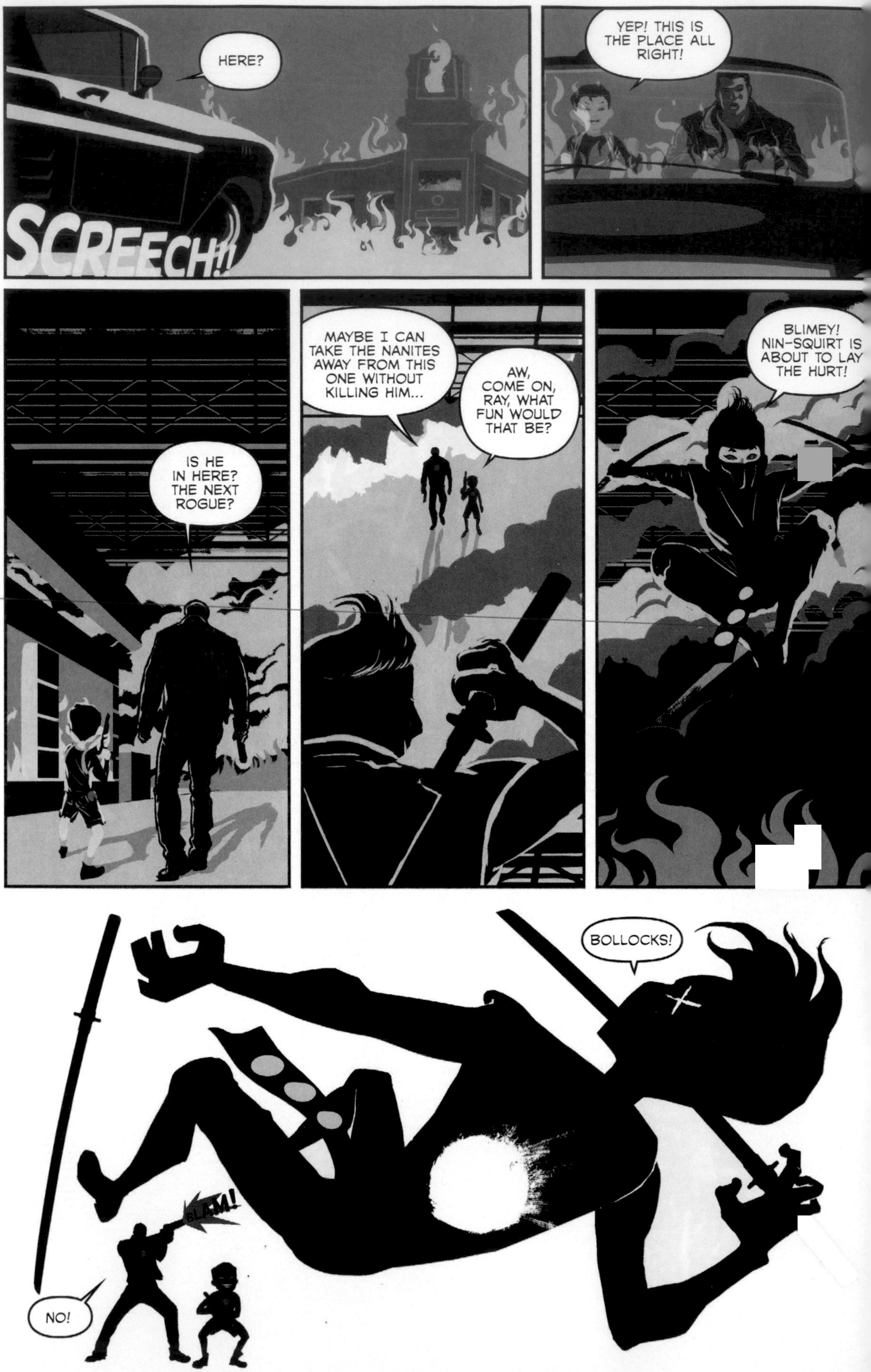
HERE?
SCREECH!!
YEP! THIS IS THE PLACE ALL RIGHT!
IS HE IN HERE? THE NEXT ROGUE?
MAYBE I CAN TAKE THE NANITES AWAY FROM THIS ONE WITHOUT KILLING HIM...
AW, COME ON, RAY, WHAT FUN WOULD THAT BE?
BLIMEY! NIN-SQUIRT IS ABOUT TO LAY THE HURT!
BOLLOCKS!
BLAM!
NO!

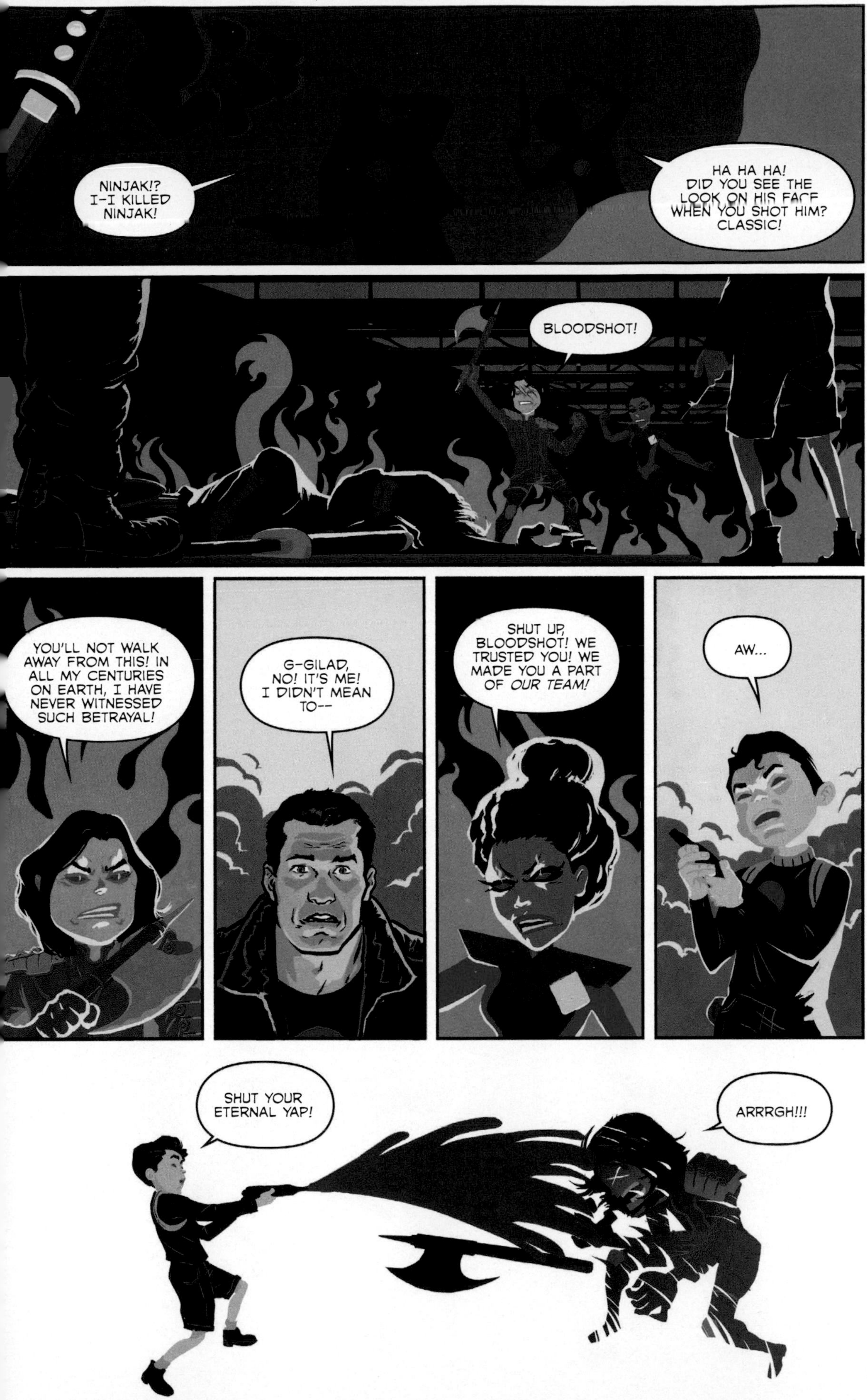
NINJAK!? I-I KILLED NINJAK!
HA HA HA! DID YOU SEE THE LOOK ON HIS FACE WHEN YOU SHOT HIM? CLASSIC!
BLOODSHOT!
YOU'LL NOT WALK AWAY FROM THIS! IN ALL MY CENTURIES ON EARTH, I HAVE NEVER WITNESSED SUCH BETRAYAL!
G-GILAD, NO! IT'S ME! I DIDN'T MEAN TO--
SHUT UP, BLOODSHOT! WE TRUSTED YOU! WE MADE YOU A PART OF *OUR TEAM!*
AW...
SHUT YOUR ETERNAL YAP!
ARRRGH!!!

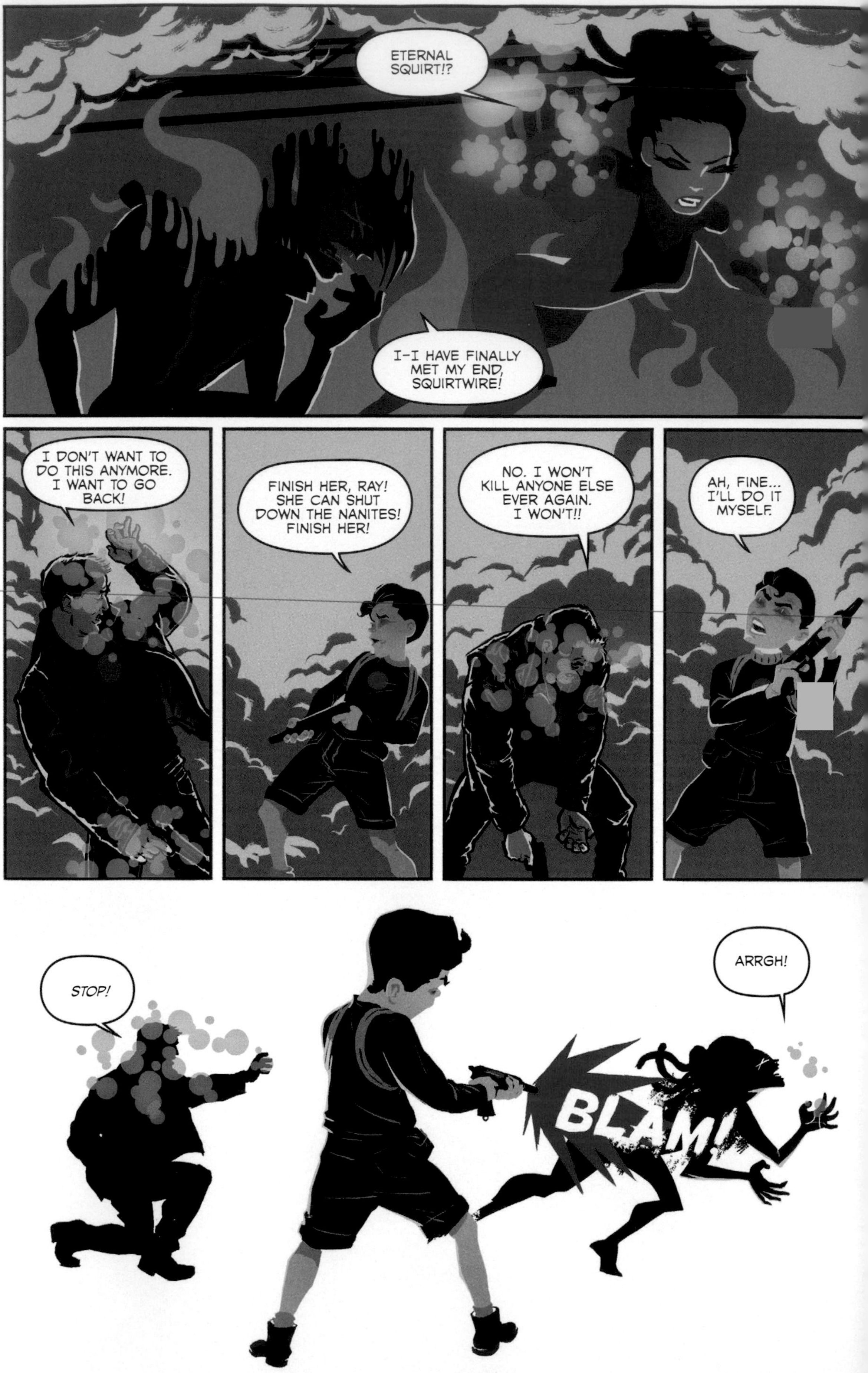
ETERNAL SQUIRT!?
I-I HAVE FINALLY MET MY END, SQUIRTWIRE!
I DON'T WANT TO DO THIS ANYMORE. I WANT TO GO BACK!
FINISH HER, RAY! SHE CAN SHUT DOWN THE NANITES! FINISH HER!
NO. I WON'T KILL ANYONE ELSE EVER AGAIN. I WON'T!!
AH, FINE... I'LL DO IT MYSELF.
STOP!
ARRGH!
BLAM!

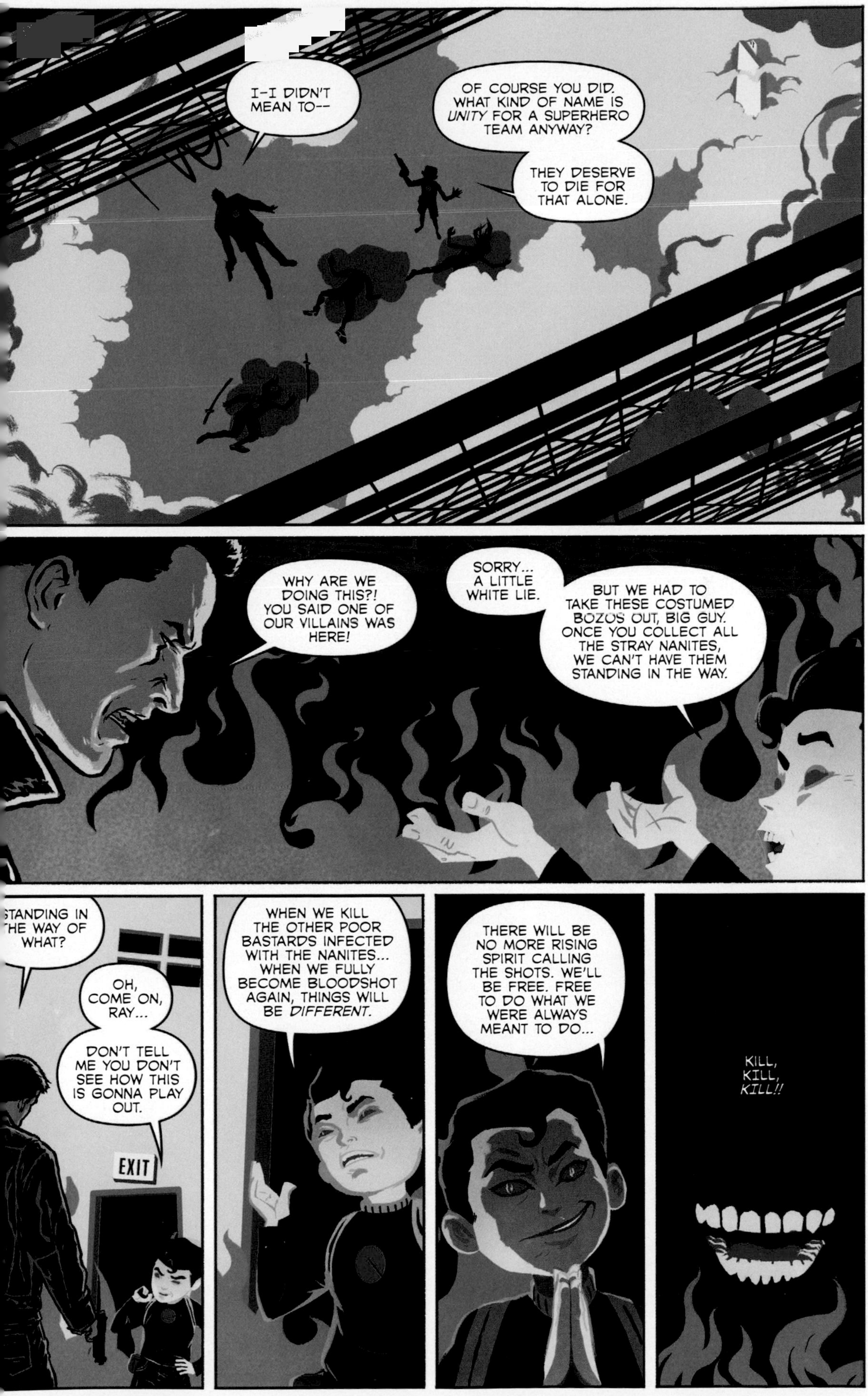
I-I DIDN'T MEAN TO--
OF COURSE YOU DID. WHAT KIND OF NAME IS *UNITY* FOR A SUPERHERO TEAM ANYWAY?
THEY DESERVE TO DIE FOR THAT ALONE.
WHY ARE WE DOING THIS?! YOU SAID ONE OF OUR VILLAINS WAS HERE!
SORRY... A LITTLE WHITE LIE.
BUT WE HAD TO TAKE THESE COSTUMED BOZOS OUT, BIG GUY. ONCE YOU COLLECT ALL THE STRAY NANITES, WE CAN'T HAVE THEM STANDING IN THE WAY.
STANDING IN THE WAY OF WHAT?
OH, COME ON, RAY...
DON'T TELL ME YOU DON'T SEE HOW THIS IS GONNA PLAY OUT.
EXIT
WHEN WE KILL THE OTHER POOR BASTARDS INFECTED WITH THE NANITES... WHEN WE FULLY BECOME BLOODSHOT AGAIN, THINGS WILL BE *DIFFERENT*.
THERE WILL BE NO MORE RISING SPIRIT CALLING THE SHOTS. WE'LL BE FREE. FREE TO DO WHAT WE WERE ALWAYS MEANT TO DO...
KILL, KILL, *KILL!!*

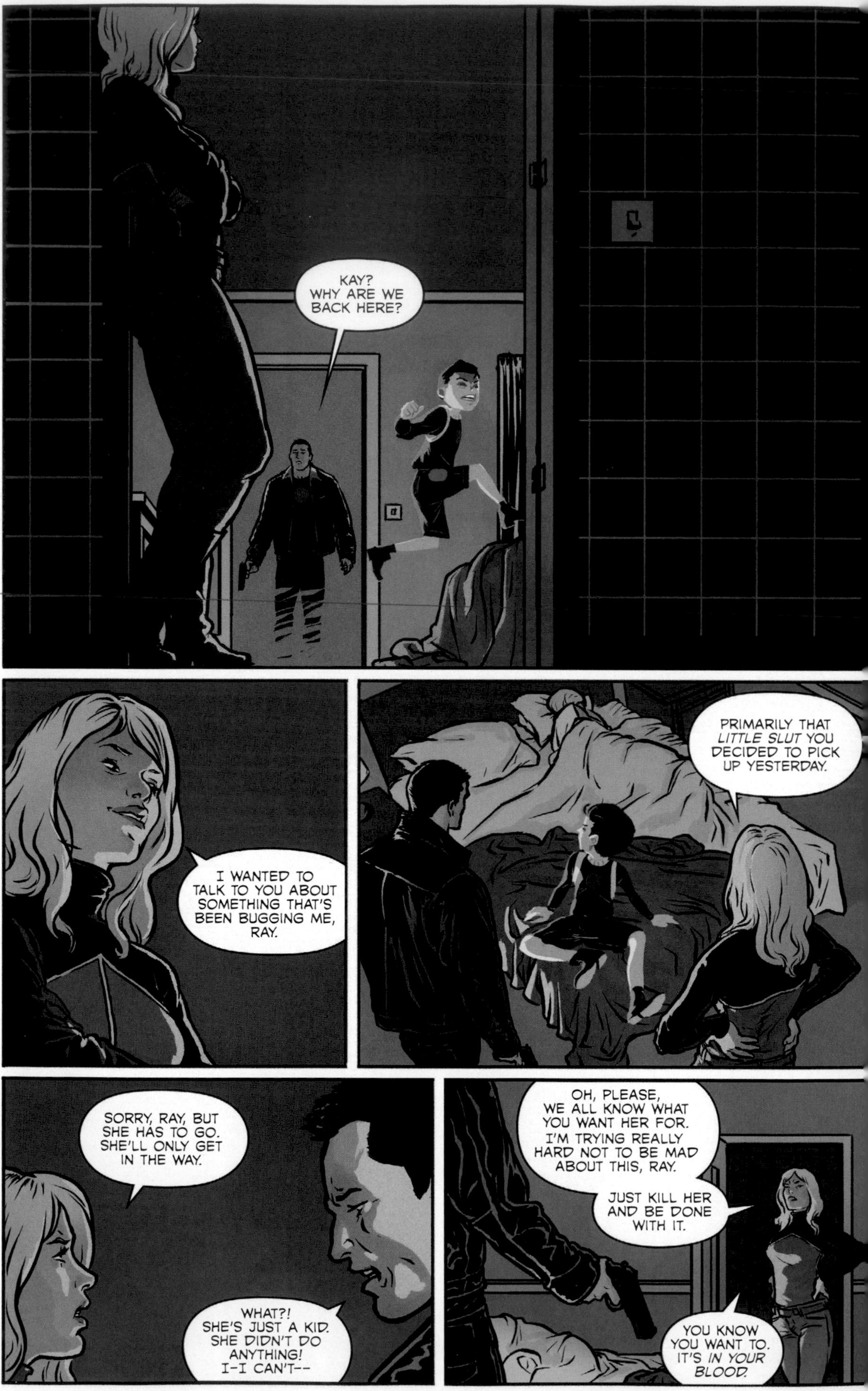

KAY? WHY ARE WE BACK HERE?
I WANTED TO TALK TO YOU ABOUT SOMETHING THAT'S BEEN BUGGING ME, RAY.
PRIMARILY THAT *LITTLE SLUT* YOU DECIDED TO PICK UP YESTERDAY.
SORRY, RAY, BUT SHE HAS TO GO. SHE'LL ONLY GET IN THE WAY.
WHAT?! SHE'S JUST A KID. SHE DIDN'T DO ANYTHING! I-I CAN'T--
OH, PLEASE, WE ALL KNOW WHAT YOU WANT HER FOR. I'M TRYING REALLY HARD NOT TO BE MAD ABOUT THIS, RAY.
JUST KILL HER AND BE DONE WITH IT.
YOU KNOW YOU WANT TO. IT'S *IN YOUR BLOOD.*

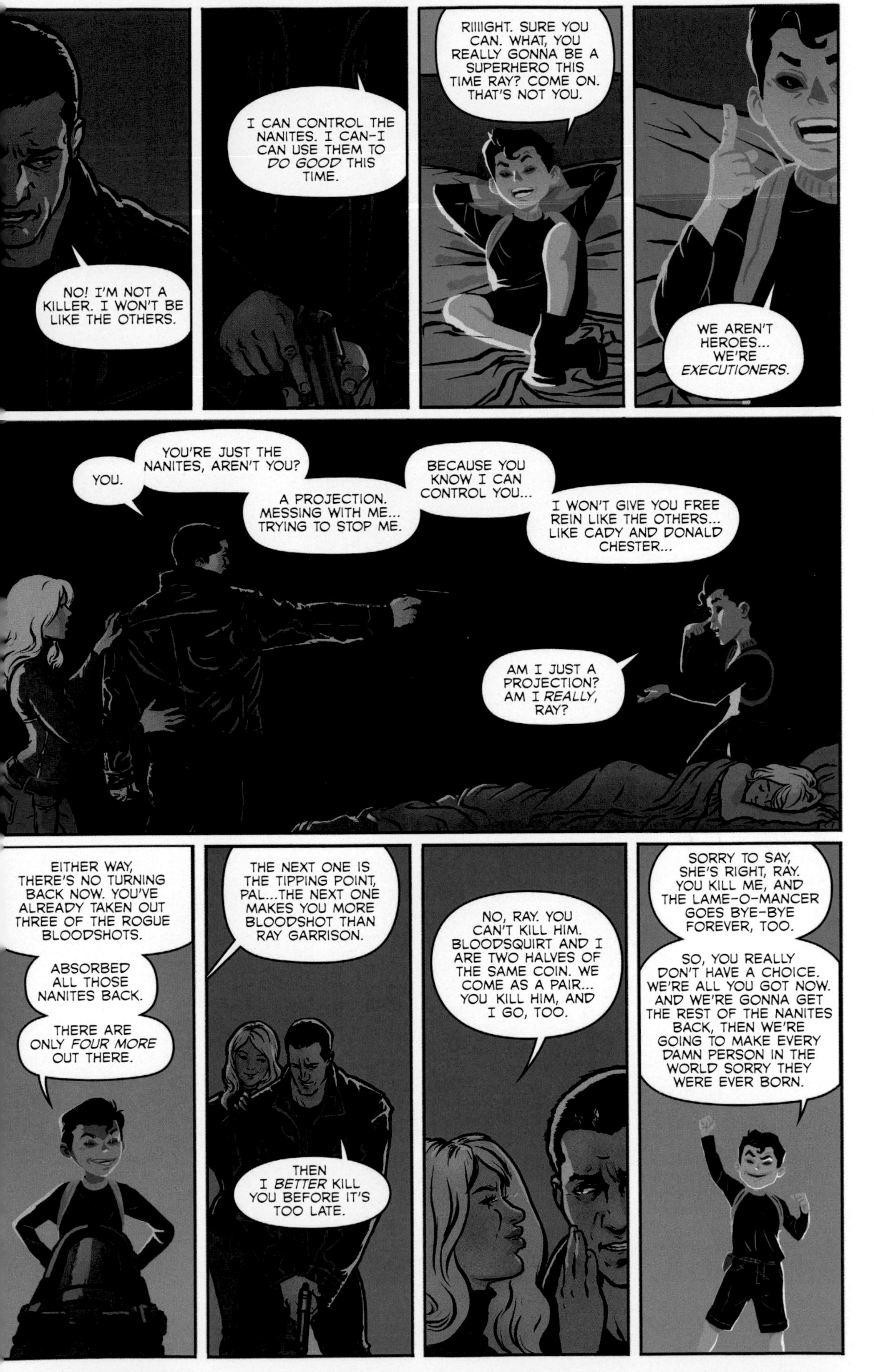
NO! I'M NOT A KILLER. I WON'T BE LIKE THE OTHERS.
I CAN CONTROL THE NANITES. I CAN-I CAN USE THEM TO *DO GOOD* THIS TIME.
RIIIIGHT. SURE YOU CAN. WHAT, YOU REALLY GONNA BE A SUPERHERO THIS TIME RAY? COME ON. THAT'S NOT YOU.
WE AREN'T HEROES... WE'RE *EXECUTIONERS*.
YOU.
YOU'RE JUST THE NANITES, AREN'T YOU?
A PROJECTION. MESSING WITH ME... TRYING TO STOP ME.
BECAUSE YOU KNOW I CAN CONTROL YOU...
I WON'T GIVE YOU FREE REIN LIKE THE OTHERS... LIKE CADY AND DONALD CHESTER...
AM I JUST A PROJECTION? AM I *REALLY*, RAY?
EITHER WAY, THERE'S NO TURNING BACK NOW. YOU'VE ALREADY TAKEN OUT THREE OF THE ROGUE BLOODSHOTS.
ABSORBED ALL THOSE NANITES BACK.
THERE ARE ONLY *FOUR MORE* OUT THERE.
THE NEXT ONE IS THE TIPPING POINT, PAL...THE NEXT ONE MAKES YOU MORE BLOODSHOT THAN RAY GARRISON.
THEN I *BETTER* KILL YOU BEFORE IT'S TOO LATE.
NO, RAY. YOU CAN'T KILL HIM. BLOODSQUIRT AND I ARE TWO HALVES OF THE SAME COIN. WE COME AS A PAIR... YOU KILL HIM, AND I GO, TOO.
SORRY TO SAY, SHE'S RIGHT, RAY. YOU KILL ME, AND THE LAME-O-MANCER GOES BYE-BYE FOREVER, TOO.
SO, YOU REALLY DON'T HAVE A CHOICE. WE'RE ALL YOU GOT NOW. AND WE'RE GONNA GET THE REST OF THE NANITES BACK, THEN WE'RE GOING TO MAKE EVERY DAMN PERSON IN THE WORLD SORRY THEY WERE EVER BORN.

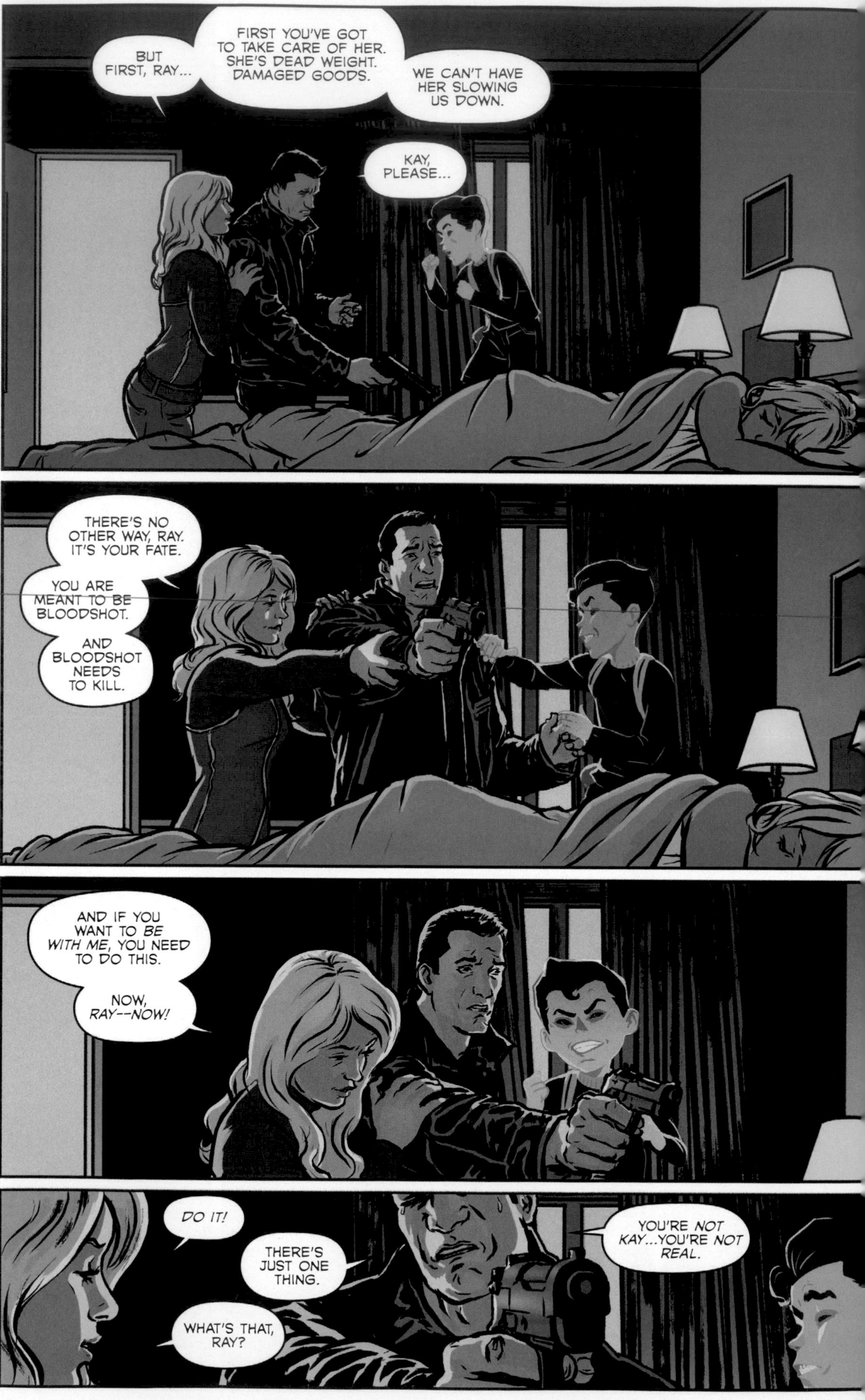
BUT FIRST, RAY...
FIRST YOU'VE GOT TO TAKE CARE OF HER. SHE'S DEAD WEIGHT. DAMAGED GOODS.
WE CAN'T HAVE HER SLOWING US DOWN.
KAY, PLEASE...
THERE'S NO OTHER WAY, RAY. IT'S YOUR FATE.
YOU ARE MEANT TO BE BLOODSHOT.
AND BLOODSHOT NEEDS TO KILL.
AND IF YOU WANT TO *BE WITH ME*, YOU NEED TO DO THIS.
NOW, *RAY--NOW!*
DO IT!
THERE'S JUST ONE THING.
WHAT'S THAT, RAY?
YOU'RE *NOT* KAY...YOU'RE *NOT* REAL.

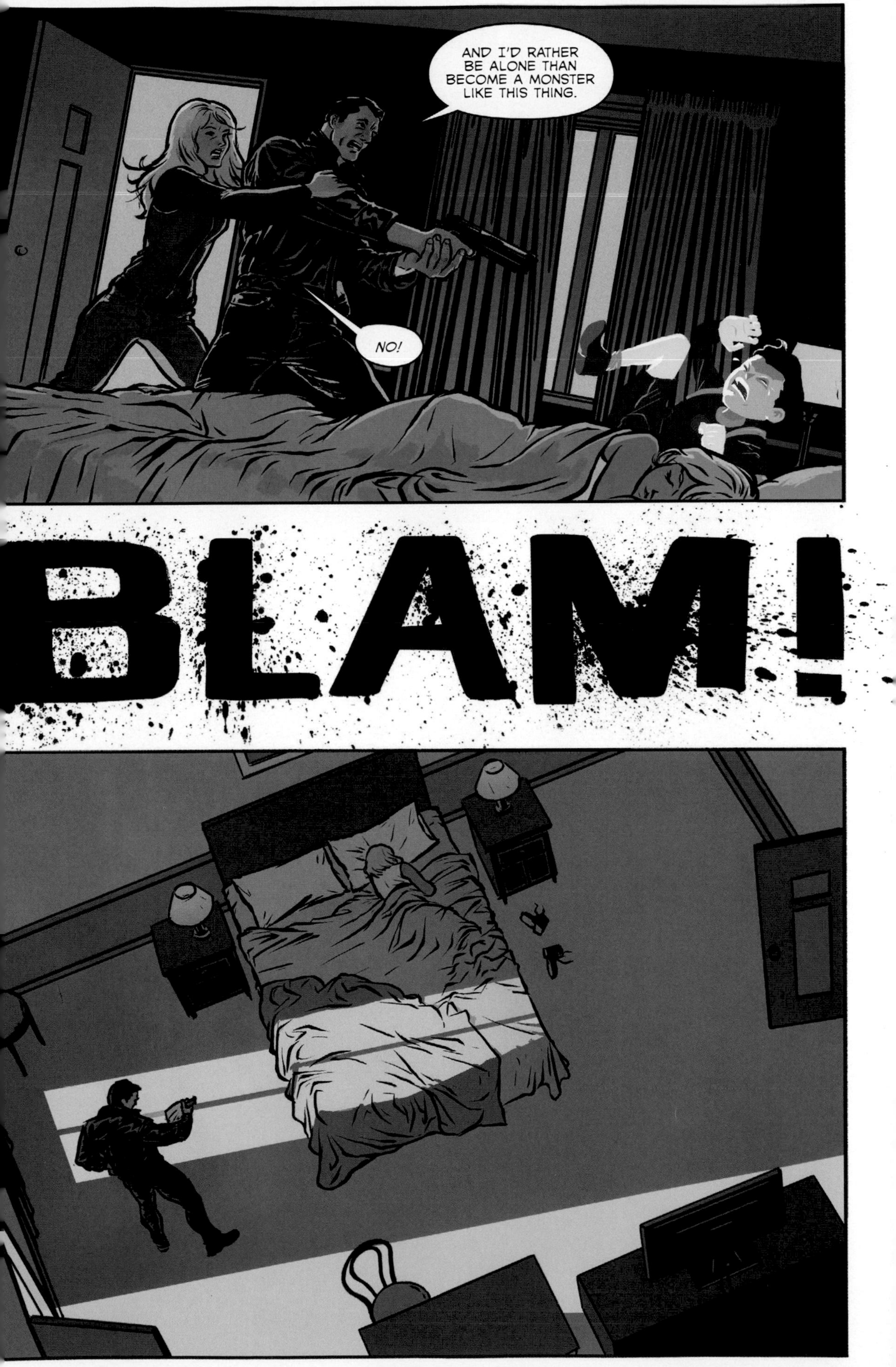
AND I'D RATHER BE ALONE THAN BECOME A MONSTER LIKE THIS THING.
NO!
BLAM!

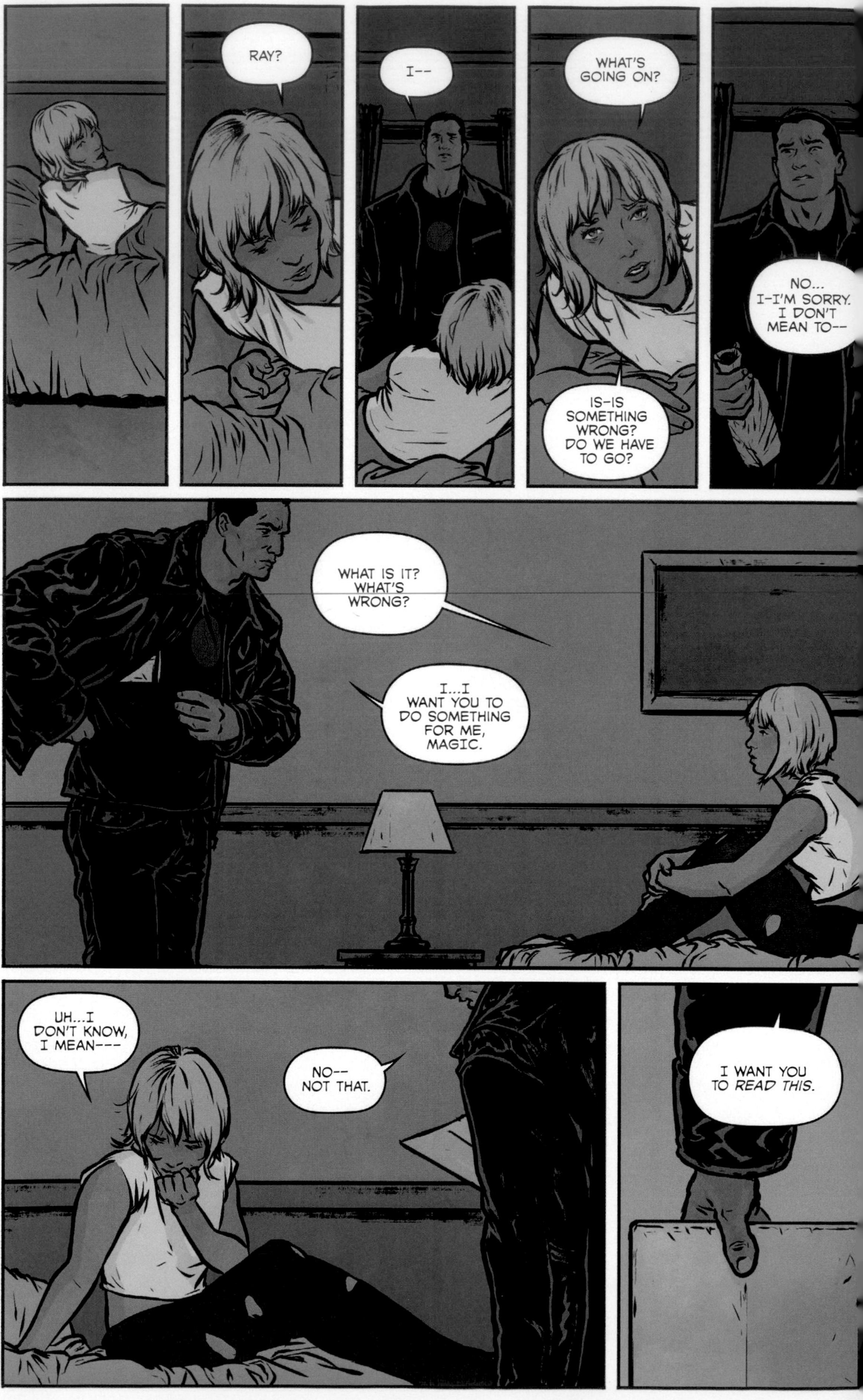
RAY?
I--
WHAT'S GOING ON?
IS-IS SOMETHING WRONG? DO WE HAVE TO GO?
NO... I-I'M SORRY. I DON'T MEAN TO--
WHAT IS IT? WHAT'S WRONG?
I...I WANT YOU TO DO SOMETHING FOR ME, MAGIC.
UH...I DON'T KNOW, I MEAN---
NO-- NOT THAT.
I WANT YOU TO *READ THIS.*

OH. OKAY.
WHAT IS IT?
IT'S ME.
IT'S WHO I WAS BEFORE ALL OF THIS.
THE MILITARY TOOK MY MEMORIES, MY PAST.
IT'S ALL IN THERE.
BUT, WHY ME?
PROJECT BLOODSHOT
CLASSIFIED
BECAUSE I'VE TRIED. I'VE TRIED TO OPEN IT EVERY NIGHT, AND I'M JUST TOO SCARED TO SEE WHAT'S INSIDE.
AND BECAUSE THE NANITES--THE MORE THAT I TAKE BACK--THE LESS OF A MAN I'LL BE. I'LL BE BLOODSHOT AGAIN. A MACHINE. I CAN-I CAN ALREADY FEEL IT HAPPENING.
AND BEFORE IT'S TOO LATE I WANT TO KNOW THAT I WAS A MAN, ONCE. THAT I HAD A LIFE ONCE...THAT I WAS GOOD ONCE.
BECAUSE, IF I WAS NEVER GOOD, I DON'T THINK I EVER CAN BE.

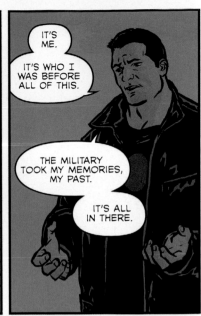

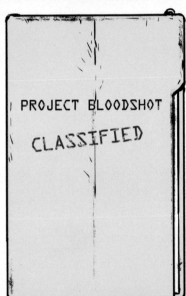

...

BUT I THINK YOU'RE GOOD *NOW*. YOU JUST DON'T KNOW YOU ARE.

PLEASE, I-I JUST *NEED* TO KNOW.

OKAY. I'LL READ IT. YOU JUST GONNA SIT THERE AND WATCH?

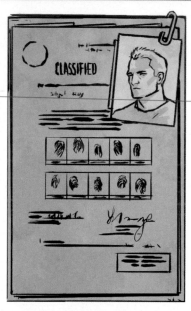

CLASSIFIED

YEAH. THAT OKAY?

YEAH. BUT I AIN'T A VERY GOOD READER. MIGHT TAKE A WHILE.

THAT'S OKAY...

I AIN'T GOT *NOWHERE ELSE* TO BE.

NEXT: *THE HUNT*

THE MAKING OF BLOODSHOT REBORN

BLOODSHOT STUDIES BY MICO SUAYAN

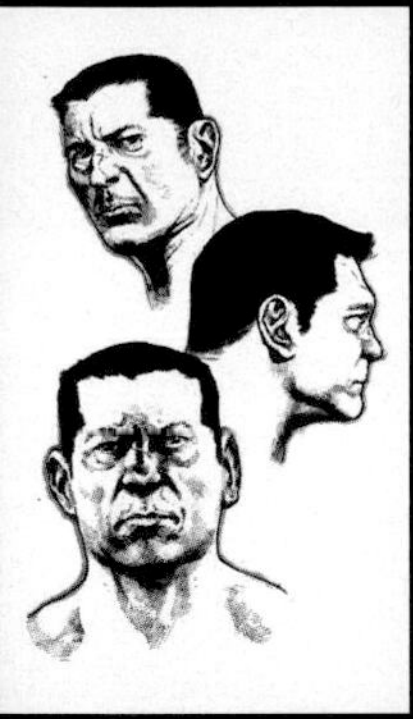
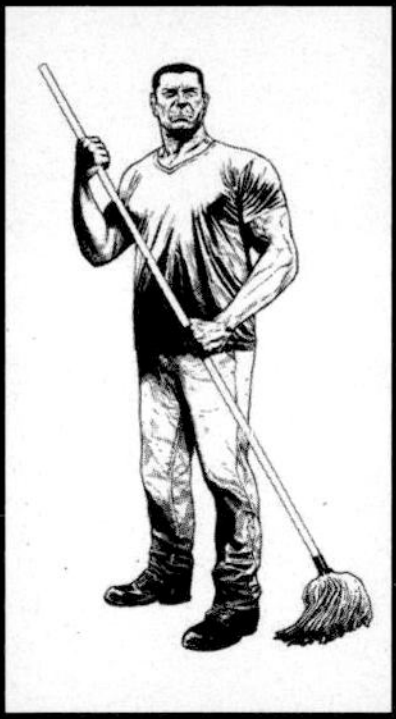
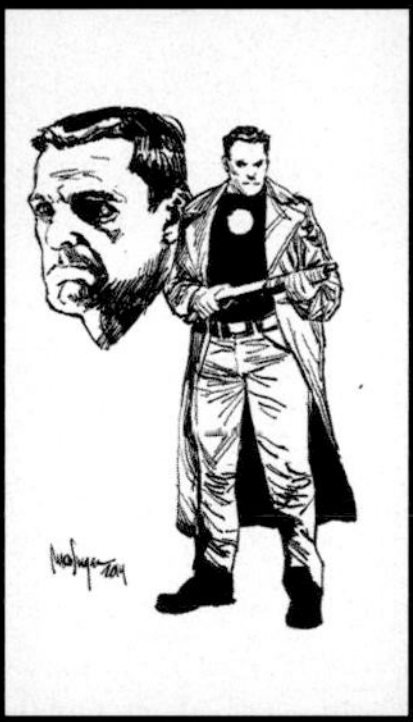
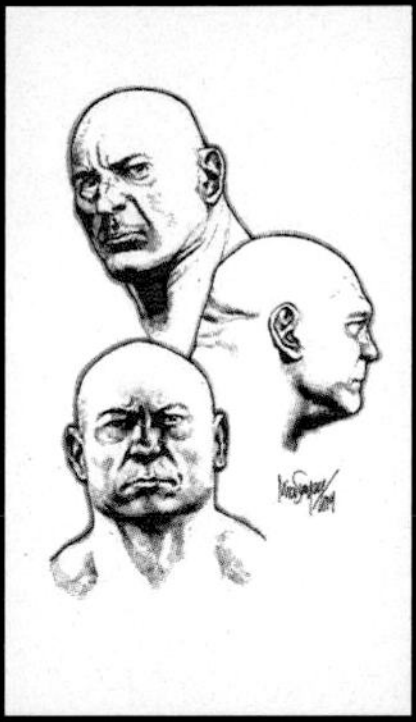
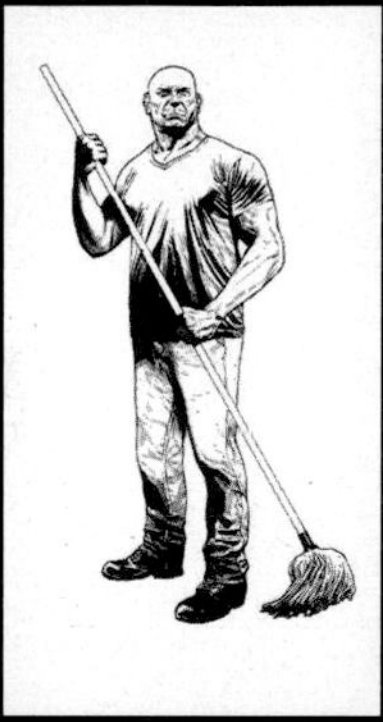

COVER STUDIES BY MICO SUAYAN

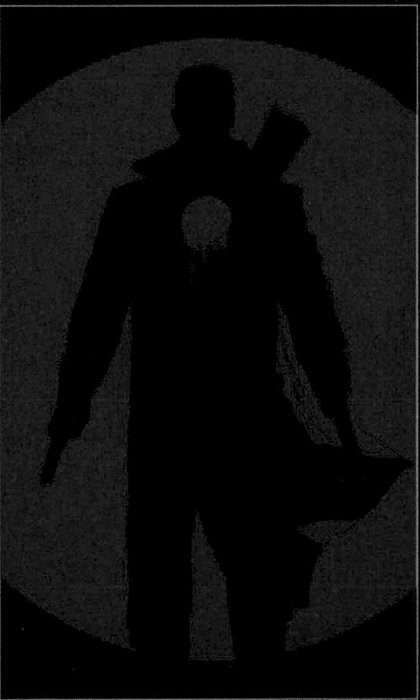
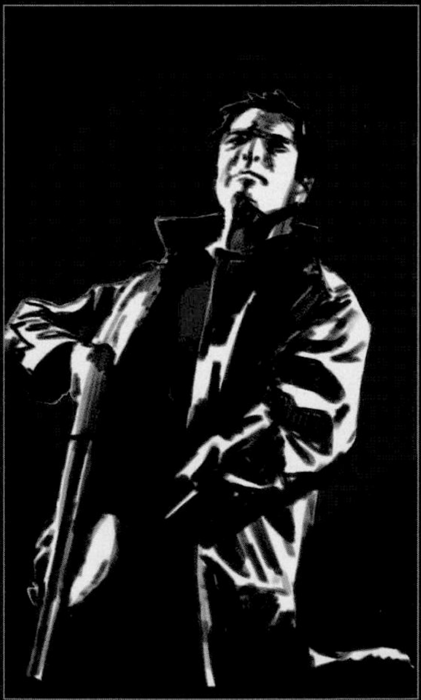
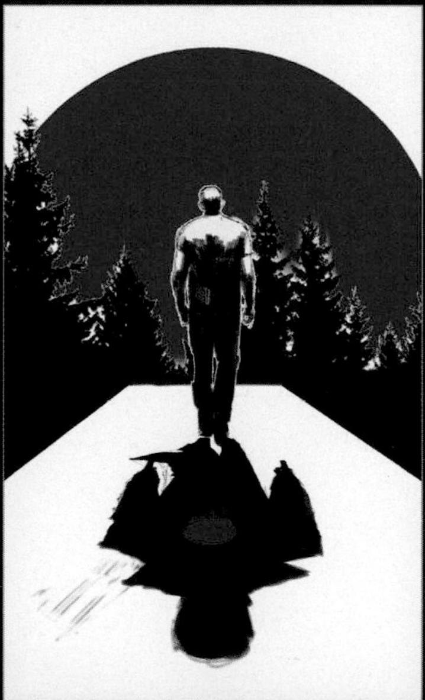

PAGE 1 SCRIPT BY JEFF LEMIRE

Mico, for this first issue, I'd like to keep the compositions simple...four widescreen panels stacked down the page.

PANEL 1 /// Black panel.

PANEL 2 /// An extreme close-up of Bloodshot's eyes. We see the whites surrounding his eyes and the blood-red eyes themselves.

PANEL 3 /// Extreme close-up of Bloodshot's chest. Shirt off, the red chest circle exposed.

PANEL 4 /// Extreme close-up of Bloodshot's hands, both at waist level, both aiming machine guns straight ahead and firing. Shell casings fly off.

PAGE 1 LAYOUT BY MICO SUAYAN

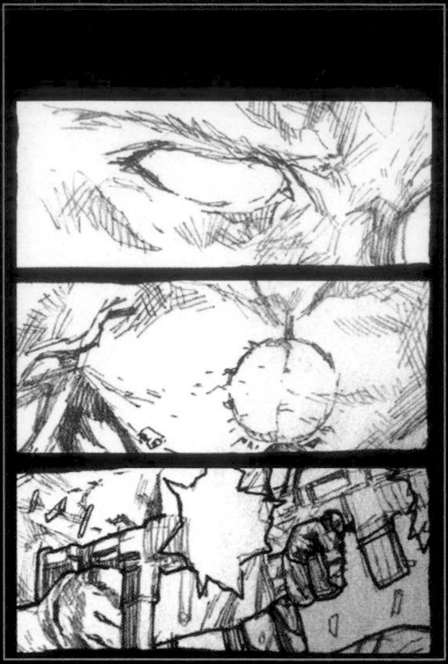

PAGE 1 INKS BY MICO SUAYAN

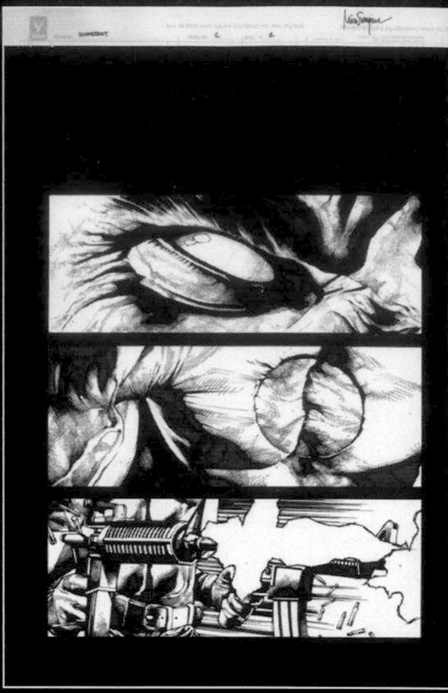

PAGE 1 COLOR BY DAVID BARON

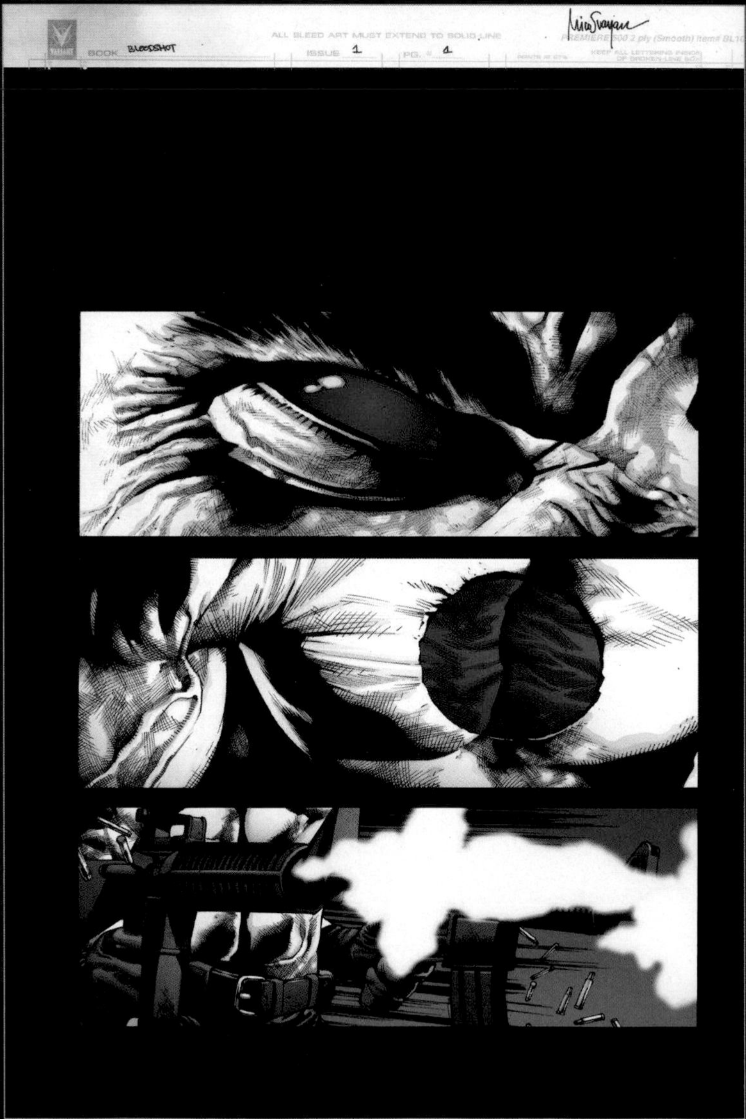
ALL BLEED ART MUST EXTEND TO SOLID LINE
BOOK BLOODSHOT
ISSUE 1
PG. 1

PAGE 2 SCRIPT BY JEFF LEMIRE

SPLASH /// A BADASS, full-body drawing of BLOODSHOT in action.

He is in a corridor in Project Rising Spirit. The bodies of ARMED GUARDS lie dead all around him. Smoke curls up from their bullet-riddled corpses.

Shell casings lie all around the floor. He aims two machine guns and fires, killing two more guards in the foreground.

PAGE 2 LAYOUT BY MICO SUAYAN

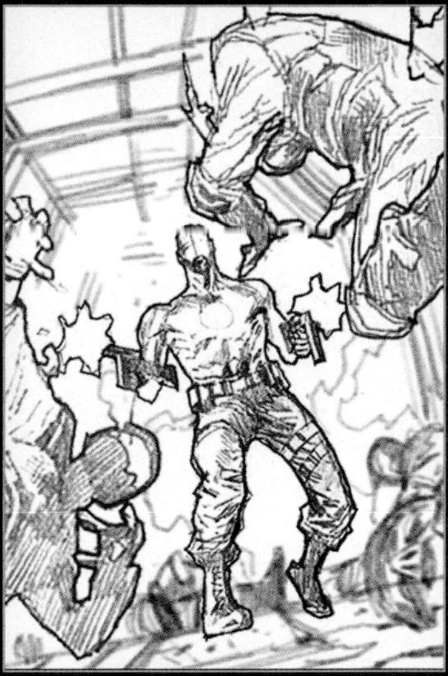

PAGE 2 INKS BY MICO SUAYAN

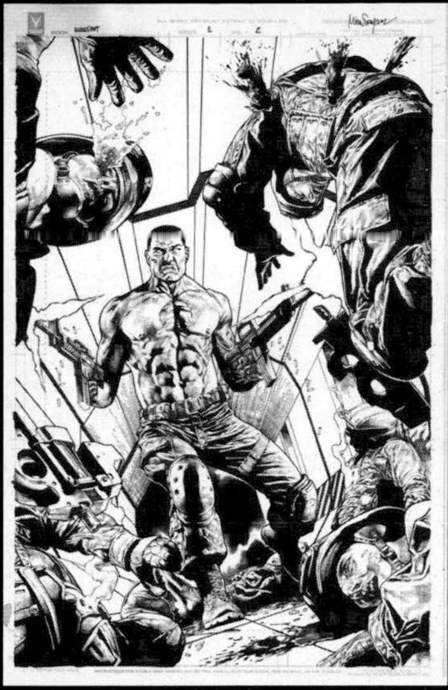

PAGE 2 COLOR BY DAVID BARON

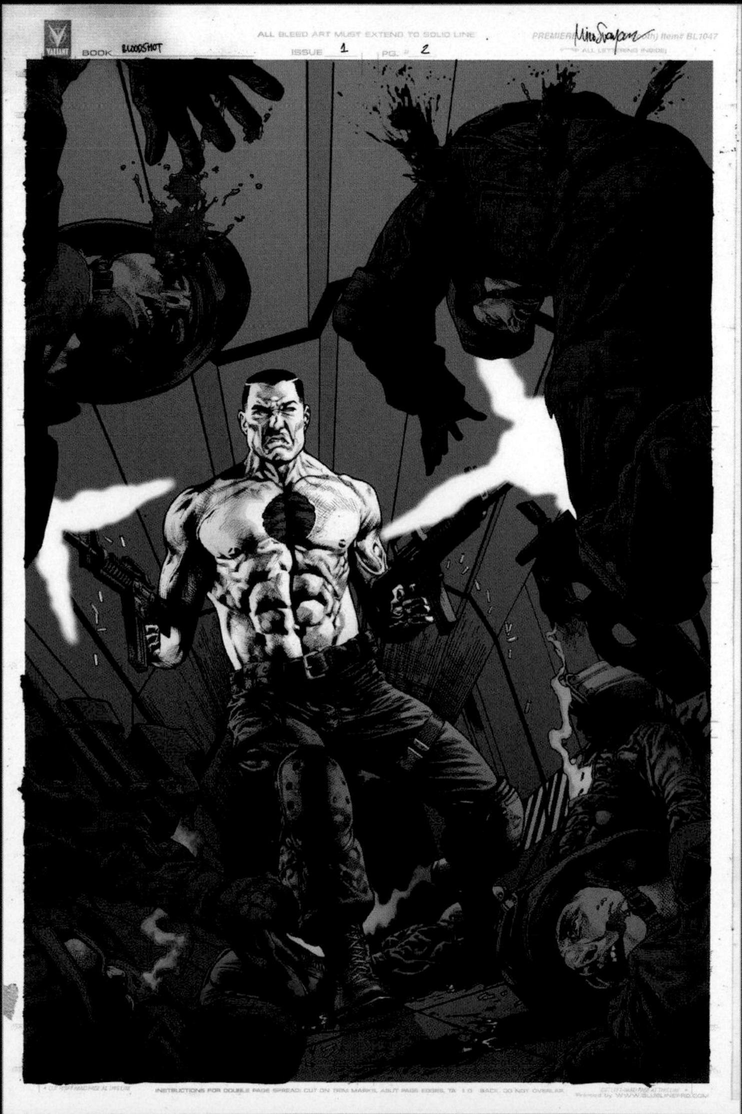
ALL BLEED ART MUST EXTEND TO SOLID LINE
BOOK BLOODSHOT
ISSUE 1
PG. 2

PAGE 3 SCRIPT BY JEFF LEMIRE

Mico, for this page I was envisioning the silhouette of BLOODSHOT from page 2, but now we see his circulatory system inside of the silhouette. A dense network of red veins and arteries filling his silhouette. And branching off from this central silhouette are a number of inset panels showing his "origin."

PANEL 1 /// The first inset panel is an EXTREME close-up of one of the Nanobots. A spider-like robot.

PANEL 2 /// Closer on Bloodshot in action. He breaks the neck of one soldier as another steps up behind Bloodshot and fires a pistol at point-blank range right into the back of his head. Bloodshot's forehead explodes with blood and guts.

PANEL 3 /// We are behind Bloodshot as he turns to the man who shot him. We see the man through the gaping hole in Bloodshot's head. The man puts his hands up in defense, terrified.

PANEL 4 /// Same, but the wound is healed. We only see the back of his head.

PANEL 5 /// Bloodshot kills the man. The man is off panel. Blood splatters up in his sneering face.

PAGE 3 LAYOUT BY MICO SUAYAN

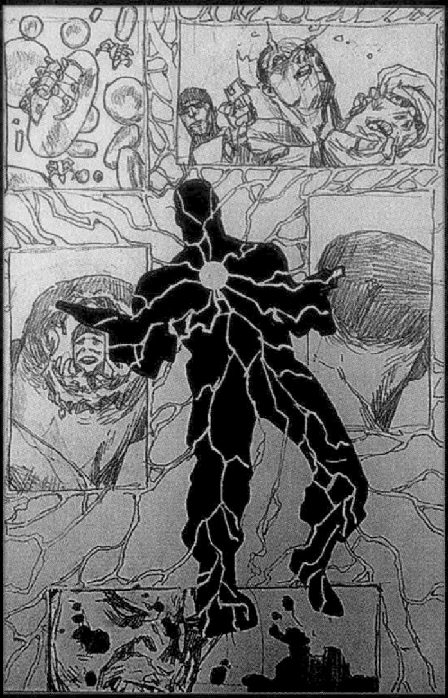

PAGE 3 INKS BY MICO SUAYAN

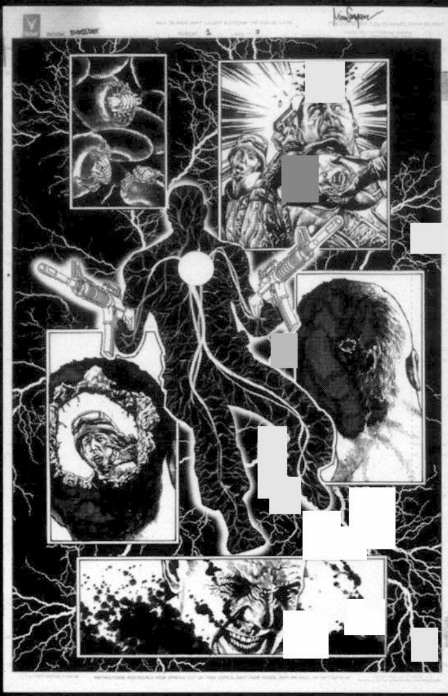

PAGE 3 COLOR BY DAVID BARON

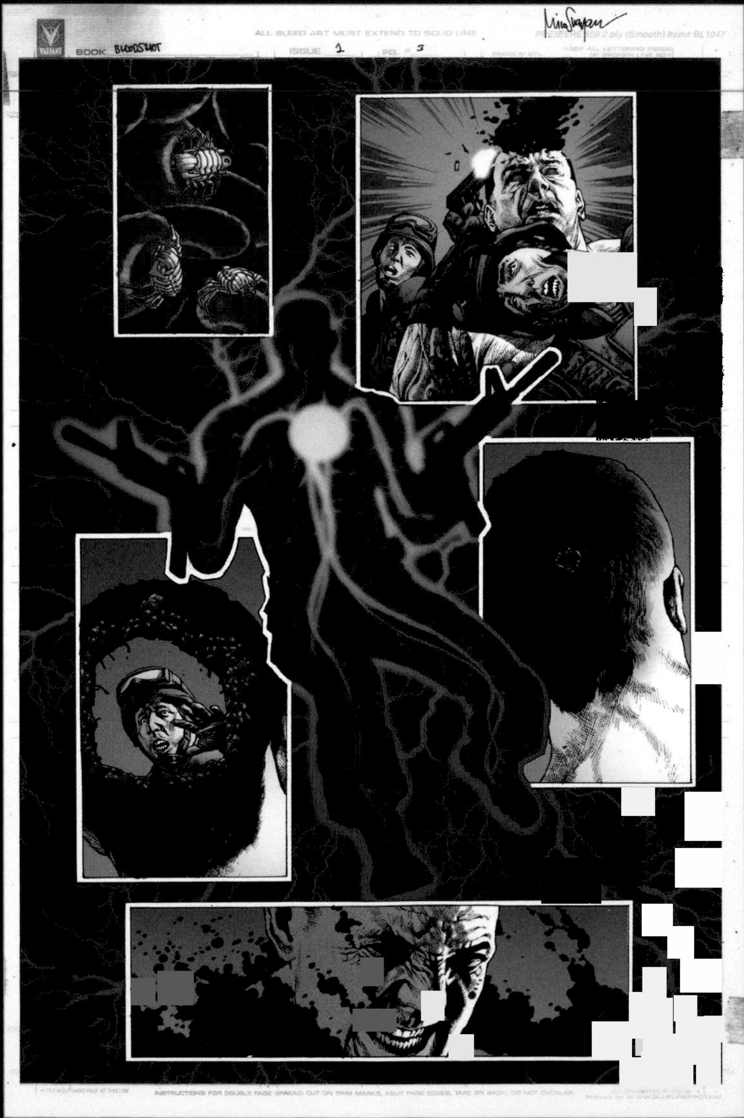
ALL BLEED ART MUST EXTEND TO SOLID LINE
BOOK BLOODSHOT
ISSUE 1
PG. 3

GALLERY

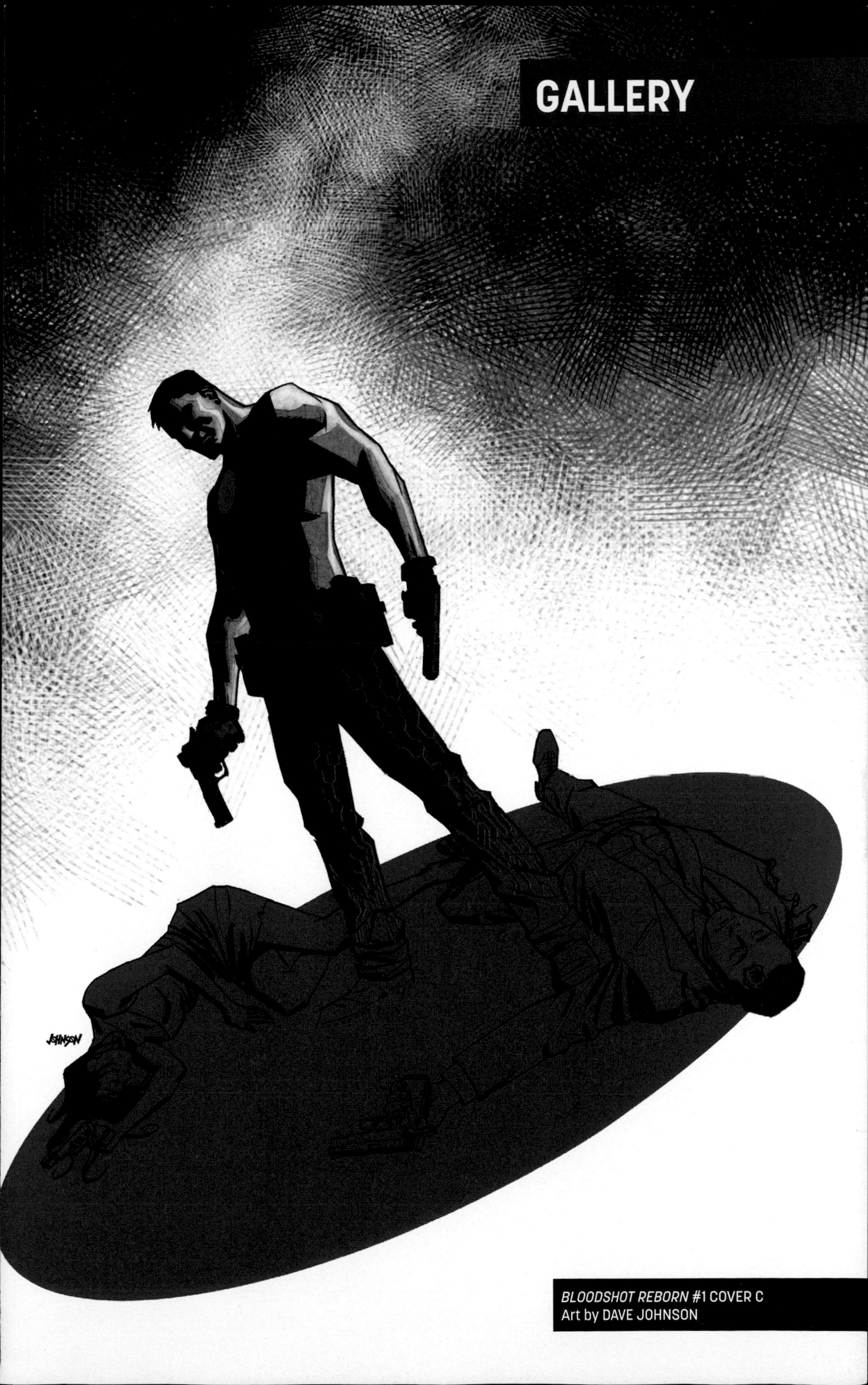
JOHNSON

BLOODSHOT REBORN #1 COVER C
Art by DAVE JOHNSON

BLOODSHOT REBORN #2 VARIANT COVER
Art by MARGUERITE SAUVAGE

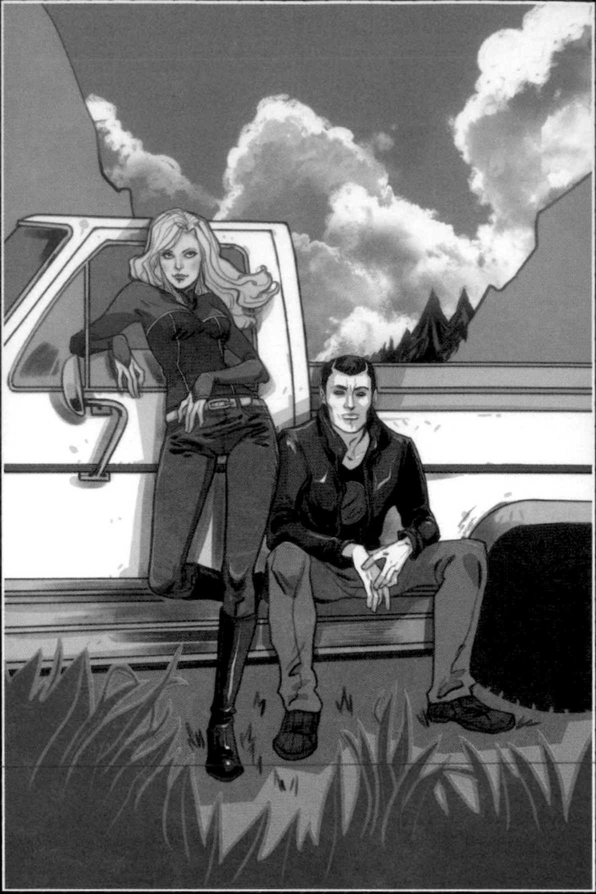

BLOODSHOT REBORN #3 COVER B
Art by LEWIS LAROSA with BRIAN REBER

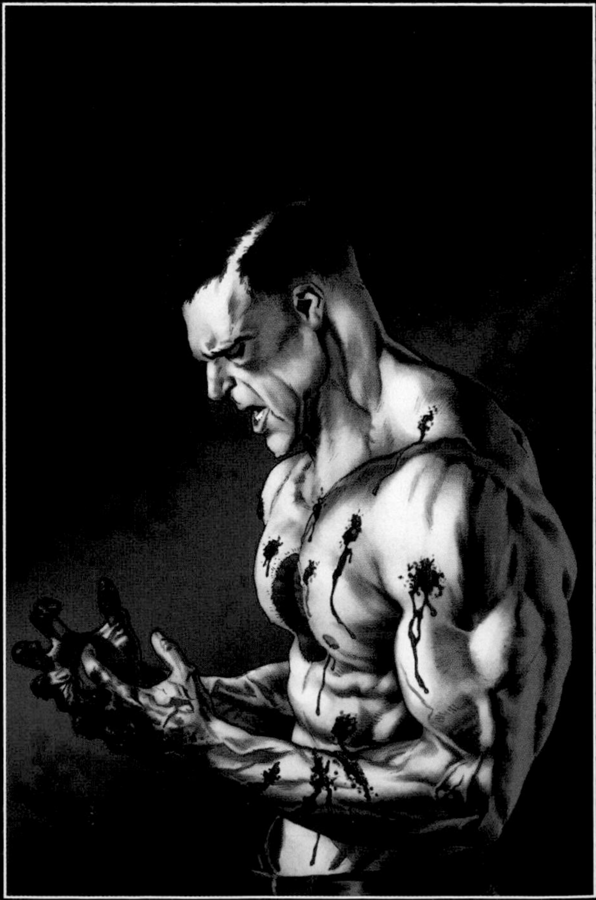

BLOODSHOT REBORN #5 VARIANT COVER
Art by KANO

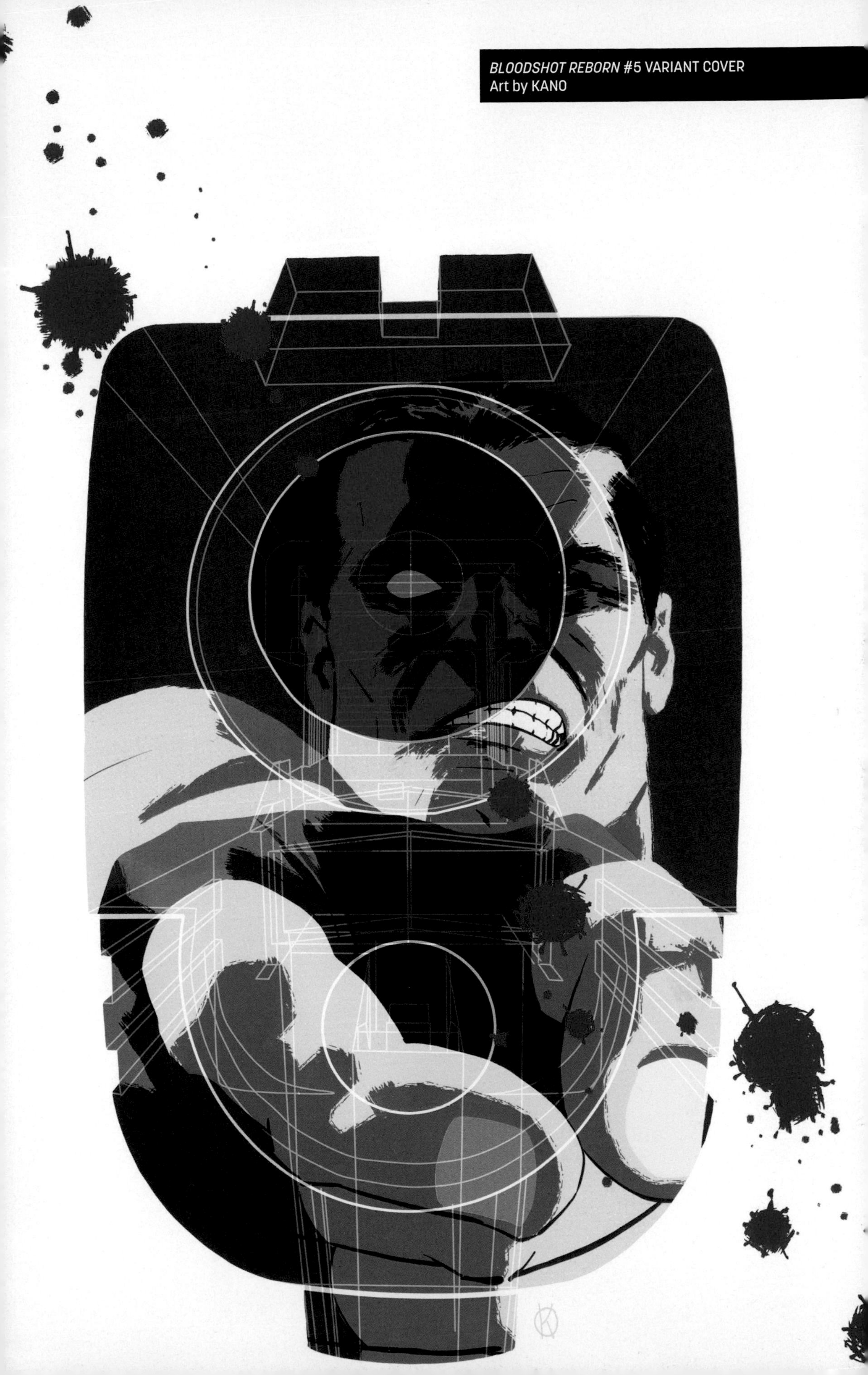

BLOODSHOT REBORN #1, p.3
Art by MICO SUAYAN

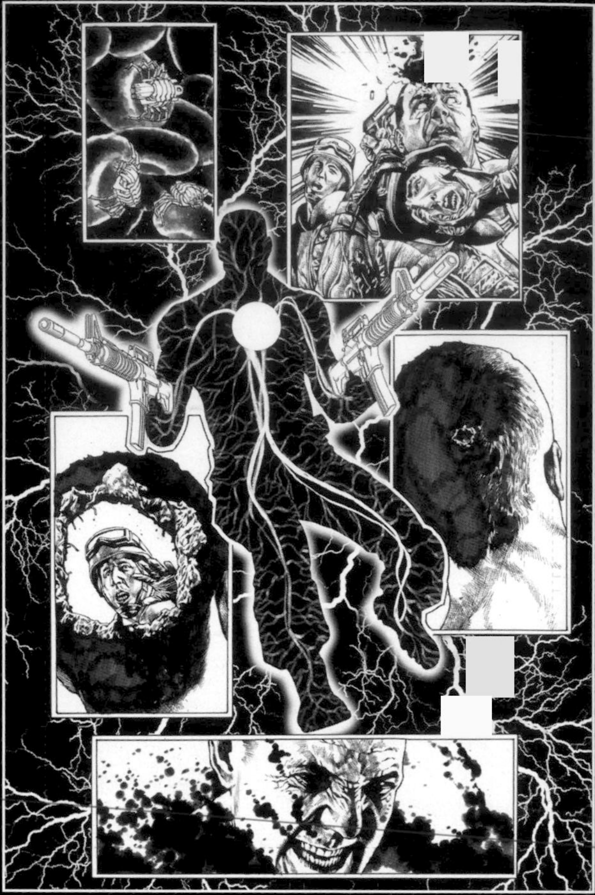

BLOODSHOT REBORN #1, p.10
Art by MICO SUAYAN

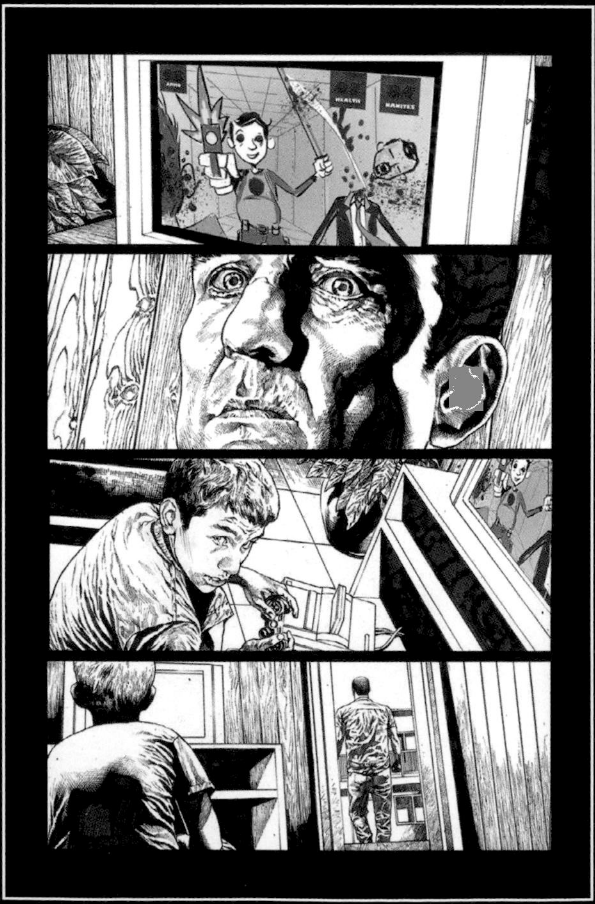

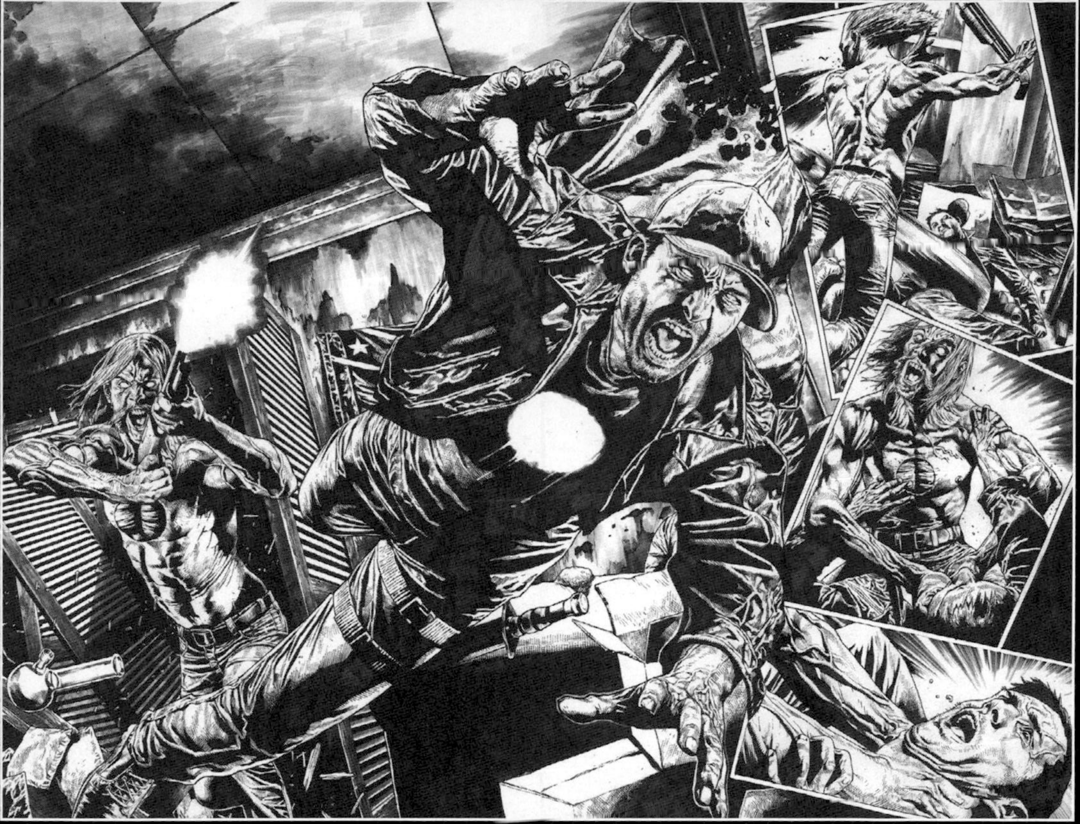

BLOODSHOT REBORN #4, pages 8-9
Art by MICO SUAYAN

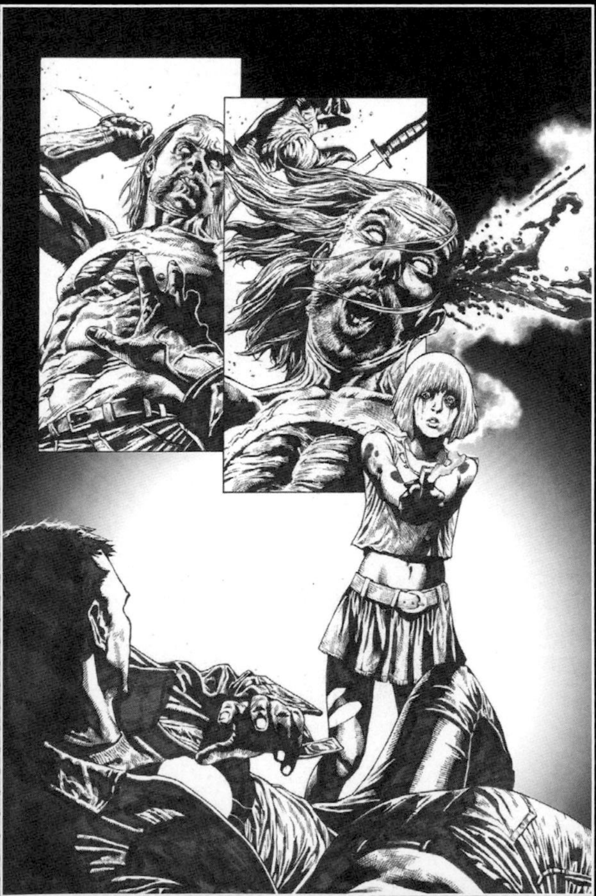

BLOODSHOT REBORN #4 p.10
Art by MICO SUAYAN

EXPLORE THE VALIANT UNIVERSE

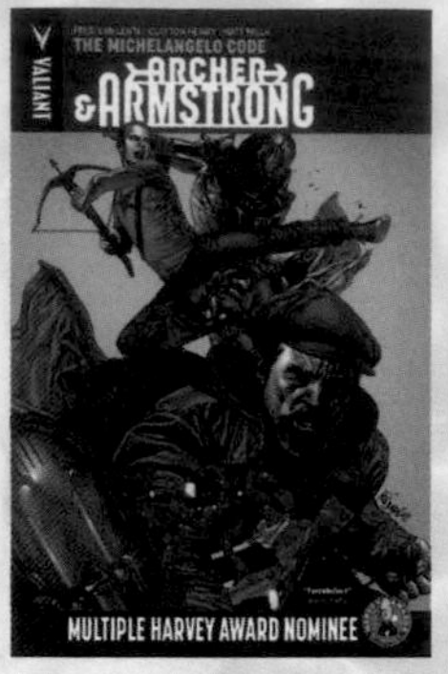
VALIANT
THE MICHELANGELO CODE
ARCHER & ARMSTRONG
MULTIPLE HARVEY AWARD NOMINEE

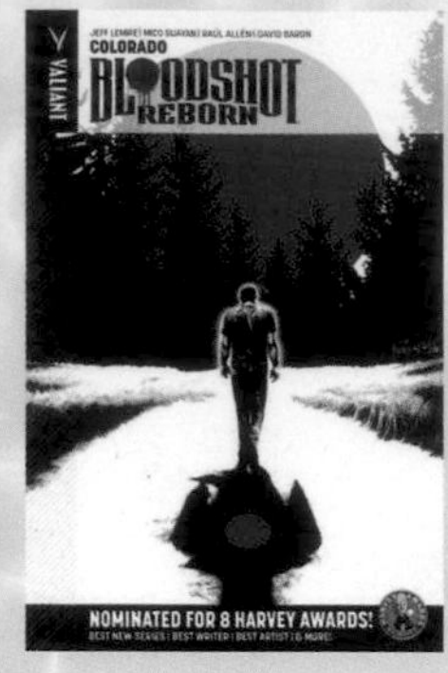
VALIANT
COLORADO
BLOODSHOT REBORN
NOMINATED FOR 8 HARVEY AWARDS!

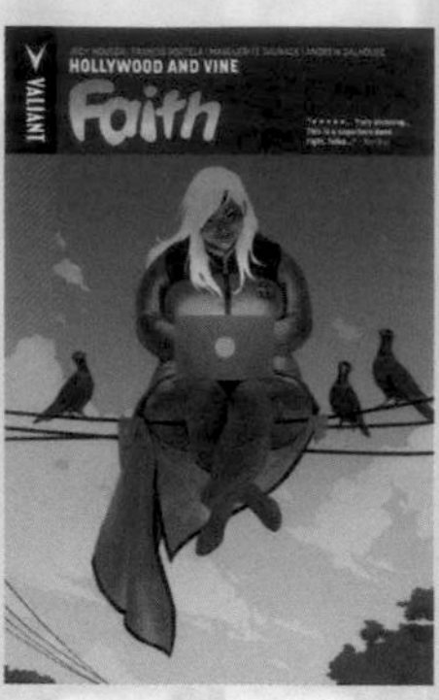
VALIANT
HOLLYWOOD AND VINE
Faith

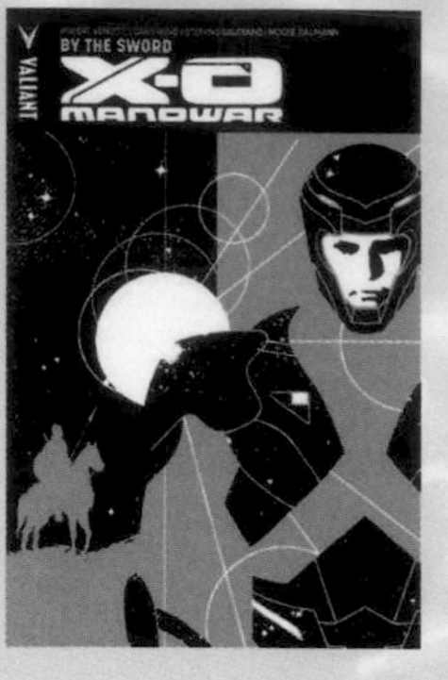
VALIANT
BY THE SWORD
X-O MANOWAR

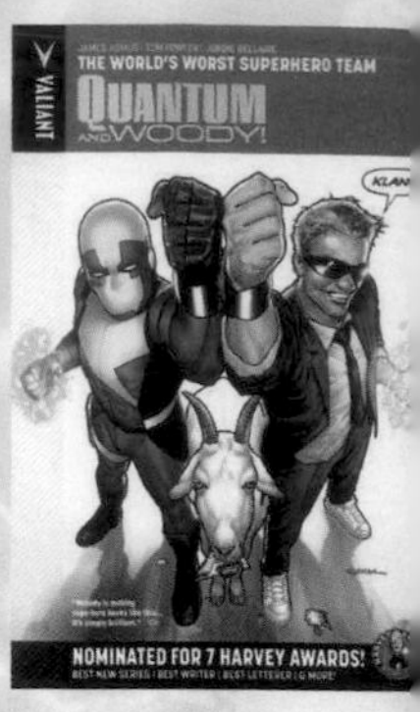
VALIANT
THE WORLD'S WORST SUPERHERO TEAM
QUANTUM AND WOODY!
NOMINATED FOR 7 HARVEY AWARDS!

A&A: THE ADVENTURES OF ARCHER AND ARMSTRONG

Volume 1: In the Bag
ISBN: 9781682151495

ARCHER & ARMSTRONG

Volume 1: The Michelangelo Code
ISBN: 9780979640988

Volume 2: Wrath of the Eternal Warrior
ISBN: 9781939346049

Volume 3: Far Faraway
ISBN: 9781939346148

Volume 4: Sect Civil War
ISBN: 9781939346254

Volume 5: Mission: Improbable
ISBN: 9781939346353

Volume 6: American Wasteland
ISBN: 9781939346421

Volume 7: The One Percent and Other Tales
ISBN: 9781939346537

ARMOR HUNTERS

Armor Hunters
ISBN: 9781939346452

Armor Hunters: Bloodshot
ISBN: 9781939346469

Armor Hunters: Harbinger
ISBN: 9781939346506

Unity Vol. 3: Armor Hunters
ISBN: 9781939346445

X-O Manowar Vol. 7: Armor Hunters
ISBN: 9781939346476

BLOODSHOT

Volume 1: Setting the World on Fire
ISBN: 9780979640964

Volume 2: The Rise and the Fall
ISBN: 9781939346032

Volume 3: Harbinger Wars
ISBN: 9781939346124

Volume 4: H.A.R.D. Corps
ISBN: 9781939346193

Volume 5: Get Some!
ISBN: 9781939346315

Volume 6: The Glitch and Other Tales
ISBN: 9781939346711

BLOODSHOT REBORN

Volume 1: Colorado
ISBN: 9781939346674

Volume 2: The Hunt
ISBN: 9781939346827

Volume 3: The Analog Man
ISBN: 9781682151334

BOOK OF DEATH

Book of Death
ISBN: 9781939346971

Book of Death: The Fall of the Valiant Universe
ISBN: 9781939346988

DEAD DROP

ISBN: 9781939346858

THE DEATH-DEFYING DOCTOR MIRAGE

Volume 1
ISBN: 9781939346490

Volume 2: Second Lives
ISBN: 9781682151297

THE DELINQUENTS

ISBN: 9781939346513

DIVINITY

Volume 1
ISBN: 9781939346766

Volume 2
ISBN: 9781682151518

ETERNAL WARRIOR

Volume 1: Sword of the Wild
ISBN: 9781939346209

Volume 2: Eternal Emperor
ISBN: 9781939346292

Volume 3: Days of Steel
ISBN: 9781939346742

WRATH OF THE ETERNAL WARRIOR

Volume 1: Risen
ISBN: 9781682151235

HARBINGER

Volume 1: Omega Rising
ISBN: 9780979640957

Volume 2: Renegades
ISBN: 9781939346025

Volume 3: Harbinger Wars
ISBN: 9781939346117

Volume 4: Perfect Day
ISBN: 9781939346155

Volume 5: Death of a Renegade
ISBN: 9781939346339

Volume 6: Omegas
ISBN: 9781939346384

HARBINGER WARS

Harbinger Wars
ISBN: 9781939346094

Bloodshot Vol. 3: Harbinger Wars
ISBN: 9781939346124

Harbinger Vol. 3: Harbinger Wars
ISBN: 9781939346117

EXPLORE THE VALIANT UNIVERSE

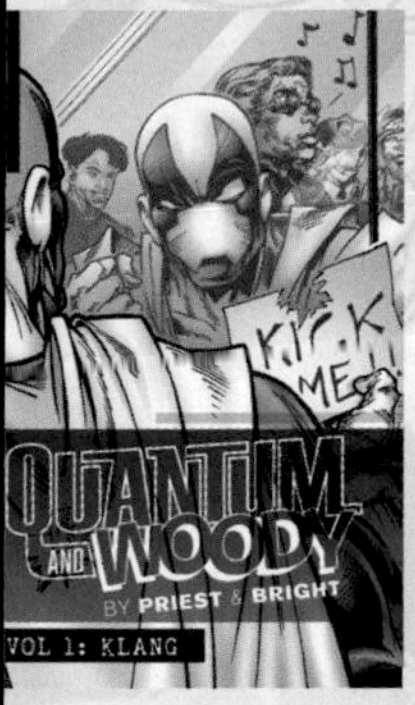
QUANTUM AND WOODY
BY PRIEST & BRIGHT
VOL 1: KLANG
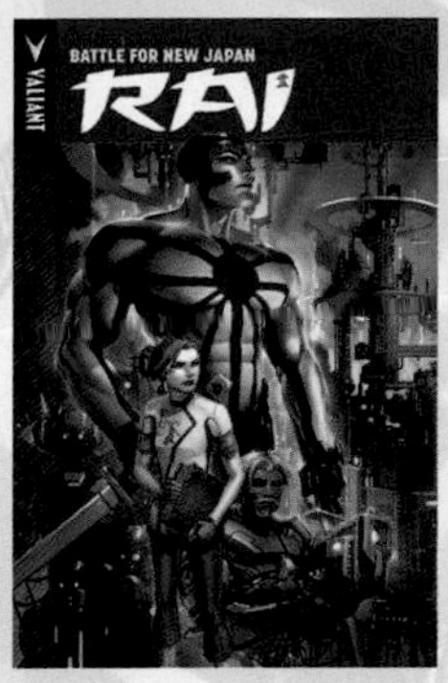
BATTLE FOR NEW JAPAN
RAI
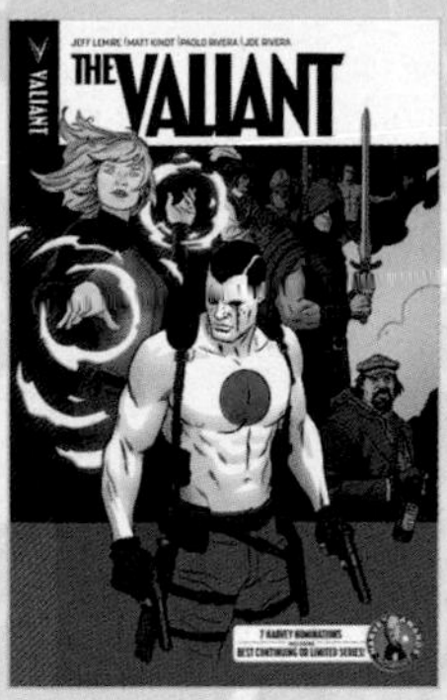
THE VALIANT
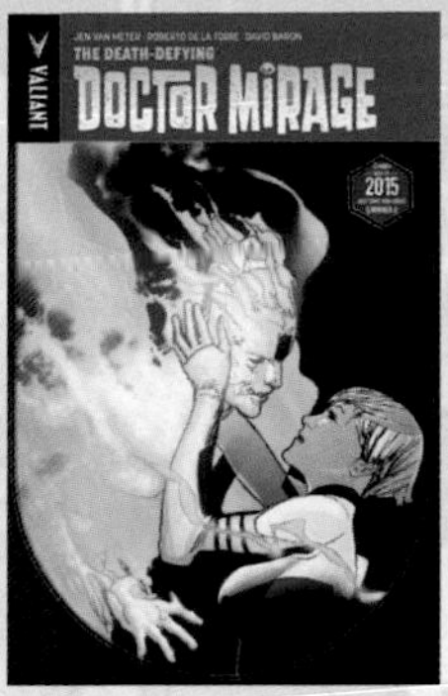
THE DEATH-DEFYING
DOCTOR MIRAGE
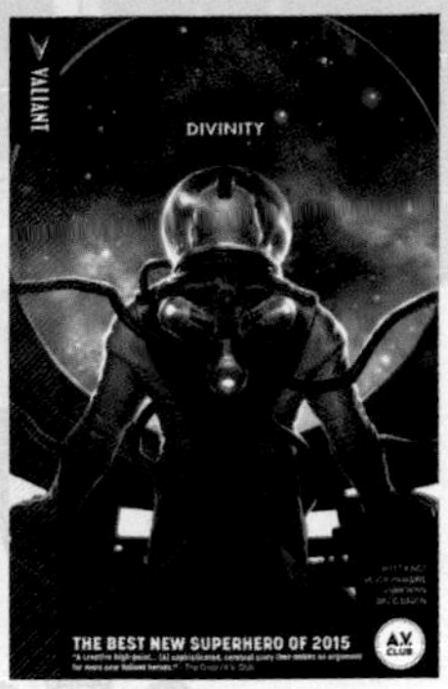
DIVINITY
THE BEST NEW SUPERHERO OF 2015

MPERIUM

olume 1: Collecting Monsters
BN: 9781939346759

olume 2: Broken Angels
BN: 9781939346896

olume 3: The Vine Imperative
BN: 9781682151112

olume 4: Stormbreak
BN: 9781682151372

INJAK

olume 1: Weaponeer
BN: 9781939346667

olume 2: The Shadow Wars
BN: 9781939346940

olume 3: Operation: Deadside
BN: 9781682151259

olume 4: The Siege of King's Castle
BN: 9781682151617

UANTUM AND WOODY

olume 1: The World's Worst Superhero Team
BN: 9781939346186

olume 2: In Security
BN: 9781939346230

olume 3: Crooked Pasts, Present Tense
BN: 9781939346391

olume 4: Quantum and Woody Must Die!
BN: 9781939346629

UANTUM AND WOODY Y PRIEST & BRIGHT

olume 1: Klang
BN: 9781939346780

olume 2: Switch
BN: 9781939346803

olume 3: And So...
BN: 9781939346865

olume 4: Q2 - The Return
BN: 9781682151099

RAI

Volume 1: Welcome to New Japan
ISBN: 9781939346414

Volume 2: Battle for New Japan
ISBN: 9781939346612

Volume 3: The Orphan
ISBN: 9781939346841

SHADOWMAN

Volume 1: Birth Rites
ISBN: 9781939346001

Volume 2: Darque Reckoning
ISBN: 9781939346056

Volume 3: Deadside Blues
ISBN: 9781939346162

Volume 4: Fear, Blood, And Shadows
ISBN: 9781939346278

Volume 5: End Times
ISBN: 9781939346377

SHADOWMAN BY ENNIS & WOOD

ISBN: 9781682151358

IVAR, TIMEWALKER

Volume 1: Making History
ISBN: 9781939346636

Volume 2: Breaking History
ISBN: 9781939346834

Volume 3: Ending History
ISBN: 9781939346995

UNITY

Volume 1: To Kill a King
ISBN: 9781939346261

Volume 2: Trapped by Webnet
ISBN: 9781939346346

Volume 3: Armor Hunters
ISBN: 9781939346445

Volume 4: The United
ISBN: 9781939346544

Volume 5: Homefront
ISBN: 9781939346797

Volume 6: The War-Monger
ISBN: 9781939346902

Volume 7: Revenge of the Armor Hunters
ISBN: 9781682151136

THE VALIANT

ISBN: 9781939346605

VALIANT ZEROES AND ORIGINS

ISBN: 9781939346582

X-O MANOWAR

Volume 1: By the Sword
ISBN: 9780979640940

Volume 2: Enter Ninjak
ISBN: 9780979640995

Volume 3: Planet Death
ISBN: 9781939346087

Volume 4: Homecoming
ISBN: 9781939346179

Volume 5: At War With Unity
ISBN: 9781939346247

Volume 6: Prelude to Armor Hunters
ISBN: 9781939346407

Volume 7: Armor Hunters
ISBN: 9781939346476

Volume 8: Enter: Armorines
ISBN: 9781939346551

Volume 9: Dead Hand
ISBN: 9781939346650

Volume 10: Exodus
ISBN: 9781939346933

Volume 11: The Kill List
ISBN: 9781682151273

EXPLORE THE VALIANT UNIVERSE

VALIANT
HARBINGER DELUXE EDITION 2

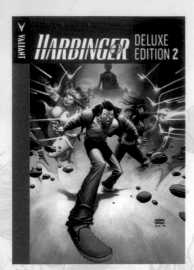

OMNIBUSES

Archer & Armstrong: The Complete Classic Omnibus
ISBN: 9781939346872
Collecting ARCHER & ARMSTRONG (1992) #0-26, ETERNAL WARRIOR (1992) #25 along with ARCHER & ARMSTRONG: THE FORMATION OF THE SECT.

Quantum and Woody: The Complete Classic Omnibus
ISBN: 9781939346360
Collecting QUANTUM AND WOODY (1997) #0, 1-21 and #32, THE GOAT: H.A.E.D.U.S. #1, and X-O MANOWAR (1996) #16

X-O Manowar Classic Omnibus Vol. 1
ISBN: 9781939346308
Collecting X-O MANOWAR (1992) #0-30, ARMORINES #0, X-O DATABASE #1, as well as material from SECRETS OF THE VALIANT UNIVERSE #1

DELUXE EDITIONS

Archer & Armstrong Deluxe Edition Book 1
ISBN: 9781939346223
Collecting ARCHER & ARMSTRONG #0-13

VALIANT
ARMOR HUNTERS DELUXE EDITION

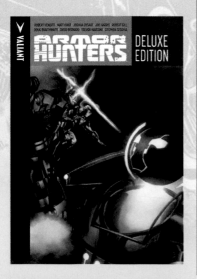

Armor Hunters Deluxe Edition
ISBN: 9781939346728
Collecting ARMOR HUNTERS #1-4, ARMOR HUNTERS: AFTERMATH #1, ARMOR HUNTERS: BLOODSHOT #1-3, ARMOR HUNTERS: HARBINGER #1-3, UNITY #8-11 and X-O MANOWAR #23-29

Bloodshot Deluxe Edition Book 1
ISBN: 9781939346216
Collecting BLOODSHOT #1-13

Harbinger Deluxe Edition Book 1
ISBN: 9781939346131
Collecting HARBINGER #0-14

Harbinger Deluxe Edition Book 2
ISBN: 9781939346773
Collecting HARBINGER #15-25, HARBINGER: OMEGAS #1-3, and HARBINGER: BLEEDING MONK #0

Harbinger Wars Deluxe Edition
ISBN: 9781939346322
Collecting HARBINGER WARS #1-4, HARBINGER #11-14, and BLOODSHOT #10-13

Quantum and Woody Deluxe Edition Book 1
ISBN: 9781939346681
Collecting QUANTUM AND WOODY #1-12 and QUANTUM AND WOODY: THE GOAT #0

Q2: The Return of Quantum and Woody Deluxe Edition
ISBN: 9781939346568
Collecting Q2: THE RETURN OF QUANTUM AND WOODY #1-5

VALIANT
JAMES ASMUS TOM FOWLER MING DOYLE
KANO JORDIE BELLAIRE DAVE LANPHEAR
QUANTUM AND WOODY!
DELUXE EDITION 1
MEH!

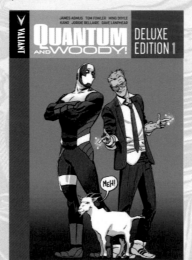

Shadowman Deluxe Edition Book 1
ISBN: 9781939346438
Collecting SHADOWMAN #0-10

Unity Deluxe Edition Book 1
ISBN: 9781939346575
Collecting UNITY #0-14

X-O Manowar Deluxe Edition Book 1
ISBN: 9781939346100
Collecting X-O MANOWAR #1-14

X-O Manowar Deluxe Edition Book 2
ISBN: 9781939346520
Collecting X-O MANOWAR #15-22, and UNITY #1-4

VALIANT
JIM SHOOTER | DAVID LAPHAM
CHILDREN OF THE EIGHTH DAY
HARBINGER
VALIANT MASTERS

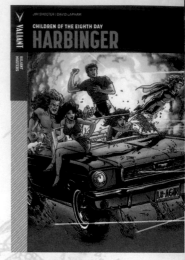

VALIANT MASTERS

Bloodshot Vol. 1 - Blood of the Machine
ISBN: 9780979640933

H.A.R.D. Corps Vol. 1 - Search and Destroy
ISBN: 9781939346285

Harbinger Vol. 1 - Children of the Eighth Day
ISBN: 9781939346483

Ninjak Vol. 1 - Black Water
ISBN: 9780979640971

Rai Vol. 1 - From Honor to Strength
ISBN: 9781939346070

Shadowman Vol. 1 - Spirits Within
ISBN: 9781939346018

VALIANT
KEVIN VANHOOK | DON PERLIN
BLOOD OF THE MACHINE
BLOODSHOT
VALIANT MASTERS

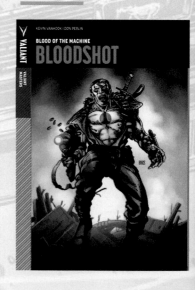

BLOODSHOT REBORN READING ORDER

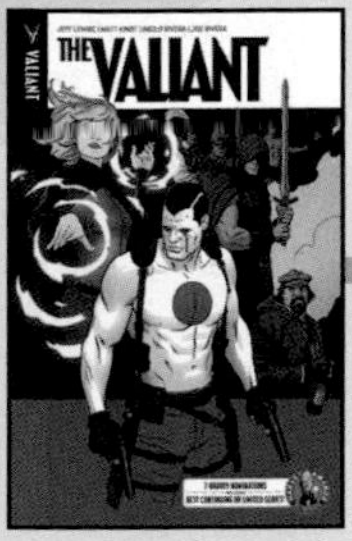
THE VALIANT

The Valiant
(OPTIONAL)

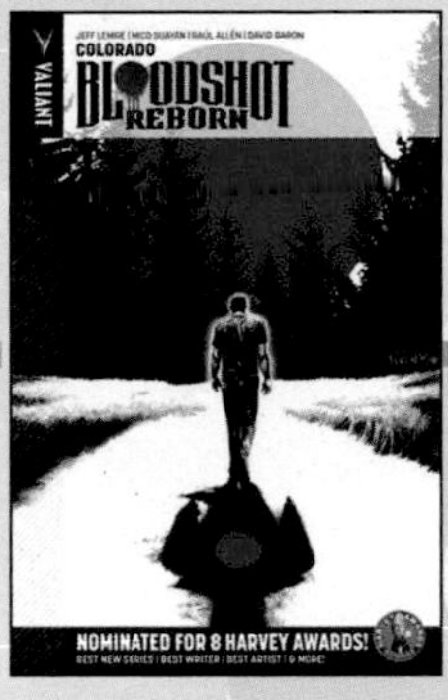
COLORADO
BLOODSHOT REBORN
NOMINATED FOR 8 HARVEY AWARDS!

Bloodshot Reborn Vol. 1: Colorado

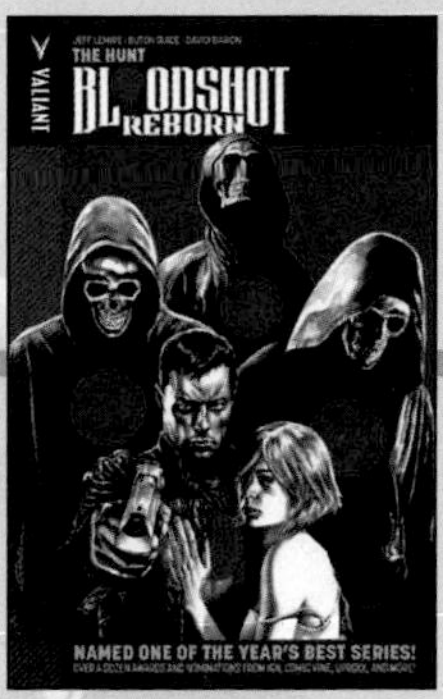
THE HUNT
BLOODSHOT REBORN
NAMED ONE OF THE YEAR'S BEST SERIES!

Bloodshot Reborn Vol. 2: The Hunt

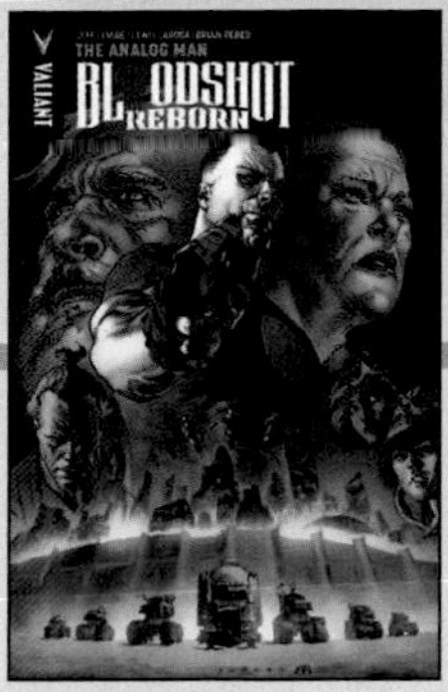
THE ANALOG MAN
BLOODSHOT REBORN

Bloodshot Reborn Vol. 3: The Analog Man

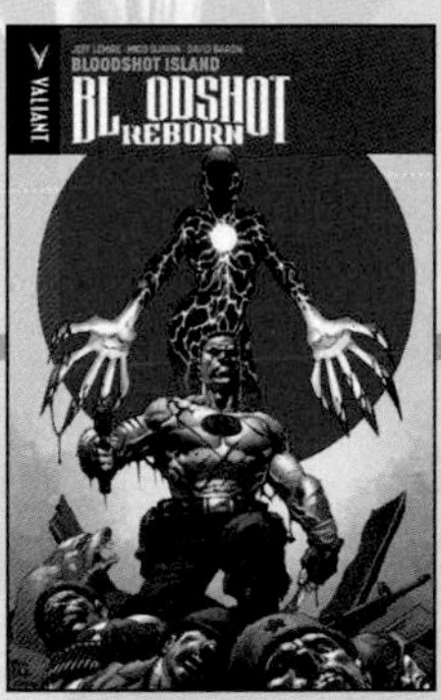
BLOODSHOT ISLAND
BLOODSHOT REBORN

Bloodshot Reborn Vol. 4: Bloodshot Island

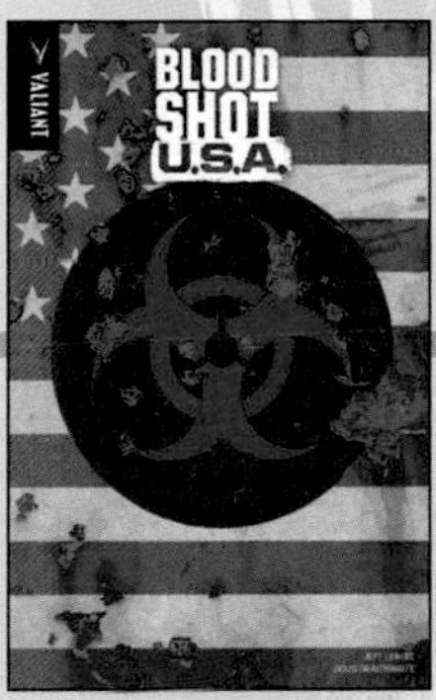
BLOOD SHOT U.S.A.

Bloodshot U.S.A.

Who was Bloodshot? Discover the origins of the man from Rising Spirit in the pages of his self-titled series that lead to the epic events of THE VALIANT!

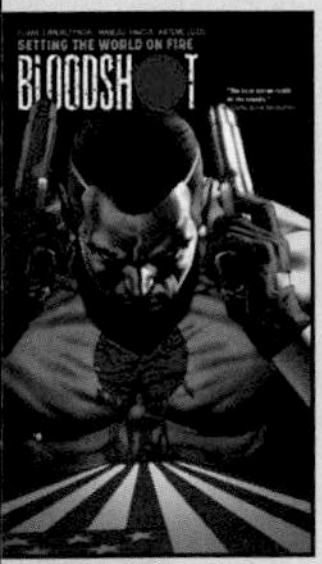
SETTING THE WORLD ON FIRE
BLOODSHOT

Bloodshot Vol. 1: Setting the World on Fire

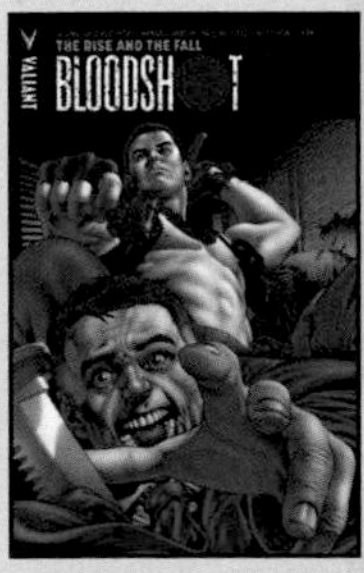
THE RISE AND THE FALL
BLOODSHOT

Bloodshot Vol. 2: The Rise and the Fall

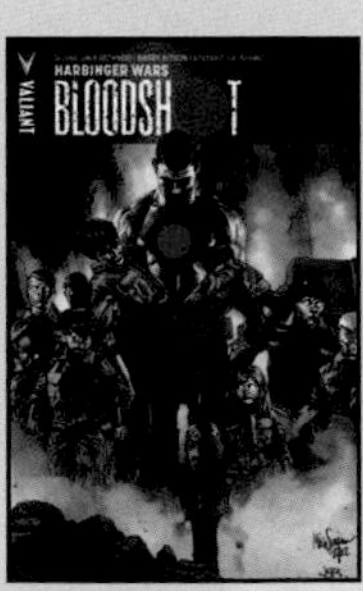
HARBINGER WARS
BLOODSHOT

Bloodshot Vol. 3: Harbinger Wars

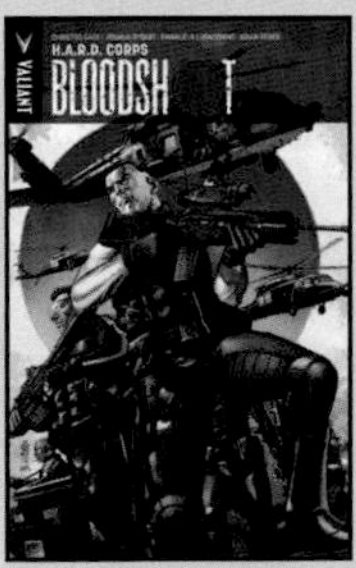
H.A.R.D. CORPS
BLOODSHOT

Bloodshot Vol. 4: H.A.R.D. Corps

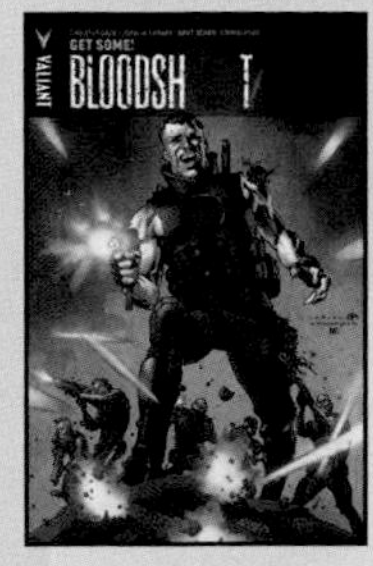
GET SOME!
BLOODSHOT

Bloodshot Vol. 5: Get Some!

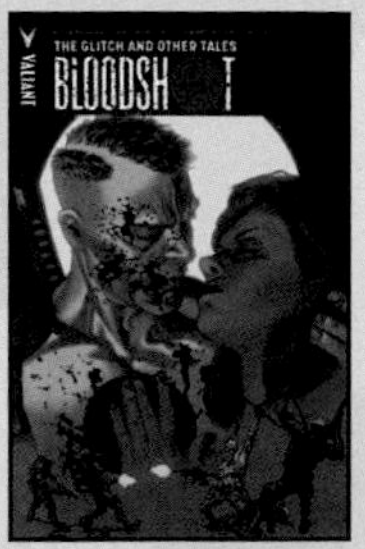
THE GLITCH AND OTHER TALES
BLOODSHOT

Bloodshot Vol. 6: The Glitch and Other Tales

BLOODSHOT REBORN

VOLUME TWO: THE HUNT

"THE HUNT" IS ON!

Bloodshot is on the hunt. Determined to stop the violent
reign of terror that plagues Colorado, Bloodshot journeys
across the Rocky Mountains to destroy the remaining
nanites that have caused mass murderers to spring up
across the state. But will the drugs, booze, and insane
visions rattling around his head put an end to his journey
before it begins?

Start reading here as New York Times best-selling writer
Jeff Lemire (THE VALIANT, *Descender*) and modern master
Butch Guice (NINJAK, *Captain America: The Winter Soldier*)
begin the second staggering story arc of the chart-
topping new series that Entertainment Weekly calls "a
subversive new take on Valiant's resident unkillable killing
machine." Collecting BLOODSHOT REBORN #6-9.

TRADE PAPERBACK
ISBN: 978-1-939346-82-7

JEFF LEMIRE | BUTCH GUICE | DAVID BARON
THE HUNT
BLOODSHOT REBORN